NUCLEAR AMBIGUITY

NUCLEAR AMBIGUITY

The Vanunu Affair

Yoel Cohen

SINCLAIR-STEVENSON

First published in Great Britain by
Sinclair-Stevenson
7/8 Kendrick Mews
London SW7 3HG England

British Library Cataloguing in Publication Data
A CIP catalogue record for this book is available from the
British Library.

ISBN: 1 85619 150 8

Typeset by Rowland Phototypesetting Limited
Bury St Edmunds, Suffolk

Printed and bound in Great Britain by
Clays Ltd, St Ives plc

CONTENTS

PROLOGUE

Engineering a successful press leak means ensuring that the target audience responds in the desired manner and that there are no undesirable reactions from other quarters. By this standard, Mordechai Vanunu's sensational leak to the London *Sunday Times* in October 1986, describing his work at Israel's nuclear research centre at Dimona, could not be acclaimed a total public relations success. In making his disclosure, Vanunu, who had worked at Dimona as a technician for nine years, wanted to alert his countrymen and the world at large to the nuclear danger. For the first time somebody with direct knowledge of the Israeli nuclear programme had spoken in public about it. Previous estimates that Israel possessed about twenty nuclear warheads were much lower than the 100–200 warheads which the *Sunday Times* and its scientific advisers estimated after hearing Vanunu's account. He also claimed that Israel was developing a thermonuclear bomb. But Vanunu's hope that ordinary Israelis and the international community would bring pressure upon the government to dismantle its nuclear capability was not to be.

Vanunu's disclosure ricocheted in a number of directions. It raised Israel's nuclear deterrent posture against the Arab world in general and Iraq in particular. Israeli officials felt freer to allude to the nuclear programme than they had before Vanunu; there was little worth to a nuclear capability which could not be seen or at least hinted at. Rather than

1

quoting the stock Israeli position that it would not be the first to introduce nuclear weapons into the region, Jerusalem responded to Iraqi threats made throughout 1990 to attack the Jewish state with its chemical weapons by promising to hit Iraq '100 times over', an allusion to an attack of mass destruction. Prime Minister Itzhak Shamir, speaking to CNN in October 1990, said, 'Somebody threatening you with the most terrible weapons in the world has to think about certain responses to the use of such weapons.' Vanunu's disclosure contributed to deterring Iraq from deploying non-conventional warheads in the thirty-nine Scud missiles it launched against Israel during the Gulf War. Baghdad correctly calculated that Israel would not respond with a nuclear attack as long as Iraq did not cross the threshold from conventional weapons to non-conventional.

Popular concern in Israel in 1990 and 1991 about the Iraqi threat stimulated public and media discussion about it – and the options for Israel of a non-conventional military response – than had ever occurred. At no time was Israeli military censorship as liberal on this point as during this period. Blunt allusions in the media to an Israeli nuclear capability, which in the past would have been blue-pencilled, were not prevented by the military censor. As Dan Margalit, a columnist on *Haaretz* remarked, 'While the government has to keep quiet, the media will do the government's job.' Yet, when the war ended so did the censor's short-lived liberal approach.

Another unintended consequence of Vanunu's revelations was to encourage Iraq to redouble its efforts to rebuild its nuclear bomb programme damaged by the Israeli air attack on its nuclear reactor at Osiraq five years earlier. Vanunu's story may have contributed to Iraq's brief flirtation with the Jewish state towards the end of the eighties when, faced with defeat in its war with Iran, Baghdad put out diplomatic feelers to Jerusalem which resulted in a series of meetings between Israeli and Iraqi officials. But this, and a debate within the Israeli intelligence establishment over the real – as opposed to the psychological – threat of mass destruction weaponry, resulted in Israeli military intelligence lowering the priority which had earlier been given to information about Iraq. As a result, when the Gulf War broke out Israel did not possess such basic information as whether Iraq had chemical warheads for its missiles. To be on the safe side, the entire population were given gas masks rather than (as later proved a better defence) instructed to use below ground bomb shelters which are more effective against conventional bomb attacks.

The disclosure also affected the sensitive US–Israeli relationship. Publicly, during the war US Defense Secretary Dick Cheney reacted to Iraqi missile attacks on Israel by stating that Israel had the nuclear option. However, behind closed doors the Bush administration viewed Israel's nuclear development with concern. Bush placed priority on dealing with the danger of non-conventional arms particularly in the Middle East, and arms control figures prominently in the US-sponsored Middle East peace talks, which began in Madrid in November 1991. Washington recognises that in the short-term Israel should not give up its nuclear deterrent capability particularly at a time when it is being pressured by the US as well as the Arab states themselves to make territorial compromises. The US administration knows that such a deterrent will play a crucial role if and when Israel loses part of her territorial advantage. All that the Bush proposal expects is that the programme will be interrupted, and controlled, for example by inspection and controls of raw materials like uranium. Washington banned the sale to Israel of a supercomputer which can be used for simulating nuclear explosions. Low-level measures were introduced, like banning visits by Israeli scientists to US nuclear laboratories.

The chances of an arms control agreement, if not of Vanunu's goal for a nuclear-free zone in the region, were considerable after the Gulf War. Iraq had been vanquished. Iran, the other major military power in the Persian Gulf, is still recovering from its war with Iraq. With only one real nuclear power in the region, Israel, the problem of controlling nuclear proliferation does not appear daunting. Israeli interest in winning recognition and peace from her neighbours, as well as the need to reduce a crippling defence budget to absorb over one million Soviet Jews, adds to the chances of a regional arms control agreement. Iran, Libya and Syria are dependent upon imports to improve their respective missile capabilities. The willingness of the US, the Soviet Union, France, China and Britain – which between them control 85 per cent of world arms sales – to sell to them has declined. The Bush administration placed restrictions upon the export of materials used in the production of chemical and biological weaponry and missile delivery systems. However, without the cooperation of all countries involved in the arms trade, a sole US embargo would have little effect. Moreover, the chances of controlling conventional arms was limited to specific countries. Following the war the US agreed to supply its coalition partners – Saudi Arabia, Egypt, Bahrein, the United Arab Emirates and Turkey – with military hardware worth over $23bn.

The dismantling of Iraq's non-conventional capability – nuclear, chemical and biological – was made a condition of the US-led coalition ceasefire agreement. Notwithstanding that it subsequently became clear that much of Iraq's armoury escaped unscathed from the war, that part which was destroyed was from Israel's perspective achieved without the Israeli forces becoming embroiled on Iraqi soil. And international concern was focused specifically upon Iraq, rather than on Israel's own capability. More comprehensive control of the region's armouries requires to be linked to the political issues and conflicts which have caused the arms proliferation, yet the obstacles are awesome. From the Arab perspective, the present situation is not even-handed, but

Israel's nuclear programme is a fundamental element in its security. No Israeli government will entrust the country's fate to others, so it is most unlikely that any government will negotiate away its strategic superiority, although Israeli security might eventually be ensured through a defence system comprising non-offensive weapons such as the Patriot and Arrow anti-missile systems.

Israel's nuclear programme has been mirrored by a low-level diplomatic stance favouring a regional free zone. An Egyptian proposal for a nuclear freeze in the region, made at the 1978 Camp David meeting which produced the Egyptian–Israeli peace agreement, was rejected by Israel. Given the refusal of some of the major Islamic nations to end their war with Israel, there is little likelihood of Israel giving up its weapon of last resort. Vanunu miscalculated in making his disclosure because many Israelis favour possession of a nuclear weapon. He underestimated the role which the nuclear capability has played in deterring Arab states: it was, for instance, an important factor in Egypt's decision to make peace in 1977.

Yet not all Israeli politicians would insist upon full peace agreements with all Arab states, characterised by the exchange of ambassadors and the plethora of economic, social and political contacts which distinguish normal diplomatic ties, prior to Israel's giving up its nuclear capability. But a minimum requirement would be the renunciation of war and directly negotiated agreements.

The Gulf War and its aftermath placed a question-mark over the future viability of Israel's posture of ambiguity about her nuclear capability. The predicament facing its officials was that the veil over its nuclear programme, having been lowered at different moments over the years, could not easily be raised again in the face of international pressure for arms control. Already in 1986, following Vanunu's revelations, all the denials in the world failed to convince most people that Israel was not a nuclear power. The only

5

question was the detailed breakdown, type and number, of the nuclear capability. The Vanunu story was a watershed in the lifespan of the nuclear posture.

In addition to revealing the man behind the disclosure, and how the *Sunday Times* checked its informant's claims, this book explores the evolution of the nuclear programme and the policy of nuclear ambiguity. The leak produced some diplomatic cliff-hanging by Jerusalem. Israel wanted Vanunu, who was in London, to face trial in Israel for divulging one of the country's most important secrets. His abduction – via a third country, Italy – meant the disappearance of somebody who had talked to an internationally-respected newspaper. The book also probes Vanunu's abduction and the closed-doors trial he faced.

I wish to thank the many people – nuclear proliferation experts, intelligence officers and other officials, journalists and individuals close to Mordechai Vanunu – who saw me in researching the book. Some of those spoke on condition that they remained anonymous.

I am grateful to Vernon Futerman for his support and encouragement. My thanks for editorial assistance to Evelyn Grosberg, Michael Hareven and Emily Mallaby of Sinclair-Stevenson, and for his early efforts to Joshua Tadmor. Aaron S. Cohen and Sefton Cohen were unstinting with advice and help throughout the preparation of the book.

The Israeli military censor made brief deletions to the text. The author, an Israeli citizen, was required to state that 'the book is based on foreign sources, which in no way implies the veracity or non-veracity of the information in the book.'

February 1992

1. GOING NUCLEAR

'Israel will not be the first to introduce nuclear weapons into the region.' This time-honoured phrase, enunciated by six successive prime ministers from various political parties, has been the Jewish state's sole declared position on the nuclear option. 'Israel has no nuclear weapons, will not resort to using nuclear weapons and will not be the first to introduce such weapons into the region,' Prime Minister Itzhak Shamir told American reporters in 1983. On the day after the *Sunday Times* report it was repeated yet again by Prime Minister Shimon Peres.

Israel has never admitted to possessing nuclear weapons. She has, however, intimated more than once that she is quite capable of producing them, and has played up her scientific and nuclear energy achievements.[1] This seemingly contradictory posturing has been described as the 'bomb in the basement' policy, with the result that Arab states suspect or are convinced that Israel has stockpiled nuclear weapons and would be prepared to use them if faced with annihilation.

Although the phrase 'Israel would not be the first . . .' could be considered by foreign observers a bare-faced lie, like a Bible tract it may be talmudically interpreted in many ways to cover precise information regarding nuclear capability. 'The first to introduce' allows Israel to be the second. The term 'nuclear weapons' is consummate hairsplitting. Does it mean only assembled nuclear warheads (the 'bomb in the basement' school) or does it extend to unassembled

7

components or even nuclear arms infrastructure (the nuclear options school)? Are 'weapons' only offensive or are they also those intended for the 'peaceful' purpose of deterring an enemy? A nuclear weapon is defined by the proliferation treaty, and by others, as one which has been tested. To this day the claim that Israel has tested a nuclear device remains speculative.

'In the Middle East' need not refer simply to Arab countries which, with the exception of Iraq, have been many years away from producing nuclear weapons. It could include United States bases and ships. The Middle East may be defined as extending from Morocco to Afghanistan and including India and Pakistan. That Israel will not be the first to introduce nuclear weapons into the region remains as true today as it was thirty years ago.

It was to 'create doubt – and eventually resignation and despair – about the Arab dream of exterminating Israel from the world's map', as former Israeli foreign minister Abba Eban put it, which moved David Ben-Gurion, the country's first prime minister, to launch a nuclear research programme. In terms of territory, Israel's size may be compared to the American state of New Jersey, the British region of Wales, the West German *Land* of Hesse, the French region of Picardy, the island of Sardinia, or one-third of the Australian state of Tasmania. Israel's borders prior to the 1967 war narrowed to some thirteen kilometres between the Mediterranean Sea and Jordan. The goal was to guarantee the country's survival through Arab acceptance of the Jewish state, leading to an end of the state of war. Its partly disguised nuclear capability has over the years served to impress on Arab neighbours Israel's determination to survive by whatever means necessary.

The nuclear deterrent proved itself in the Arab–Israeli war in October 1973.[2] After the Egyptians repulsed the first Israeli counter-attack along the Suez Canal, causing heavy casualties, and Israeli forces on the Golan Heights were retreating in the face of a massive Syrian tank assault, thirteen nuclear bombs were hastily assembled by the Israelis during a seventy-eight-hour period.[3] At 10 p.m. on 8 October, the northern commander, Major-General Itzhak Hoffi, informed his superior, 'I am not sure that we can hold out much longer.' After midnight, Defence Minister Moshe Dayan solemnly warned Prime Minister Golda Meir: 'This is the end of the Third Temple': a symbolic comparison between the state of Israel and the first two Jewish temples destroyed by the Babylonians in 586BC and by the Romans in AD70. Mrs Meir gave Dayan permission to activate the nuclear weapons. As each bomb was assembled, it was rushed to waiting air force units, but before any triggers were set the battle on both fronts turned in Israel's favour, and the thirteen bombs were sent to desert arsenals.[4]

At the beginning of the 1982 Lebanon war, Defence Minister Ariel Sharon proposed that Israel launch a nuclear strike against Syria because, he said, Syria was about to attack the Golan Heights. But Prime Minister Menachem Begin flatly rejected the proposal.[5]

In becoming the world's sixth nuclear power after the US, the USSR, Britain, France and China,[6] Israel's nuclear development reads like a defence technology success story. Early on, a research and planning branch was established in the fledgling state's defence ministry, whose functions included the extraction of uranium from phosphate.[7] A pilot plant also enabled the production of heavy water, which is used in the separation of plutonium from uranium. In 1952 an atomic energy commission was established. In 1954 an agreement was signed with France for cooperation in heavy water and uranium production; another with the United States involved the building of a nuclear research centre for civilian purposes at Nahal Soreq. The official 'lineage' stops there.

In September 1956 France and Israel signed a secret agreement whereby France would supply Israel with a sizable plutonium-producing reactor to be built at Dimona.[8] Two months later Israel, France and Britain mounted a co-ordinated campaign to gain control of the Suez peninsula and canal. On the night that Israel was considering the United Nations request for a ceasefire, Ben-Gurion despatched Shimon Peres and Golda Meir to Paris to seek guarantees that France would help Israel develop the atomic bomb.[9] French Premier Guy Mollet, who had previously opposed France's own efforts to acquire nuclear arms, was an ardent admirer of Israel and anxious both to secure Israel's defence and to provide France with a counter-balance to Egypt in the Middle East. He agreed to France's own nuclear programme and to help Israel. Even though the Mollet government fell in spring 1957, a number of his top aides, who were also admirers of the young Jewish state, made good Mollet's commitment.[10] When Charles de Gaulle took power in June 1958 he authorised continuation of the work on the reactor but sought to slow construction of the plutonium processing plant, given its crucial role in bomb-making. However, partly on the instruction of Jacques Soustelle, de Gaulle's Minister for Atomic Research and another admirer of Israel, the work continued. Israeli scientists also observed a nuclear weapons test at a French site in the Algerian part of the Sahara desert[11] and France benefited from data provided by Israeli nuclear research.[12]

Raw materials have been obtained from a variety of sources: uranium supplies have reportedly come from Argentina, the Central African Republic, Gabon, Niger and South Africa, and heavy water for research purposes has come from Norway and the US.[13] Not infrequently, Israel employed covert means of acquisition.[14] In 1984 over forty tons of uranium which had been supplied by British companies to a Luxembourg company ostensibly for steel-making found its way to Israel. In 1985 an American was indicted by a Los Angeles court for illegally exporting to Israel 800 high-speed electronic switches, known as krytons, used in the triggering mechanisms of atomic weapons.[15]

The sensational information about Israel's nuclear pro-gramme given to the London *Sunday Times* in 1986 by former Dimona technician Mordechai Vanunu confirmed Israel's nuclear dominance of the region, and the newspaper estimated that Israel has between 100 and 200 nuclear weapons. She was believed to have delivery systems, manned aircraft and ballistic missiles for her nuclear stock-pile,[16] and reportedly as many as 100 nuclear-capable Jericho missiles. In 1989 Israel was said to have launched a Jericho missile which travelled 1,300km, and a joint Israeli–South African missile reportedly reached over 1,500km, bringing any Arab country as well as the Soviet Union within range. The Shavit missile being developed is, according to the Inter-national Institute for Strategic Studies, intended to have a 7,000km range.

Israel's reported possession of the nuclear bomb fills the vacuum created by developments in non-conventional arms in Arab countries. In the early sixties the Soviets built for Iraq an entire nuclear complex, including laboratories, at Tuwaitha, some twenty kilometres south-east of Baghdad, and trained 100 students in nuclear physics. Even as he plot-ted his rise to power in the mid-1970s when he was still vice-president, Saddam Hussein laid the foundation for Iraq's acquisition of nuclear weaponry. Gaining a nuclear capability was one aspect of the country's quest for domi-nance of the Persian Gulf and of the Arab world as a whole. In the 1970s Iraq purchased 250 tons of yellowcake – uranium-bearing ore – of which some 3 per cent of fission-able uranium is separated from the remaining non-fissionable element. A concentration of 90 per cent of fissionable uranium is required to make the bomb. The Soviets supplied a second research reactor in 1980, but neither this nor the earlier reactor had military significance because of their low megawattage. In 1980, however, France constructed at Osiraq a reactor with a higher megawattage which Israeli scientists calculated would be capable of producing one or two nuclear bombs a year.

But what was to be Iraq's giant leap into the nuclear club was halted a year later, on 7 June 1981, when the Israeli air force bombed the Osiraq reactor just before completion of its construction. Fourteen aircraft took part in the raid: eight F-16 Falcons, each carrying two 1,000kg bombs, escorted by six F-15 Eagles. Even though the reactor and its fuel were under the safeguards of, and subject to inspection by, the International Atomic Energy Authority, Israel was critical of these safeguards and believed Iraq was preparing to use the reactor for military purposes. Israel gave notice that it would not allow any Arab country with whom it was in a state of war to develop a nuclear arms capability. The policy was criticised within Israel as being problematic, including the difficulty of implementing such a policy after other states had already developed nuclear capability. It is also politically costly to carry out attacks on reactors supplied by western countries and the policy cannot be implemented against countries with whom Israel has peaceful relations.

When France refused to rebuild the reactor in the face of international pressures, Iraq tried to buy plutonium on the black market. In 1982 it paid $60m to several Italians who claimed to have access to stores of plutonium and highly-enriched uranium. The offer was a hoax and the Iraqis walked away empty-handed. Stung by this and by other setbacks, Iraq turned to enriching its own uranium by gas centrifuges. Up to 500 centrifuges, arranged in batteries called a cascade, are needed to produce the enrichment. Iraq's attempts to obtain the centrifuges in the US, Britain, Germany, France and Holland were blocked by the governments concerned. Iraq then embarked on producing its own. Hussein Kamal, Saddam's son-in-law, who headed the Technical Corps for Special Projects, ran a network of agents in front companies around the world to purchase seemingly innocuous machine parts for use in the manufacture of centrifuges and other stages in making the bomb. By 1987 Iraqi scientists had assembled a complete centrifuge laboratory from equipment bought in France, Germany, Switzerland and Liechtenstein. There was no shortage of uranium. About thirty pounds of enriched uranium, enough for one bomb, had been recovered from the 1981 air raid. Yellowcake had earlier been purchased from Brazil, Niger and Portugal. In addition, a sealed-off area in the Chiya Gara mountains, a region near Iraq's Turkish border, holds an open-cast uranium mine, which Saddam visited seven times in 1990 alone.

Until the 1990 Gulf crisis, American officials had estimated that it would take Iraq 5–10 years to acquire anything more than a single low-yield bomb given, as they believed, that Iraq lacked the facilities for separating uranium. But after the crisis broke, the Defense Intelligence Agency – which correctly forecast Saddam's plan to invade Kuwait – reduced its estimate from five to two years following information received from two agents inside Iraq and new details about Hussein Kamal's secret purchases of nuclear technology. Within weeks of the allied military operation against Iraq, the latter's nuclear arms potential was weakened. Early US claims that Iraq's non-conventional capability had been nullified proved exaggerated. Teams from the International Atomic Energy Authority subsequently combed Iraq for its nuclear and other non-conventional armaments facilities and for its enriched uranium. While much was discovered, there remain suspicions that Iraq has succeeded in moving weapons' parts and uranium to secret locations, with the intention of restarting its nuclear programme in the future.

Other Arab countries remained far behind Iraq in gaining a nuclear arms capability. While Egypt was the first Arab country to become interested in nuclear energy – by 1961 it had an operational nuclear reactor and plans for eight reactors by the end of the century – her attempts to gain nuclear

13

weapons have been limited. Syria is behind all the major Arab countries due to technological and budgetary limitations. The Soviet Union refused to give Syria nuclear arms, but undertook to come to her assistance if attacked. But with closer USSR–US ties, Syria felt less able to rely on Moscow. Libya flip-flopped from failing in a bid to obtain a nuclear bomb from China to opposing its acquisition on principle, but changed back again in 1987 with a declaration by Colonel Gadafy that 'the Arabs must possess the atomic bomb to defend themselves until their numbers reach one billion, until they learn to desalinate sea water, and until they liberate Palestine. We undertake not to drop the bomb on any state around us, but we must possess it.' After failing to obtain nuclear materials from a number of countries, Libya reportedly gave Pakistan some $200m to help finance its nuclear arms programme, but apparently received few benefits. Nor did a 1978 agreement with India fulfil Libyan hopes for technology or a nuclear device. Revolutionary Iran developed a small nuclear research reactor at Isfahan but, while it has succeeded in obtaining equipment and weapons-grade materials, particularly from Argentina, it has yet to achieve assembly of a plutonium processing plant.

Pakistan is the most advanced Muslim state in the field of nuclear arms, partly motivated by a need to counter India's nuclear option; India exploded a nuclear device in 1974. Pakistan began producing weapons-grade uranium in 1986 and notwithstanding reservations about supplying Libya with nuclear weapons, it is willing in the long term to share its nuclear arms achievements. 'When we acquire the technology, the entire Islamic world will possess it with us,' said then President Zia ul-Haq in 1986. Saudi Arabia, which has Silkworm missiles with a range of 2,000km, enough to reach Israel, and which are nuclear-carrying, has poured funds into Pakistan's nuclear programme, impressed by 'the development of the first Islamic and Arab nuclear bomb'. So

14

concerned is Israel at Pakistan's nuclear advances that it approached the Indian government for permission to use an Indian air base as a refuelling stop for Israeli planes en route to bomb the reactor.[17] But India turned Israel down. Israel then offered to supply the Indian air force with advanced high-explosive bombs which would be effective against the uranium plant. But this would have adversely affected India's relations with the Arabs and her position in the developing world, as well as exposing her own nuclear research centre to a Pakistani counter-strike.[18]

Implausible as it may sound, another worst-case scenario concerned the possibility of a Palestinian group gaining a nuclear device and holding Israel hostage. That groups practising terrorism might use nuclear devices to gain publicity or to achieve other results has long been a nightmare for western officials. The Palestine Liberation Organisation unsuccessfully tried to purchase some twelve kilograms of plutonium in the Sudanese black market.

Difficulties in producing nuclear weaponry have encouraged some Arab states to opt for the poor man's bomb: chemical weaponry. In addition to Iraq, countries believed to possess chemical weapons include Libya, Egypt and Iran. Iraq's missile programme was designed to use chemical-carrying warheads. Egypt was the first Arab country to use chemical weapons in the Yemeni civil war in the mid-sixties. As a result, on the eve of the 1967 Arab–Israeli war, Israel arranged for emergency shipments of gas masks from West Germany to be distributed among the population. Religious authorities in Israel went through the process of dedicating certain parks as graveyards, fearing massive casualties from Egyptian chemical attacks on civilian targets, but their fears were unrealised as the Egyptian air force was destroyed within hours of the opening of the war. In 1989 Egypt purchased equipment for a chemical gas plant from a Swiss company. In the mid-1980s Iraq produced an estimated sixty tons monthly of mustard gas

15

and four tons of the deadly nerve agents, Sarin and Tabun, at a secret plant forty kilometres south of the city of Samarra. The programme gained importance after the Israeli destruction of the Osiraq reactor.

Iraq began using chemical weapons in its war with Iran in 1984. Both mustard gas and Tabun were used on many occasions. In February 1986 about one in ten of the soldiers in a large Iranian force attacking Fao were killed or injured by chemical weapons. Iraq has been accused of using cyanide and mustard gas against Halabja, an Iraqi border city 240km north-east of Baghdad which had been overrun by Iranian forces in 1988. Foreign journalists who visited the city saw streets strewn with hundreds of corpses of civilians slain in a gas attack. Iranian officials estimated that 5,000 perished and a further 4,000 were wounded. Not much is known about Syria's chemical weapons capability, although she imported some from the Soviet Union, and these are located north of Damascus. Libya used chemical weapons during its incursions into Chad and the Sudan, having obtained the necessary materials from West Germany.

Little information is available concerning Arab biological weaponry, but both Iraq and Syria have been at different stages of development. Iraq had manufactured biological capabilities to spread cholera, typhoid, anthrax and other diseases. These can be delivered through missile or bomb but, unlike chemical substances, biological agents take a long time to disable the target population. Moreover, medications and vaccines exist for many of the viruses spread in biological warfare.

The logic behind the Israeli policy that nuclear capability should remain a matter of supposition can best be understood by considering the consequences of Israel going public. In the event of Israel's disclosing a nuclear capability, it would rally the Arab world, further complicate an uneasy Egypt–Israel relationship, and create internal pressure on

16

Arab governments to balance Israel's capability. Given the Arab states' technological and economic limitations, they would certainly lean on their supplier states, which would be under certain pressure to provide parity. Going public could also seriously complicate the US aid package to Israel. According to the 1976 Symington Clause of the Foreign Assistance Act, a US administration must cut off economic aid and military grants or credit to any country which imports uranium enrichment technology or materials without accepting the safeguards of the International Atomic Energy Authority on its nuclear facilities.

While Israel is a member of the Vienna-based International Atomic Energy Authority, only the nuclear reactor at Nahal Soreq, which Israel declares is used for peaceful purposes, is open for inspection to the IAEA. Like most of the other nuclear states, Israel has not signed the non-proliferation treaty which requires signatories to open all nuclear facilities to inspection. (These other states include France, China, India, Pakistan, Brazil, Argentina.) Most of the signatories are those without the bomb; Arab signatories have added the reservation which denies any change in their state of war with Israel.

Total ambiguity about the Israeli nuclear option had a very short lifespan. Impairment of the image occurred at two levels: the political declaratory one and the technical. In 1956, when Israel and France signed the secret agreement for the construction of the nuclear reactor at Dimona, all the members of Israel's Atomic Energy Commission, except its chairman, resigned because they thought that Israel's nuclear priorities should be economic rather than defence orientated.[19] And when the Eisenhower administration asked about the construction of the reactor at Dimona and the establishment of a strict security zone around it, Prime Minister Ben-Gurion assured Washington that it was a textile plant. This was later amended to a water-pumping station.[20]

The posture of ambiguity emerged as a result of a compromise between those Israeli ministers and officials who backed going public with a nuclear option and those, including Levi Eshkol, Yigal Allon and Ariel Sharon, who said that Israel's defence should be based on conventional arms. It remains unclear exactly when the line that 'Israel will not be the first to introduce nuclear weapons into the region' was first conceived. Some say Ben-Gurion pulled it out of his sleeve when he met President de Gaulle in Paris in June 1960. The two conversed relaxedly about the future of Algeria, the global political situation and the doctrines of the great philosophers. Suddenly de Gaulle shifted gear, fixed Ben-Gurion with a hawk-like stare and roared: 'Tell me honestly, Mr Ben-Gurion, why do you need a nuclear reactor?' Taken aback, Ben-Gurion assured the French president that Israel would not manufacture an atomic weapon at the reactor and that it would not be the first to introduce nuclear arms into the Middle East.

The first serious challenge to the country's nuclear ambiguity occurred when, in December 1960, an American U-2 spyplane photographed the reactor. The CIA revealed to an emergency session of the Nuclear Energy Congressional Committee that what the Eisenhower administration had been led to believe was a textile plant was a large and tightly guarded nuclear facility. 'Israel was on its way to becoming the fifth nuclear power,' the CIA staffer told the committee. It led to a crisis in US–Israel relations. Washington was upset that it had been lied to and that the CIA had failed to detect it for over three years: CIA head Allan Dulles was sacked partly for this, although the error was so embarrassing that his dismissal by President Kennedy was delayed.[21] The US asked Israel whether it was planning to go into nuclear weapons production. Ben-Gurion had to acknowledge to the Knesset that a thermal reactor was being constructed in the Negev with French assistance, but said that it would be devoted to peaceful ends. Yet surprisingly Deputy Defence

Minister Shimon Peres was still claiming in 1963 that Dimona was a water desalination plant 'intended to turn the Negev into a garden'. To verify that the reactor was being used for civilian purposes only, the Kennedy and Johnson administrations insisted on inspecting Dimona, making weapons sales conditional on these. American nuclear scientists visited the reactor in 1961 and 1963, while it was being built, and reported that no chemical separation plant was being constructed. So did inspectors between 1964 and 1967, although these added that adequate inspection was not possible because of the hurried and limited nature of the visits allowed. A team which visited the facility in 1969 submitted a written complaint that it 'could not guarantee that there was no weapons-related work at Dimona in view of the limitations imposed by the Israelis on its inspection procedures'. Vanunu told the *Sunday Times* about a false wall built on the ground floor of Machon 2 to disguise the service lifts to the subterranean floors beneath which plutonium was separated and bomb parts manufactured.

Nuclear ambiguity was further undermined after a number of unauthorised statements by senior Israeli officials. While serving as president of Israel (a mostly symbolic office), Ephraim Katzir, himself a scientist of some international renown for his work in physical chemistry and biology on polyelectrolytes and an important figure in Israel's Atomic Energy Commission, told a group of American and European scientific journalists in December 1974 that 'Israel has a nuclear potential'. A reporter followed it up with a question about the capability and time limit for realising the nuclear potential, to which Katzir retorted: 'Do you think I'd state a date here in these circumstances?' Another asked whether Israel's nuclear potential was not a worrisome phenomenon. Katzir replied: 'Why should this matter worry us? Let the world do the worrying.' His remarks set off a chain reaction around the world, and Israel's Foreign Ministry quickly got the president's office to put out a clarifier that Katzir was referring to 'the general potential in Israel of scientists and general scientific-technological experience that objectively could be implemented if so desired'.

Two years later, Moshe Dayan, who had resigned as defence minister in the aftermath of the 1973 Yom Kippur War, told French TV, 'For Israel, the future should include the option and possibility of possessing nuclear weapons without any external control. I think we have the possibility of manufacturing the bomb now. I believe that if the Arabs introduce an atomic bomb into the Middle East sometime in the future, we ought to have a bomb before they do, yet naturally not in order to use it first.' Dayan was one of Israel's political elite who favoured Israel's going public, arguing that a military deterrent comprised solely of conventional weaponry had a crippling effect on the national economy. A political row broke out with Moshe Arens claiming that Dayan's remark could severely harm Israel. A few months later, Dayan said during a visit to Canada, 'Israel possesses the scientific and technological capability to produce an atomic bomb, should the Arabs threaten to use such a bomb, but Israel will never be the first to launch nuclear warfare in the Middle East.'

It is not difficult for this sophistry to take on the air of double-talk. Dayan, then foreign minister, told a visiting delegation from the US House of Representatives Armed Services Committee in February 1978, when asked about an Israeli nuclear capability, 'We won't be the first to use nuclear weapons, but we wouldn't like to be the third element to do so.' Itzhak Rabin, who has stuck closer to the official formula, was once asked, after reiterating that Israel would not be the first to introduce nuclear weapons, 'How fast will Israel succeed in becoming the second state to do this?' 'Well, it's difficult to answer that,' he replied, 'I hope the other side won't be tempted to introduce nuclear weapons. I believe we can't afford to be the second, yet we'll have to be neither the first nor, at the same time, the second.

And this depends on when one of the sides decided to do it.'

Ambiguity was also impaired by international speculation on whether Israel had carried out any nuclear tests. In September 1979 US satellites recorded a double flash of light originating from the South Atlantic–Indian Ocean area. Both the CIA and the Defense Intelligence Agency (DIA) concluded that it had come from a joint South African–Israeli testing of a nuclear device. But a scientific panel set up by President Carter suggested that the flash probably resulted from the impact of a small meteorite on a satellite. Israel reportedly carried out underground nuclear tests in the Negev as early as 1963,[22] and it has been suggested that Israeli nuclear scientists are competent enough to design nuclear weapons using implosion techniques that do not need full-scale tests.[23] Testing of the Jericho missile's warhead and its nuclear explosion potential is said to have been carried out by computer simulation, obviating the need to detonate the weapon.[24] But thermonuclear weapons require some type of tests.

On 5 October 1986 Vanunu's structural details of the nuclear research centre at Dimona were published in the *Sunday Times*, and he described what his work comprised and what he had seen. He provided data about the plutonium production process, which enabled the newspaper and its scientific advisers to draw up their estimate of 100–200 Israeli warheads. Yet it was not the first time that an estimate of this size had been made. In 1981 Israel was said to possess 100 nuclear devices and in 1985 *Aerospace Daily* quoted unnamed sources that Israel might possess 200 nuclear weapons. According to Dr Frank Barnaby, who debriefed Vanunu for the newspaper, the significance of his allegations was threefold.

'First, the actual size of the Dimona reactor is much larger, five or six times larger, than we first thought. Israel has produced a great deal more plutonium than we first thought

21

– thirty-two kilograms a year which is enough for about eight nuclear weapons.' Accordingly, Israel may have 150 nuclear bombs, or enough plutonium for them, each equivalent to one dropped on Nagasaki, Barnaby said. 'The most interesting thing that Vanunu told us is that Israel is producing lithium deuteride and tritium, the material needed for thermonuclear weapons.' Tritium's value in nuclear weapons is based on its high rate of fusion with deuterium and the large numbers of high-energy neutrons released in this reaction. The fusion of deuterium and tritium produces ten times as many neutrons as fission for the same energy release. These can produce an explosion equal to hundreds of thousands of tons of TNT, capable of destroying an entire city. 'The third interesting thing is that his story and photographs prove that the French provided the Israelis with not only the Dimona reactor but also the plutonium processing plant.' Even more information would have come out, denting further the image of ambiguity, had Vanunu not been abducted back to Israel. The *Sunday Times* planned to follow up the initial exposé, but were unable to check the reports with their informer.

Given the considerable strategic benefit to Israel's military posture gained from the estimate that it possesses 100–200 nuclear warheads, the *Sunday Times* and Barnaby suspected that Vanunu was given just enough rope to take the photographs inside the reactor and make his disclosure to the newspaper. After all, the Mossad reportedly knew about Vanunu while he was still in Australia before coming to London for a month to be debriefed by the newspaper.[25] On the day after the *Sunday Times* published its exposé Yaakov Kirschen, then the cartoonist of the *Jerusalem Post*'s 'Dry Bones', drew a cartoon showing President Assad scowling at a newspaper and saying, 'Israel has the N-bomb? I don't believe it! Obviously, a lie planted by Zionist agents to scare us! On the other hand maybe they leaked the truth so that we would think that it was a trick and not believe it!' And, if Barnaby and the *Sunday Times* were correct that Vanunu was being used by the Israeli authorities, it follows that Barnaby and the *Sunday Times*, owned by pro-Israel Rupert Murdoch, were if not knowing at least unknowing participants in an Israeli disinformation plan. All this assumes Israel's willingness to have the most sensitive details about Dimona's structure and the plutonium production process published,[26] as well as estimates to be calculated of the capability itself.

To what extent have Vanunu's allegations been accepted by nuclear scientists and, more importantly, by Arab states and other foreign governments? Vanunu said that his own involvement was limited to certain sections of the Dimona complex. He had not seen a completed weapon, nor did he have direct knowledge of any Israeli nuclear arsenal. It is therefore possible that the fusion components Vanunu photographed are experimental weapons and that simple atomic bombs of more certain reliability form the backbone of Israel's nuclear arsenal, according to Leonard Spector of the Nuclear Proliferation Program at the Carnegie Endowment Fund. In its own estimate made in 1987 that Israel possessed up to 100 nuclear weapons, the London-based International Institute of Strategic Studies had agreed to a considerable extent with the *Sunday Times* estimate. (This estimate has not altered since then.) US officials, however, while accepting the authenticity of Vanunu's technical data, challenged the *Sunday Times* estimate because it was inconsistent with other relevant information in their possession suggesting that Israel had no more than 50–60 plutonium-using devices. (Five years later, US intelligence estimates were that Israel possessed 60–80 nuclear devices.)

US officials questioned the *Sunday Times*'s claim that the reactor's megawattage increased six times from twenty-four megawatts to 150 megawatts. The French–Israeli agreement allowed for only a twenty-four megawatt reactor. Yet

Vanunu's claim that forty kilograms of plutonium were produced annually would require a 150 megawattage. This led the *Sunday Times* to conclude that the reactor had been enlarged six times. But US officials were sceptical because that would require a very large number of additional cooling units. They believed that the original twenty-four megawattage was not changed substantially, but may have operated at about forty megawatts because of cooling efficiencies permitted by the desert climate. Accordingly, they claimed that Israel had 50–60 warheads rather than the 100–200 estimated by the *Sunday Times*. The US estimate is based on the nine-year period when Vanunu worked at Dimona – the only solid information available. Barnaby argues that reprocessing did not just begin on the day Vanunu walked through the doors at Dimona; his estimate includes some sixty warheads for the earlier period. Had Barnaby based this solely on the nine years Vanunu was there, he would agree with the US figure: ninety warheads, or a conservative estimate of sixty, which assumes that the optimum quantity of plutonium is not reached due to factors such as wastage.

Unnamed experts, quoted by *The Economist Foreign Report*, expressed surprise that Israel's plutonium processing plant was underground since the operation is highly toxic and radioactive; a minor accident could endanger the whole operation. However, Dr Perrin told the *Sunday Times* that France had built the underground facility. There was also surprise when the components for bombs were said to be assembled beneath the reprocessing plant in Machon 2's underground facility, involving unnecessary risk.

Vanunu's allegations aroused much interest in the Arab world, but attention was focused less upon the precise details of his claims than on the general issue and history of Israel's nuclear capability. Many Arabs did not regard the information as anything new but rather as confirming what was already known. 'Vanunu is no Columbus,' the Abu Dhabi daily *Al-Atihad* wrote. In 1966 Nasser condemned Israeli

24

efforts to build an atomic bomb and threatened preventive action. During the historic Sadat visit to Jerusalem in 1977 Egyptian Prime Minister Mustapha Khalil told Israeli minister Ezer Weizman, 'What have you got to be afraid of. You've got nuclear weapons . . .' The possibility was raised among some Arab commentators that Vanunu's leak was part of a Mossad plot to raise Israel's military posture. But most saw the *Sunday Times* report as the result of a genuine security leak. Arab leaders did not rush to release statements condemning Israel, wishing neither to show they were 'being deterred' nor to arouse internal public calls for an Islamic bomb. According to William Eagleton, former US ambassador to Damascus, Syrian President Hafez el-Assad appears to accept Israel's nuclear potential as a matter of fact, but he will not refer to it in conversation with western diplomats.

Post-Vanunu reaction also took on a prescriptive tone, namely the question of how the Arab world should counter the perceived nuclear threat from Israel. A Radio Damascus commentator said, 'the nuclear weapon does not need to exist in one place, or be the monopoly of one particular people.' Seeing the Vanunu disclosures 'as proof that conflict with Israel is unavoidable', the Egyptian opposition paper *Al-Shaab* said that Israel's nuclear potential 'obligates Egypt to adopt a nuclear option'. In republishing the report from the *Sunday Times, Al-Shaab* wrote, 'our intention is not to arouse fears because of Israel but to arouse Egyptian public opinion and to declare to our government the iniquities successive Egyptian administrations since Sadat have committed against the country's national security in giving a one-sided advantage to Israel.' According to the head of Israeli military intelligence, General Amnon Shahak, 'the Vanunu affair and publications about Israel's ballistic capability accelerated Syria's construction of a non-conventional capability in the sphere of chemical weaponry.'

Arab will was mainly translated into diplomatic action. An Arab resolution – similar to those passed in recent years

– calling for the United Nations to investigate Israel's nuclear programme, and for nuclear cooperation with other countries, was passed in the UN General Assembly by a majority of ninety-two to two (the United States and Israel), with forty-two abstentions. A UN report published in October 1987 said that while it had no proof there is 'a strong impression that Israel possesses the potential to make nuclear arms'. It offered as evidence Israel's reluctance to confirm or deny a nuclear arms capability, its contradictory statements regarding nuclear arms, and its refusal to sign the non-proliferation treaty. A confidential report of the International Atomic Energy Authority on Vanunu's disclosure sounded an urgent alarm, and warned that Israel's nuclear programme 'had torn apart the fabric of the international atomic control system'.

The story had little impact on official United States policy: 'We are concerned by the existence of unsafeguarded nuclear facilities and have made our concern known to Israel. We have urged Israel to accept comprehensive safeguards,' Charles Redman, the State Department spokesman, said at a briefing on the day after the *Sunday Times*'s publication. This repeated the standard position taken by successive US administrations, but within official circles the revelations had considerable significance. President Reagan convened the Jason Committee – the administration's highest scientific advisory group which meets behind closed doors to analyse major scientific national security developments – to assess the impact on US strategy. Arms analysts at the Los Alamos and Livermore nuclear laboratories examined Vanunu's testimony, including much not published in the newspaper, and fifty-seven photographs Vanunu had taken inside the Dimona centre. They reconstructed replicas from the photographs showing warheads,[27] and officials were surprised at the scope of the Israeli programme. They accepted the newspaper's claim that Israel was producing the neutron bomb, but they disagreed with the estimate of Israel's warheads, arguing that the statistics reflected the peak rate of production. A change occurred in the attitude of the Bush administration, whose concern about nuclear and chemical arms proliferation was high among its international priorities. Stiffer procedures for visits by Israeli scientists to American nuclear laboratories were reportedly introduced.[28]

One area in the Jewish State's relationship with the United States which might have been affected by the *Sunday Times*'s allegations was Congressional approval of the Administration's foreign aid package to Israel. Observers pointed to the 1975 case when Congress held up the planned sale to Israel of Pershing surface-to-surface missiles which, they noted, could be fitted with nuclear warheads. While the Vanunu disclosures were examined in the Joint Congressional Committee on Nuclear Policy, there was no major initiative to cut off foreign aid. In fact, the quantity of US financial aid, and type of military hardware, did not change in the two years following the report. It also had less impact on the American peace movement than on the European peace movement where Vanunu became one point of focus in the anti-nuclear campaign, due to the closer ties between the United States and Israel, as well as to the considerable number of Jews in the American peace movement. Israel was later to face another potential challenge from the US after the NBC television network claimed in October 1989 that Israeli–South African nuclear cooperation included the joint testing of an intercontinental missile over a 1,500km range. Questions were asked whether Israel had given South Africa access to US missile technology.

Most congressional attempts to control nuclear proliferation have failed. One case where it succeeded was in Taiwan, which in 1987 began constructing a small-scale plutonium extraction unit. In March 1988, under US pressure, Taiwan agreed to halt work and dismantle the Canadian-supplied research reactor. The US has applied a double standard in implementing congressional controls on foreign aid among the new nuclear nations. 'India, which exploded a nuclear device in 1974, and Israel, which is generally assumed to have the bomb, are somehow exempt from US punitive actions,' Pakistani journalist Mushahid Hussain argued. By contrast, 'Pakistan, a closed ally that has not tested a weapon, is periodically pushed around.'

The nuclear issue had been played by both sides. In 1961 President Kennedy offered Israel Hawk missiles in return for an undertaking not to develop nuclear weapons.[29] The climax of the policy of 'nuclear exchange' was the US agreement in 1966 to sell Israel Patton tanks and Skyhawk fighter bombers.[30] Shortly after the Vanunu exposé, Amos Rubin, Prime Minister Shamir's economic adviser, told the *Christian Science Monitor*, 'If left to its own Israel will have no choice but to fall on a riskier defence which will endanger itself and the world at large. To enable Israel to abstain from dependence on nuclear arms calls for $2-3bn in US aid.'

There was also no reaction from the Soviet Union, which followed the Soviet practice of discouraging Arab states from requesting help with non-conventional hardware. The most Moscow has done has been to supply Arab states with advanced conventional weaponry, such as Scud missiles, and vague promises of protection in the event of nuclear attack.

West European governments, anxious not to encourage Arab nuclear arms proliferation, also played down the revelations. The French Foreign Ministry spokesman had 'no comment, none' regarding the claim by Dr Francis Perrin that France had helped construct a plutonium processing plant at Dimona. Jean-Bernard Raymond, the French foreign minister, said, 'Vanunu's exposé repeats what has been well known for many years. The cooperation ended in 1959; thirty years is certainly enough time for Israeli scientists to gather enough nuclear information without any connection to the French–Israeli cooperation of the 1950s.'

The only diplomatic relationship significantly affected was with Norway. In 1959 Israel purchased twenty-two tons of heavy water from a Norwegian company. Heavy water allows nuclear reactors to run on natural uranium, which is widely available, rather than on enriched uranium fuel, which is scarce and tightly controlled. Norway had imposed what were at the time unusually strict controls over the material, getting Israel's pledge to use it exclusively for peaceful purposes and obtaining the right to inspect it to verify that Israel was adhering to its pledge. But Norway conducted only one inspection, in 1961, prior to completion of the Dimona reactor.[31]

After the *Sunday Times* story Norwegian politicians and other public figures demanded to know the fate of the heavy water, pressing the government to take up Norway's right of inspection. Initially Israel rejected Norwegian requests that the heavy water be inspected by the IAEA on the grounds that the Norwegian supply had become mixed with other supplies, and that the IAEA was biased. But as parliamentary and public pressure increased, the Norwegian government told Jerusalem that unless it could inspect the heavy water, Oslo would insist on its being returned. In April 1988 the two governments initialled an agreement under which Norwegian inspectors would be allowed to see the heavy water in the first year, and in subsequent years the IAEA could inspect. (IAEA inspections are considered more rigorous than Norway's.) It was also a compromise for Norway: under the terms of the agreement they would be unable to determine whether in the long years intervening Israel had used the heavy water to manufacture nuclear weapons. However, the Norwegian parliament's Foreign Affairs Committee rejected the compromise formula, insisting on knowing what had happened to the heavy water. This could only be discovered, the Norwegians said, if they had access to Israel's nuclear research facilities. After renewed negotiations Israel agreed in April 1990 to return to Norway the remainder of the heavy water which she had, 10.5 tons.

In October 1988 Norway, one of the world's chief suppliers, announced a ban on exports of heavy water, apart from tiny amounts required for scientific research. The decision was a culmination of the Norwegian–Israeli crisis and of the suspected diversion to India of fifteen tons of heavy water supplied to a West German company, and to Israel of 12.5 tons supplied to Romania in 1986.

Within the international scientific community, the revelations raised the level of discourse about Israeli nuclear capability. Israel's programme, according to one nuclear proliferation expert, was 'always hush-hush. Everyone was uncomfortable about mentioning it – everybody agrees there is no benefit in publishing it.' But 'it was out of the closet now', he added. Government officials opened up. 'Before Vanunu, the Israeli programme was treated with enormous secrecy by US officials, off-limits in even off-the-record conversations,' another expert remarked. 'Afterwards, though they wouldn't go into classified information, there was still enough in the public domain to start an educated discussion on the direction of the programme and the implications of the veracity of Vanunu's allegations.'

The exposé had little impact on Israeli nuclear policy itself. 'Israeli policy has not changed. We will not be the first to introduce nuclear weapons into the region,' Prime Minister Peres told the Israeli Cabinet meeting on the morrow of the *Sunday Times* report. 'The government is used to sensational press reports on the subject of the nuclear research centre at Dimona, and we are not accustomed to relate to them,' he added. Moreover, addressing fellow Labour Knesset members, Peres said that the story 'did not weaken us'. There was increased reference in official Israeli declaratory policy to non-conventional deterrence. General Amnon Shahak said in December 1986, 'It was obvious to the Arabs that because of Israeli military strength and the backing it enjoys from the United States they will not be able to annihilate Israel in a military strike. The Arabs believe Israel also has a non-conventional power.'

The option of Israel going public with any nuclear capability has long been debated within the informed elite of Israeli and other strategic thinkers. Adherents of going public point to a variety of arguments in favour. A logical mutual deterrence system would replace random decision-making. An undisguised deterrent would not only be clear and precise but credible. A mutual deterrence system requires a second strike force to hit back after the enemy force has destroyed some of a country's nuclear forces: the *Sunday Times* suggests that Israel possesses such a second strike capability. Any public nuclear deterrent could also enable Israel to make territorial concessions towards resolving the Arab–Israeli dispute without jeopardising its security. In addition, it might be a counter to any superpower attempting to expand influence in the region.

A major argument of some who favour incorporating a nuclear capability into Israel's formal military deterrent is one of economics. It would relieve conventional weaponry of the brunt of deterring the enemy, enabling qualitative improvements in conventional weaponry to be carried out and reducing the crippling defence budget. The $64,000 question is twofold. First, what effect would this have on the foreign aid budget from the United States? Is the bilateral relationship so important and crucial to the United States that the US administration would agree to the same volume of defence and economic aid when Israel had acknowledged nuclear capability? Would – and could – the US administration push legislation through Congress which would put the onus on Arab states by requiring their chemical weaponry capability to be placed under international supervision before US aid assistance could be interrupted? In the face of congressional pressure to cut off US aid to Pakistan

31

after Pakistani officials hinted that their country possessed the bomb, the Reagan administration enacted legislation in December 1987 which would have required India to place its nuclear facilities under international supervision before any suspension of economic assistance to Pakistan.

The second and even more difficult question concerns Arab reaction to an Israeli decision to go public about something they have long believed exists. The *Sunday Times* allegations do not appear to have triggered a major Arab arms race. This was also true in 1960 after the American U-2 spyplane photographed the construction of the nuclear reactor at Dimona. Given economic and technological limitations to achieving a nuclear potential, it did not become a major issue in Arab domestic agendas. Israel's going public with a nuclear capability when both Arab world attention and superpower attention were otherwise occupied could be as important as any other factor in influencing short-term regional and international reaction.

Supporters of the existing ambiguity policy point, first, to the seemingly crazy actions of some Arab states where decision-making is often centralised in the hands of one (not always rational) person. A mutual deterrent system assumes rationality on the part of the two sides concerned. Second, an Israeli bomb could pressure Arab states to pursue nuclear parity, increasing the Middle East arms race. Third, a deterrent involving nuclear forces would reduce the flexibility which conventional forces enjoy: nuclear weaponry cannot deal with the problem of terrorists and terrorism. It can serve only as a weapon of last resort. Fourth, going public would add to the diplomatic difficulties in Israel's overt and covert actions against Arab attempts to develop a nonconventional capability, such as the 1981 air strike on the Iraqi nuclear reactor. And fifth, ambiguity has been shown to work. The Arabs have been deterred, as evidenced in the 1973 war when, after crossing the Suez Canal, Egyptian forces took the Sinai but did not continue into the Israeli headland. Furthermore, it is the incalculability of the irreversible step of going public which leads ambiguity's backers, like Alan Dowty of Notre Dame University, to conclude that 'the current situation is comprehensible, familiar and – in a sense – secure!'

2. THE LIFE AND TIMES OF MOTTI VANUNU

Shlomo and Mazal Vanunu lived comfortably in Marrakesh, Morocco in the 1950s. They were Jews raised in poverty who struggled to improve their lot. Shlomo ran their grocery store and Mazal, his wife, moonlighted as a dressmaker. This earned them enough for a house with running water and drainage, a backyard for the children, and an Arab servant. It was life in an Arab country, speaking Arabic and dressing in long Arab gowns and desert sandals, but Shlomo, whose father-in-law Rabbi Ben-Abu was a widely respected scholar, wanted his children to receive a fine Jewish as well as a general education.

Their son Mordechai was born to this Jewish–Arab existence on 13 October 1954. He was educated at the Alliance, a French-language, secular Jewish school. He helped out a lot at home and was also close to his grandfather, daily taking to him the food Mazal had prepared. It was a life which, if not idyllic, was peaceful and better than that enjoyed by many other Jews in the Arab world.

Life for Moroccan Jews, however, was changing. Unbeknown to the Moroccan authorities, Jewish Agency officials had been in the country since the 1950s encouraging families to emigrate to the young state of Israel. Small and large groups of emigrants were secretly organised. The Vanunus were among the last to decide to leave Marrakesh, delayed by their reluctance to leave behind the grandfather, who had become ill. But after he died in 1963 they decided to leave.

Shlomo sold the grocery store and the one-storey house. On the day the Vanunu family were ready to leave, Mazal dressed the six children in French-style clothing and straw hats. After reaching Casablanca by train, the family travelled by ship to Marseilles. Shlomo took the opportunity there to buy a refrigerator, washing machine, radio, tape recorder, and even carpets, to take with them to their new home.

When the family arrived in Israel they were sent to Beersheba, Israel's fourth largest city. Situated in the south of the country on the edge of the Negev desert, its population of 70,000 comprised new immigrants, many from north Africa. Others came from Iraq, India and east Europe. Large suburbs to the north and north-west of the city were built to absorb the new arrivals. But the Vanunus' dreams of the good life in the land of their forefathers were quickly dashed. They were given a large hut with collapsible beds and mattresses. There was no dividing wall. To this day the children remember being told to put the refrigerator and carpet in the middle of the hut. It took the family a number of months, perhaps half a year, to resign themselves to their way of life in Israel. They felt as though they had traded the Garden of Eden for the wilderness. Shlomo contacted relatives living in Migdal Haemek in the north of Israel, and an uncle suggested they go there to a small vacant apartment owned by the state-subsidised housing company, Amidar. They did, but were evicted from it and sent back to Beersheba.

The ingathering of the Jews may have been a foundation of the Zionist dream, but it was not easy for the young Jewish state to absorb so many immigrants in so short a time. The houses for new immigrants were small, often hopelessly inadequate for the many large families. The veterans, mostly Israelis of European stock, had improved their skills and occupied most of the senior administrative and managerial positions. Elementary education was free and universal, but standards were lower in the new immigrant areas where it was difficult to find good teachers. Perhaps the most serious aspects of the problems surrounding Israel's absorption of the oriental Jews were the psychological ones. The wide gap between the status and achievements of the European Ashkenazi and the oriental Sephardi communities was in part due to favouritism and prejudice. Immigrants were popularly labelled with different degrees of disdain: the east Europeans as robbers, the Americans as having dollars, and so on. The Moroccans were held in lowest esteem, as primitives coming from beyond the Atlas Mountains.

The Vanunus were soon moved to a small house in Beersheba's 'Daled' neighbourhood, where they were to stay for the next eight years. Daled was a conservative area, with many religious people who were politically to the right. But it was also the city's drug centre. It was not easy to bring up a family in an area where so many had at one time or another been charged with criminal offences. Entertainment consisted of a film every couple of months which would be shown on one of the outer walls of a building. Even though Beersheba was an industrial centre, producing ceramics, pesticides and textiles, the only work Shlomo found was in share-cropping and heavy labour – quite a letdown from running a grocery store. The father of seven cried about the way he was treated in his homeland. He eventually became ill and was hospitalised. Twenty-five years later he had a stall selling religious artefacts in the city market.

'My parents had much to despair about and most of it fell on their children. We should not have received the treatment we received,' Mordechai would write one day. The children, though, did make their way, and Mordechai himself received a university education and earned a respectable salary at a nuclear research centre.

The family life-style became more religious in accordance with the practice of the Ashkenazi-led religious establishment in Israel. The radio was no longer left on during the

Sabbath as it had been in the more relaxed atmosphere prevalent in Morocco. Mazal modestly covered her hair all the time instead of only when going to synagogue. Shlomo was looked upon as a rabbi at the small *shul*, or synagogue, where he prayed daily. Mordechai was put by his father in the junior Bet Yaakov school, an independent network of schools which provided a more intensive Jewish religious education than the state-administered school system.

The choice of schooling by orthodox Jewish parents is of considerable importance. For a son to be given an intense grounding in the Torah and the books of Jewish law, to grow up observant and perhaps even spend his entire life studying the Torah, is the dream of very orthodox parents. At least, should the son take a secular job, he should have a complete grounding in these subjects, which would form the basis of the family fabric. The state religious system taught the entire spectrum of general subjects in addition to the religious ones, thereby preparing students for the matriculation exams required for university entrance, but did not ensure that all students remained religious. It was not surprising therefore that after three years, when Mordechai completed junior school in 1966, Shlomo put his son in a *yeshiva katanah*, a high-school version of a talmudical college, where boys concentrated in the main on studying the Talmud. In spending most of their time with one religious instructor, the boys, who slept away from home, were under the influence of an educator rather than a teacher in the narrower sense. But Mordechai failed to become absorbed in it.

His father transferred him to the Wolfson *yeshiva*, which was a new boarding school providing a more modern education with many of the secular studies and preparation for matriculation, but also intensive religious studies. 'Vanunu's problem was the same as all the children of the big wave of Moroccan immigrants,' according to Rabbi Joshua Shalkovsky, then a religious studies teacher at Wolfson. 'There was a cultural gap between the parents and the children. Israeli culture was very different in terms of values, interests and mannerisms. The idols of the new state were the ones which captured the attention of the youth. They looked on their parents as primitive, backward, even if they had lived in cities and towns in North Africa.' According to one of Mordechai's brothers, Asher, 'When I was in a religious framework I was full of doubts and questions. I didn't have the opportunity to understand what was happening on the other side of the fence. I wanted to look at forbidden places. But I am not a rebel.'

'Wolfson was not the best possible choice,' Meir, another brother added. 'It was a compromise. My father wasn't interested in secular studies and general education. His dream was a more religious education.' Initially, Mordechai's photographic memory proved ideal for memorising passages from the Torah and the Talmud, but after some time he became withdrawn, associating with the less religious boys, becoming one of the so-called Gang of Three in the class. At one stage the principal, Rabbi Silbert, suggested to Shlomo Vanunu that he find another school for his son. Mordechai was discovered shaving with an open razor in contravention of Jewish religious law which requires a closed blade shaver. The turning point was when he was caught listening to the radio on the Sabbath.

The reaction of the school authorities was a microcosmic consequence of the pressures placed by the modern environment on the religious school. A staff meeting was specially convened. 'We were faced with an acute dilemma,' one of the teachers remarked. 'On the one hand, to throw out the boy would ensure that he understood the seriousness of the matter. If we didn't do anything our esteem in the eyes of the religious boys would go down tremendously. On the other hand, it would mean that he was lost for good. There were among us some who did not believe in throwing a boy out.' While in some cases pressures came from fathers not to ask a boy to leave, in this case some staff members had sympathy for Mordechai's father because he was religious and was trying to improve his children's upbringing. Another difficulty was that the school was not yet sufficiently established to be able to send its drop-outs to other schools.

The educators were not unaware of the underlying problems. For one, many of the boys came from Beersheba's Daled neighbourhood, the very influence Shlomo, in sending his son to the boarding school, had hoped to avoid. Beersheba Daled's problems were in effect imported into a school which had wanted to be isolated from them. Another difficulty was that Mordechai's class was the amalgamation of two classes because one of the teachers became sick. The teacher was not replaced and the forty boys did not receive the personal attention which they might otherwise have received. Yet another may have been the very long school day resulting from the combined secular and religious studies programme.

By the time Mordechai left Wolfson after matriculation there was, according to Meir, 'a continuous conflict at home, a conflict which was to reach to the very foundations of the family framework. As with other families, there were noisy arguments. Father and mother lost their traditional authority.' It was a far cry from Mordechai's younger days, when his good nature endeared him to his father, making him his favourite, and when he was a role model for the younger brothers and sisters who treated him with a certain deference.

Mordechai hoped to get into the air force for his three-year national service and become a pilot, but he failed the exams. Instead, he joined the Engineering Corps, rising to be a squad commander. According to his army certificate, 'He was a very good NCO, carried out his task as required, and possessed initiative.' He turned down the option of signing on as a commissioned officer in favour of university. He was accepted to major in physics at Tel Aviv University in 1975, but left at the end of the first year because of his need to work to support himself. His work in a bakery and then as a guard at a lunar park, together with the forty days' compulsory reserve service, upset his academic study. He returned to Beersheba.

After answering an advertisement for trainee technicians at the Dimona nuclear research centre, he was asked at his first interview about his political affiliations. At that time, Mordechai supported Menachem Begin, who the following year led the Herut Party to political victory, ending thirty years of Labour Party rule. Typical of many oriental Jews, he looked to Herut to liberate them from the Labour Party's hold on Israeli bureaucracy and public life, but his support was not more than that of a passive participant. He was also asked about any criminal offences, drug or alcohol problems, as candidates with social problems were not accepted. He had previously been rejected in a job application to Shin Bet, Israel's domestic intelligence service, on psychological grounds. Yet Dimona security was apparently unaware of this rejection.

Accepted as a candidate, he was sent back to school for a crash course in physics, chemistry, maths and English. He passed the exams in January 1977 together with thirty-nine of the forty-five candidates. Those who were to work in Machon 2, described by Vanunu as an eight-storey underground structure housing a plutonium separation process, were given four months to familiarise themselves with the work. In addition to the general pass given to all those working at Dimona, he had Pass No. 320 which gave him entry to Machon 2. On his first trip to Dimona after acceptance, in February 1977, the first thing Vanunu and other trainees had to do was to sign the Official Secrets Act, the penalty for infringement being fifteen years' imprisonment. And it does seem that he did not reveal to even his closest associates the exact nature of his work, despite his pride at beginning work in the highly sensitive installation. 'He spoke only in general terms. We knew that he worked in the nuclear

40

research centre,' Meir said. 'Never did he let out a word about his work. We just knew that he worked there,' his mother said. A girlfriend, Judy Zimmet said, 'I knew it had something to do with atomic projects. I had figured that out, but he only spoke of chemicals and controls.'

On 7 August, he began work as a controller on the night staff. It was the start of a nine-year stint which was to take him through every department in the Machon, giving him a complete overview of the processes which he said later were used for the manufacture of thermonuclear weapons. He worked hard, rarely missed a day, and not infrequently stood in for his colleagues. His monthly salary of some $800, relatively good by Israeli standards, enabled him to buy a flat and a car, as well as to save, although he lost much of his savings in the Israeli bank shares crash in October 1983. After working for two years Vanunu felt bored by his routine. He decided to return to university.

He started an engineering degree at Beersheba's Ben-Gurion University while still working at the Dimona reactor, some forty kilometres away, but then decided that he did not want to invest the five years required to complete such a degree. He moved to economics, but did not settle down there either, and finally began a joint degree in philosophy and geography. Students at Ben-Gurion used to kid him, 'So what are you studying now?' It is not surprising that he finally plumped for philosophy; he had been reading Nietzsche at the age of seventeen. One of the courses he attended was Professor Avner Cohen's on philosophy and nuclear issues. He defined his goals as 'acquisition of linguistic abilities, to read more and more books, and to develop orderly thinking and a stable way of life'. He was not a brilliant university student. 'Let us say he didn't shine intellectually,' Dr Evron Polkov, one of his philosophy lecturers, remarked. 'He was an above average student; at once reliable and hard-working,' according to Dr Lurie, head of the philosophy department. But he went on to commence a

master's degree in philosophy and became an assistant to Dr
Haim Marantz, a position which consisted mostly of marking
undergraduate students' papers.

Vanunu's politicisation came suddenly, with a vengeance.
The 1982 Lebanon war, and the controversial invasion spearheaded by Defence Minister Ariel Sharon, was the turning
point. He attended demonstrations against the war. When
Dr Polkov, whose course on metaphysical realism Vanunu
was later to attend, was imprisoned for conscientious objec-
tion to serving in Lebanon, Vanunu organised a demonstration for him outside the gaol. Opposition to the war
widened into a general sympathy for the Arabs on the West
Bank, whose situation Vanunu equated with that of
Sephardi Jews. In his own army reserve service he preferred
to work in the kitchens, not wanting to have anything to do
with the military machine. According to Musa Fawzi, head
of the Arab student body at Ben-Gurion, and a friend of
Vanunu, 'Motti believed that mutual respect of the Arab
and Jewish peoples would enable them to live together. But
as long as there was discrimination against an Arab minority
this he believed could not be achieved.'
    Through Jewish settlement, Vanunu later wrote, 'Israel
made the first error. If they would have tried to create a
link with the Arabs in the land and not try to make Jewish
settlements, push the Arabs out and acquire territory, then
one could have found a way to establish a united state.' At
an evening of eastern folklore at the university student club
in November 1985, attended by over 100 Arab students,
most of whom wore the *kefiah* scarf, Vanunu called from
the stage, which was bedecked with the PLO flag, for the
establishment of a Palestinian state. The only other Jewish
student at the evening was a representative from the student
union's comptroller's committee attending in an official
capacity.
    He became his department's representative on the stu-

dents' union. He later helped to found Campus, a student group which aimed to improve Arab student rights including dorming on campus, as well as the conditions for university scholarships for Arab students. In the legal cases of two Arab students he sought assistance from two leading Israeli civil rights lawyers, Dr Amnon Zichroni and Avigdor Feldman, both of whom were later to figure in Vanunu's defence when he was charged with treason and espionage. In one instance Vanunu travelled to a university on the West Bank to photocopy the philosophy classics in the Arab language for some fellow Arab students in his department. He managed to get an Arab elected to the student council by ensuring that many Arab students voted in the elections, usually characterised by an apathetic turnout. Even the Left's control of the student union did not contribute to an improvement of Arab student rights, he told the student newspaper, *Berberane*, in a 1984 interview. Only electing an Arab would enable this to be achieved.

By 1984 Vanunu was moving towards communism. In June he attended a meeting in Paris of students from different countries. 'He threw out the labels of somebody who had recently turned to the Left and was at the stage of being more "like the Pope than the Pope himself"', another Israeli delegate, Shlomo Slotzki noted. At Ben-Gurion, together with another philosophy student, Yoram Peretz, he organised a left-wing circle to discuss issues of the day from a philosophical perspective. He also affiliated it to the Israel Communist Party.

Had Vanunu held these views when he applied for the post at Dimona in 1976, he clearly would not have been accepted. One problem for security officials is to monitor any changes, political or psychological, which occur after an applicant has been accepted and which subsequently make him unsuitable for a specific job.

He was questioned by his employers about his political activities. He felt he was being followed Vanunu wrote in his diary as early as May 1983. When he was interviewed by *Berberane* he asked its editor, David Youssof, not to mention that he worked at Dimona. Whether this was because he feared the authorities at the nuclear research centre would discover his political leanings or whether he was concerned that his image on campus as a left-wing supporter might be damaged by that publicity is unclear. In any case the authorities do not seem to have had any problems in gathering information on Vanunu. Meir Boznack, who worked at the university while Vanunu was a student, was alarmed at the political views expressed by someone working at the nuclear research centre, and in July 1985, some six months before Vanunu was dismissed, Boznack alerted a 'reliable source' and the university's security officer. Students who knew that Vanunu worked at the nuclear research centre were also concerned. In 1984 he had planned to join the Israel Communist Party, Rakah, which has 2,000 members of whom some 250 are Jews, but 'my place of work warned me that they know exactly what goes on in the Communist Party's branch in Beersheba', Vanunu wrote to a friend. A CIA report on Israel's intelligence community claimed that the Shin Bet had thoroughly penetrated the party and followed its activities through informants, surveillance and technical operations.

In May 1985 Vanunu was summoned to a meeting with the Shin Bet at Israeli defence headquarters at Hakirya, Tel Aviv. There, according to Judy Zimmet, he was asked to sign a declaration admitting that he was friendly with Arabs, including those close to the PLO, and that he had passed them state secrets. He refused to sign it, arguing that while he had many Arab friends, a few of whom, he said, might be linked to terrorist organisations, he emphatically denied that he had passed them state secrets. The implications of these relationships were explained to Vanunu by security officers, according to whom Vanunu undertook to discontinue them. While he delayed his application to join the

Israel Communist Party, he continued meeting his Arab friends.

The lapse in security at this point seems to be not in the lack of information that the authorities gathered but in the decision to allow Vanunu to continue working at Dimona. This error of judgement was compounded by the fact that he was not closely supervised, even though he was known to be a security risk.[1] Remarkably, even after he had been warned by the Shin Bet, he felt confident enough to bring a camera and rolls of film to work, and he managed to take pictures and detailed plans of Machon 2. On one of the days that he brought in the camera in his personal bag, the bag was bypassed in a random security check.[2] Dimona was a place where everybody knew one another: 'It was one happy family.' The security consciousness in this highly sensitive place had been weakened by the camaraderie which characterises Israeli society. Vanunu remarked that 'the authorities do not think that we Moroccan Jews are intelligent. They think that we just do a job when we are told what to do.'

Vanunu claimed that he contemplated resigning in the summer of 1985 but that he was persuaded to stay on, albeit in another section of the complex. According to him, his grade and salary were raised at the time.[3] Apart from the ideological reason which led him to decide to leave Dimona, he had been frustrated by his work.[4] 'There was no challenge. He had advanced as much as he could,' according to Meir. He believed that his lack of advancement was due to his Sephardi background. This is despite the fact that today many Sephardi Israelis occupy key positions in the civilian and military sectors of public administration.

Nevertheless, there were major weaknesses in the career management structure at Dimona. The eighties saw Dimona hit by a series of labour-management disputes including worker protest meetings, demonstrations, and even the blocking of the entrance to the centre. And, unlike nuclear reactors in other countries, no psychological testing of workers is carried out after applicants have been accepted. Frustration and embitterment were particularly prevalent among scientists, according to a 1987 survey by the personnel section at Dimona on relations between workers and the workplace. There was a feeling that after key projects were completed, alternative ones were not set up, budgets were cut, and research teams dismantled. Scientists were offered very generous terms to take early retirement, and the impression existed that those who did not accept did so because they were unable to find employment in the work market.[5]

In December 1985, 180 workers were laid off from the centre because of economic cuts.[6] US analysts speculated that Israel had trouble running the plutonium plant for a number of years, creating a backlog of spent fuel. Vanunu was hired, they reasoned, as part of a large group of technicians to deal with the backlog and the 180 were laid off once the backlog had been reduced.[7] Vanunu was one of those laid off. By agreeing to voluntary dismissal, he received compensation greater than if he had resigned. Shortly before he accepted voluntary dismissal, he finally submitted his application to join the Israel Communist Party. On the application form he put down his job as being a student. Had he written that he worked at the nuclear research centre the party would have been suspicious, Uzi Borstein, the party spokesman said. Like other new applicants to the party Vanunu was put on probation, which usually lasts six months to a year. It allows 'the new candidate to get to know the party, and the party the candidate', Borstein said. In the short period before he left Israel, Vanunu was critical of the work of the party's Beersheba branch. He questioned the ideological background of some of the branch members. He advocated the need to bring lecturers to explain what communism is, to interest the wider public regarding communist economic and political thinking, and to open new branches of the party in the region.

46

Throughout 1985 Vanunu was debating within himself what to do next in his life. All the options were open: to study law; to continue his philosophy studies at Ben-Gurion; to move to the Hebrew University in Jerusalem, the country's most prestigious university; to work in Tel Aviv, or go to the United States or South America. There was to be a new chapter in his life, he noted in his diary. Different ideas were coming to fruition. In addition to changes at work and university, Vanunu wrote of leaving the region, of leaving even the Jewish faith. A new beginning. A life of choice based on his own experiences. By October he had decided to go to the Far East in order, as he told a friend, 'to find himself'. He had a basic curiosity regarding Buddhism. In fact, his interest in religion was one of the motivations for studying philosophy. But his visa application to visit India was turned down, and instead he decided to stop off in Thailand. He planned to continue on to Australia, and from there to Boston where both Meir, to whom he was intellectually close, and Judy Zimmet, his girlfriend, lived.

In the previous fifteen years, Mordechai Vanunu may have grown intellectually, but emotionally he found considerable difficulty in relating to people. To describe him as 'quiet and introverted', as did Rahel Reiner, another assistant in Ben-Gurion's philosophy department, was an understatement. His difficulties to form human relationships are a feature of his diary. In April 1983 he bemoaned that marriage and children would not be experiences he expected to enjoy. Why, he asked in May 1984, did he circulate in places where there are people, particularly girls, if he was prevented from developing relations with them. For the meantime, he concluded, it was better to spend time with his books and writing. At one student party he suddenly stripped naked. His purchase of a new car in 1982 is a telling illustration of his difficulties. 'Why did you buy a car with headlights? You only work at night,' workers at Dimona chided him. For days he did not speak to them. Moreover, he went and sold the car at a considerable loss. Three graphologists who separately examined Mordechai's handwriting each focused on his difficulty in forming human relationships.

Yet by 1985, three months before he left Israel, Vanunu had had a serious relationship. A mutual friend introduced him to Judy Zimmet, an American volunteer midwife at Beersheba's hospital, ostensibly because he wanted to write a paper on philosophical aspects of abortion. She had been in Israel for nearly a year, spending the first part at an *ulpan* learning Hebrew at the World Union of Jewish Students at nearby Arad. 'We felt good together,' she said. 'Motti and I liked many common things. We both liked song, trying new things together, new kinds of food, restaurants and films. Motti was very curious.' According to Meir, she felt more for Mordechai than he for her. When he decided to travel to the Far East he said that he wanted to go alone: his loner side returned. 'Our relations were not clear and changed all the time,' Judy said. However, at one point in Australia he wanted to suggest that she come and join him but she had already left Israel and began computer studies at Boston University. In making Boston the last destination of his trip, Vanunu presumably planned to see her again.

Saying goodbye to his family was not difficult. His visits to his parents had become rare occurrences and when he did it was briefly. 'He was ashamed of them. There was a feeling that if he had grown up in another framework, perhaps he could have been somebody great, a major scientist, a professor and not a despairing nuclear technician,' said Tzipi Rav-Hen, a close friend. On that Yom Kippur, the holiest day in the Jewish calendar when even secular Israelis stay home, Vanunu went to the sea with Arab friends to go swimming. Apart from conversion to another religion there were few acts which could distance him more from his father's cherished religion. 'Because my parents are religious I am not only non-religious but anti-religious. I rebelled against

God and said there is no god, nothing. Only then can you examine everything afresh,' he said. Apart from Meir whom he felt closest to, and Asher, who after meeting a girl from Holland on a kibbutz went back with her, and with whom he sold posters in different European cities, the other brothers were Albert, and two younger ones Moshe and Danny who were respectively finishing and beginning their national service. Two of his sisters, Shulamit and Haviva, had married Chassidim and lived in the very orthodox city of Benei Beraq near Tel Aviv. Nanette, a trained teacher, had a job outside Beersheba, but because she was about to get married decided to stay in the city and became an assistant in a cosmetic store. Mordechai was closest then to Bruria, perhaps because she was less strictly religious than the other sisters. And it was to her that he brought his various possessions for safekeeping before leaving, including his diaries.

On 17 January 1986 he sailed from Haifa for Athens, leaving a country he intended not to see for a long time. From Athens he flew Aeroflot, the cheapest available flight, to Bangkok. It included a forty-eight-hour stopover at Moscow, and an opportunity for the aspiring communist to visit the city. The KGB lost quite an opportunity at the airport in failing to discover the undeveloped rolls of film taken inside Dimona which he had stuffed into his knapsack. From there he went to Thailand and Burma, returning to Thailand, where he stayed for a month in a Buddhist ashram. He continued to Nepal, where he spent the Passover feast with a couple of Israeli tourists; then to Singapore, and on to Australia. After trying to get employment at the Israeli consulate in Sydney and the Jewish Agency, which handles Jewish immigration to Israel – surprising, given the alienation from Israel which Vanunu felt – he took up taxi-driving.

His stay in Sydney was to begin a 'new chapter' in Vanunu's life. While he foresaw some of it, such as the break with Judaism, he could not have anticipated its ending.

Living in one of Sydney's sleazy districts, King's Cross and the parish of St John's, he felt a strong sense of fellowship with the area. Its rector, John McKnight, a large man, often seen wearing the distinctive blazer of the Church Army, was a well-known youth worker who had previously directed a drug rehabilitation centre. Under Operation Nicodemus the church opened its doors a couple of evenings a week to attract the area's socially disadvantaged for counselling. When Vanunu entered St John's one evening, he began asking McKnight, the assistant rector Stephen Gray, and the lay catechist David Smith, questions about Christianity, becoming deeply involved in conversation with them. It was not Vanunu's first contact with Christian institutions. He had visited Christian sites of interest in Israel, and through the Anglican Church in Ramallah, and its head Georges Rantasi, had obtained money for a fund for needy students at Ben-Gurion University.

It was not long before Vanunu began attending Sunday services and Bible classes, and then moved into one of the church's flats. 'I think the warmth and fellowship and love of the people of St John's just won him over,' McKnight said. Appropriately enough, Nicodemus, who is mentioned in the gospel of St John as a 'Pharisee and ruler of the Jews', was also a Jew saddled with problems who sought relief by turning to Jesus. On 17 July Vanunu was baptised by Reverend Gray and adopted the name John Crossman. Although it was less than three months between first entering the portals of King's Cross and his baptism, according to McKnight, 'the path for a convert from Judaism is easier because there is so much common ground. Vanunu believed in the essentials of the Christian faith, he believed that there was a God, and he believed that God was active in the world. He believed that God is a God of fairness and justice. I would think he believed in Jesus as the Messiah.'

Perhaps it was not surprising that Vanunu changed his religion. 'I had', he wrote in a letter to Judy Zimmet, 'chosen my religion. Nobody can decide for me. Everybody is obliged to choose his faith and find his answers to life.' Nor was it so surprising that he adopted Christianity. Universalism is a value which he would have found attractive in any framework. 'Don't consider what will happen to me if I help you but what will happen to you if I don't help you,' he wrote to a friend. 'In this life I want to help mankind, to give it all I can,' he wrote to Zimmet. That the Christian Church had taken a definite stand on the nuclear arms race made it doubly attractive. But it would be wrong to argue that the anti-nuclear platform of some branches of the Church was the primary drawing factor. 'As a caring Christian community, we were concerned about the whole range of issues – social justice, racism – and only a small group were looking at peace and justice,' said McKnight.

In contrast to some Church leaders, the rabbinate in Israel has not taken a stand on the nuclear arms question. This silence mirrors the ambiguity on the question generally in Israel. Yet, given the reality of war and, today, of non-conventional weaponry in the Middle East, this silence is inappropriate. However, in the United States, the various branches of Judaism, in particular the reform movement, have adopted positions critical of the superpowers' arms race. Though peace figures prominently in the Jewish liturgy, Judaism is not pacifist in the contemporary sense. Self-defence is an obligation: 'If a person comes to slay you, kill him first,' the Talmudic book of *Sanhedrin* argues. But, as in the Christian theory of 'just war', military action resulting in civilian casualties, whether by intention or as a foreseeable consequence, is forbidden. Consequently, Rabbi Professor Judah Bleich of Yeshiva University, New York, argues, 'the nuclear bombing of Hiroshima and Nagasaki, despite the resultant diminution of casualties among the armed forces, cannot be justified on the basis of the law of pursuit.' 'Is one person's blood redder than another's', the Talmud asks rhetorically. Some rabbinical scholars, however, attempt to

51

draw a distinction between the utilisation of weaponry and its deterrent role.

It seems obvious that Vanunu did not investigate Judaism's position on the subject of nuclear arms. Perhaps he never understood the spirit of Judaism. Orthodox Judaism has never been happy focusing simply on broad principles, on moral values which can be interpreted in many ways. Instead it has sought to map out a precise code of life, with considerable emphasis on action, or *mitzvot*. In orthodox settings, such as Vanunu's home background, there is a danger that some may lose sight of the deeper meaning of these acts.

St John's was running a number of seminars and workshops under the heading, 'Following Jesus in a Suffering World', dealing with Christian responses to such contemporary issues as poverty, race, apartheid, and nuclear arms. The message of the workshop on nuclear arms, McKnight said, was that 'Christians ought to take an active role in working against nuclear weapons and not leave it to major powers to decide for us. It was cathartic for Vanunu. It was the turning point and what he felt he had to do was as a result of the workshop.' At one of the meetings Vanunu gave a talk on his work in Israel. He produced some of the photographs he had taken inside Dimona, displaying them as if they were holiday snaps. 'He was very casual about it, and he did say this is a secret plant which he worked at. I guess I took that with a grain of salt really at the time,' one parishioner said.

The question facing Vanunu was what strategy to adopt in taking an active role against nuclear weapons. The answer came from a freelance Colombian journalist, Oscar Guerrero, who was being employed under a Commonwealth re-employment scheme to paint the church. Within four days of their meeting, Guerrero told Vanunu that he was a freelance journalist, and produced photographs which appeared to show him with such international personalities as Lech Walesa, the then president of Argentina, Alfonsin, and

Shimon Peres. He said he knew many journalists and would help to sell the story about Israel's nuclear programme. Vanunu had already attempted to contact the media while in Thailand but had it not been for the fortuitous encounter with Guerrero, there might not have been any 'Vanunu Affair'.

Initially he had second thoughts. He told Roland Sollitus, another resident of St John's who had become involved in Guerrero's plan, that he wanted to destroy the film and scrap the whole idea. Sollitus told Vanunu that he could not. Vanunu realised he was right, and immediately had the remaining film developed at a local shop.

'I had to overcome many personal barriers to do what I did,' Vanunu was to write from an Israeli prison in September 1987. 'The chief danger was the sacrifice of my personal life to exposure and slander, and of my future plans – all on this altar. But the action was worth it. By this action I pointed the path in which I believe, my own philosophy about what must be done, the way in which a man must be willing to sacrifice and risk his life for the sake of an act that is important and beneficial to all, to humanity.' The man who as a boy helped in the family, helped others in his first year at Wolfson with their Talmudic studies, helped Arab students, was – simplistically and with some political naivety – going to help those who, unlike him, were not privy to Israel's nuclear secrets. And, despite his break with the family, he wrote to Meir to apologise for the family embarrassment and hardship which would surely follow. As it turned out, Meir had since moved and received the letter after the *Sunday Times* published.

Vanunu felt that he was in a special, if not unique, position. 'I knew the basic data and material. I live my life by travel, search and examination, competing with all kinds of theories and thoughts. In the aftermath of the Lebanon war and the Shin Bet affair my inner soul doubted the country's leadership and their acts. I decided to do it like somebody

53

who sees himself responsible for all matters deciding what is good for the country. I am not a person who has got much to lose in life, a stoic who is happy with little. I had nobody to turn to for advice, nor would I have sought it had there been one.' Moreover, he saw it as a divinely ordained mission. 'All these features were gathered in one man as a bomb or mine that waited for a vehicle to explode it. I waited, I hesitated, I thought until I met the journalist. Then the mine exploded and sent me here [to an Israeli gaol]. I didn't want to offer myself for this purpose. My question is why did God, Destiny, place this function in my hands. Or, to put it another way, where would I be otherwise today?'

Despite having been sensitised during his nine years' work at Dimona to the obligation to observe secrecy and having signed the Official Secrets Act, Vanunu appears to have had few reservations as to the personal danger involved in revealing Israel's secrets. With an unrealistic world outlook it was difficult for him to distinguish the realities and he decided according to experience and impulse. Moreover, a new behavioural mode of challenging existing norms, including respect for authority, had replaced Vanunu's old set of values. In May 1983, according to his diary, Vanunu had developed his political outlook and become as extreme as was possible in that area. He also noted that he had made more acquaintances among Arabs.

Yet a number of questions regarding his motives require consideration. The most important concerns the absence from his diaries, where he put down his most intimate feelings, of the need to discuss the nuclear issue openly or of a plan to reveal information about Israel's nuclear secrets. Only Vanunu knows the reason for this, but he did decide to leave Dimona for political, among other, reasons, and he took the photographs with an apparent wish to bring the nuclear issue to public knowledge. And, he told Judy Zimmet shortly before he left his work, he was concerned that 'he was manufacturing things which could endanger humanity'. If not reflected in his diaries, the latent potential for speaking out about the nuclear programme was sown in his left-wing years of 1983 to 1985. The catalyst which sparked this was the atmosphere and discussions at King's Cross.

A second question concerns his stated goal of informing Israelis, and not just the world community, about the nuclear danger. What level of concern did he have for his countrymen if he left Judaism for another religion? Only Vanunu knows.[8] His identification with Israel was tenuous if it existed at all. 'He was very disappointed about what goes on there. He was often sarcastic,' Judy Zimmet said. A clue may lie in a letter Vanunu sent to his brother Meir Vanunu on the eve of leaving Australia for London. In it he wrote '. . . I am going to London to make an agreement with the *Sunday Times* . . . What motivates me are primarily political reasons. Despite that I have left Israel and do not wish to be involved, I am returning to being involved. I feel that it is my obligation to go public . . . I have thought a lot about this step and this appears imperative . . .'

Third, there are significant differences between civil disobedience at home and evasion of the authorities by flight to another jurisdiction. 'By submitting to the sanction of the breached law, a defendant shows himself – as well as the community – that he has deliberated; that he has weighed and measured; that he is not acting on mere impulse or whim; that he has faced his conscience squarely; that he has made a decision that is of supreme importance to himself,' Milton Konvitz, an American law professor, has argued. Vanunu did not even go abroad with the specific intent of obtaining an environment in which he could reveal the information. He went abroad because he was dissatisfied with Israel and wanted to start a new chapter in his life. While in taking the photographs of the reactor he may have wanted to direct public attention to the nuclear danger, he had no clear strategy for this: a chance encounter with a mercurial journalist resulted in the suggestion to sell his story to the media.

In addition, Guerrero's asking price to the *Sunday Times* of £250,000 for the story raises doubts as to the sincerity of Vanunu's motives. It is true that Vanunu did tell Reverend Gray he wanted 'the money used for God's work. I've asked myself, if I had something to sell, would I take it? I don't think I could resist the temptation of having half a million dollars to use for the Lord's work.' And when the *Sunday Times* told Vanunu that they would have to put his name to the story, he replied that if they did not they could have the story without payment; he was concerned for it to be told. In the final agreement drafted between the paper and Vanunu, he was to receive some of the proceeds from a book ghosted by the newspaper's Insight team. Vanunu was going to use the proceeds to begin a new life. Even if no financial deal was at any stage made between Vanunu and Guerrero in which the former would keep any of the benefits, Vanunu damaged his image by letting the matter be tainted by money for Guerrero's role. Feeling somewhat lost in the big world, Vanunu found somebody who appeared to have the right connections through which to publicise his account.

A question may also be asked whether during any part of the three months Vanunu was speaking to the media in 1986 about his big story, his exclusive information, he felt, if only subconsciously, that he was getting the attention which as a Sephardi Jew he felt deprived of. We see in this fabric the threads of Vanunu's dissatisfaction, rebelliousness, political statement, contemplation, disaffection with his country, lack of strategy, and gullibility. Quite a patchwork quilt. Yet things came out much better than Vanunu could have expected in his wildest dreams. Less than half a year after putting on a slide show about the Israeli nuclear theme to parishioners at an off-beat church, his story was front-page international news. If there were no diary entries and no clear plan beforehand, he articulated his goals after the event from his prison cell. 'The atom is a subject', he wrote in November 1987, 'which is tabooed, serious and significant, so that all citizens need to know more details regarding what is happening in the country, what the government does, in order that they shall not be surprised from a further surprise, especially after Chernobyl.' In a poem, entitled 'I am your spy', written at the same time, he wrote:

> This is not for me. It's too much for me
> Rise, read, rise and inform this people
> You are able. I the screw, the machine-operator
> the technician. You, yes. You the secret agent
> of this people. You are the eyes of the state.
> Espionage agent: Reveal what you see. Reveal to us
> what those who understand, the learned, hide from us.
> If you are not with us we are in an abyss.
> We will have a holocaust. You, only you, sit
> at the steering wheel and see the abyss
> I have no choice. I am small, citizen, your people
> But I will fulfil my obligation. I heard
> the voice of my conscience. There is nowhere to flee
> The world is small in comparison to
> Big Brother
> Behold, I am your emissary. Behold
> I fill my task. Take this
> from me. Come and judge
> Lighten my burden
> Carry it together with me. Continue
> my work. Stop the train. Get off
> from the train. The next station is Nuclear Holocaust
> The next book, the next machine, No. There is no
>   such thing.[9]

Vanunu may have articulated his tactics and even his strategy after the event but his underlying concern-cum-imprecise-objective was what existed beforehand. History is shaped by

57

deeds and events rather than by intentions. As long as a person is deemed mentally stable, be he introvert or extrovert, his actions are deemed logically motivated.

'One is totally convinced when one talks to Vanunu about his sincerity with which he holds his views against the use and possession of nuclear weapons,' Dr Frank Barnaby remarked. 'He is obviously a complex character. He's impulsive. Also he felt that he should have had faster promotion than he was getting because he was being discriminated against as an Arab Jew. These two factors are overwhelmed by his feelings against nuclear weapons and nuclear war.'

3. DEVIL'S ADVOCATE

The first that the *Sunday Times* heard about Mordechai Vanunu was when their Madrid correspondent, Tim Brown, a British journalist who had worked for many years for various foreign news organisations, told them that he had this incredible story with some photographs.

'It's right up your street', but Brown was suspicious of Guerrero, he told the paper. 'However he has some photographs which look very interesting.'

The *Sunday Times* was an ideal newspaper to approach given its investigative tradition of nearly thirty years. Many people attribute its reputation to Harold Evans's editorship of the paper spanning the period from 1967 to 1981. Many of the celebrated investigations were made during Evans's period at the helm. The paper named Kim Philby as the 'third man' in the Burgess–Maclean spy ring. Its revelations about the thalidomide affair and its campaign against the Distillers Company culminated in ten times the amount of compensation which had originally been offered to victims; when faced with a House of Lords injunction stopping the paper from publishing the story, the *Sunday Times* fought and won the case in the European Court of Human Rights. The paper investigated the DC-10 crash over Paris in 1974, and other notable causes included sanctions-busting in Rhodesia and British interrogation techniques used on suspects in Ulster. Also under Evans, the paper defied

59

government attempts to stop publication of extracts from the Crossman diaries.

But to appreciate the newspaper's brand of investigative journalism it is necessary to go back to his predecessor in the editor's chair, Denis Hamilton, and to when Insight, the paper's investigative team, was first conceived. When appointed editor in 1961, Hamilton was anxious to redefine the function of a Sunday newspaper from being simply a rehash of the week's news. Impressed by the post-war success of *Time* and *Newsweek*, he wanted to introduce two aspects of news magazine journalism: the 'back of the book' soft news pieces, on business, health and housing, for example, and the type of long cover story reportage associated with those two news magazines. In late 1962, *Topic*, an attempt to create a British equivalent of *Time*, folded. The decision was taken to hire the editor of the short-lived magazine and apply the news-background concept to weekly newspaper journalism. In its first appearance the news-background section of the *Sunday Times* had some thirteen stories, covering two pages, rather than a single long-running story. Subjects covered on the two pages, which had the title 'Insight', ranged from religion and insurance to shipping and sociology.

Originally, the idea was to use specialist correspondents, but this did not work out. Instead a unit of 'investigative' reporters was created, which would be joined, as a specific story required, by a particular correspondent. The significance of Insight, according to *The Pearl of Days*, the newspaper's official history, was that it showed 'that three or four Insight men, used to working together, could do a "crash job" on important news stories better than a large news staff used to working independently'.

One of the first major stories Insight undertook was the Profumo Affair in June 1963 involving the relationship between the navy minister and Miss Christine Keeler, who was also involved with a Soviet diplomat. In a story which ran to 6,000 words, Insight examined each of the affair's phases. The following month it carried a long investigation into the business activities of one Peter Rachman. Rachman purchased rent-controlled properties and began moving coloured people into them. This cynical exploitation of racial tensions encouraged the rent-controlled tenants to move out, enabling him to raise the price of the houses to their true market value. Its three-part series 'The Life and Times of Peter Rachman', which aired the legal and political issues of the case, launched Insight into the investigative journalism which was to make it famous.

The technique was applied to politics when, in October of that year, Harold Macmillan, the Conservative prime minister, resigned, and the party appointed a successor in its non-participatory manner of 'sounding opinion at all levels of the party'. Insight's piece that Sunday – for which political correspondent James Margach had sent the team some 10,000 words – guided the reader through the machinations of the political party.

The next year, Insight revealed the existence of an antique dealers' ring in which its members would refrain from bidding against one another. After the sale the ring would meet and reauction the items among themselves. A contributor to Insight, Colin Simpson, who had earlier been engaged in antique dealing, got into the ring at the invitation of its members after he bid items to completely unprofitable levels. A tiny microphone was placed in the reporter's clothing and the proceedings of the ring's meeting were relayed to a nearby van where another reporter and an electronics engineer recorded them. The investigation resulted in two former presidents and nine other members of the thirty-two-man council of the British Antique Dealers' Association being charged. By the mid-sixties, the paper had appointed a reporter to cover organised crime, intending that he should not have to rely upon police sources but should develop his own contacts in criminal circles.

In 1981 Rupert Murdoch purchased Times Newspapers from the Thomson Organisation. It was to mark the end of the era of major Insight investigations. Murdoch appointed Evans as editor of *The Times*, and made Frank Giles, deputy editor and previously the foreign editor, the new editor of the *Sunday Times*. Giles had for some time been concerned at how Insight had over the years become almost an empire in itself. To bring it into line he disbanded the unit. 'Insight was made up of highly adventurous and worthwhile people. It developed an internal pride of its own, breeding a certain amount of resistance to editorial control. It pretended to know and would say . . . at every moment of the day what every minister was doing,' Giles said. But Giles's appointment was temporary; he was nearing retirement.

When in 1983 Murdoch appointed thirty-six-year-old Andrew Neil, a journalist with *The Economist*, the Murdoch philosophy that newspapers exist primarily to make money was brought to bear. Among the various expenditures Neil axed were the investigations, in effect continuing a process already set in train by his predecessor. 'As far as Neil was concerned Insight was very expensive and of marginal value. In its great days Insight had become a very important strand in the *Sunday Times*'s total personality package. When people said "the *Sunday Times*" there were an awful lot of respondents who automatically said "Insight". Neil decided that the reality of Insight was hardly worth it. What he failed to see was how important the image of Insight is . . . Readers thought that the *Sunday Times* without Insight was an inferior brother . . .' an editorial executive remarked. Shortly after his appointment Neil denied that terminating the integral Insight unit was testimony to a wish to destroy the paper's investigative tradition.

'What I want to do is to approach investigative reporting by putting together ad hoc teams. My hope is that it will produce a lot more, because we will have three or four of these teams going at once. If it transpires that this slightly anarchic way doesn't work out then I will reconstitute a separate Insight team again.' Illustrative of Neil's commitment to investigative journalism was Peter Wright's MI5 *Spycatcher* memoirs. Neil flew to the US, negotiated its serialisation in the *Sunday Times* and smuggled a copy back into the country. Together with two of the paper's senior journalists, Neil – ostensibly visiting his sick mother in Scotland – edited a four-page extract which he slipped into the paper just before edition time.

In 1985, a separate Insight team was reborn. Stories covered by the team, which varied in size from three to five reporters, included the Birmingham riots, corruption in the Bahamas, and the *Rainbow Warrior* affair, which resulted in an Insight book. Vanunu could not have timed his arrival better. It was just the story to stop the decline in readership. It fitted the mould of what Insight reporting should be about: 'It should be fairly big, something of major concern,' said Phillip Knightley, a former Insight staffer. 'Not something about petty crooks.'

The *Sunday Times* was not the first news organisation which Guerrero and Vanunu had contacted. In late July they had been in touch with Carl Robinson, the Sydney-based South Pacific correspondent of *Newsweek*. Calling themselves only 'David' and 'Alberto Bravo', Vanunu and Guerrero said they could prove that Israel had the bomb. Robinson wanted to check 'David's story' through sources and asked him to provide additional evidence, including photographs. *Newsweek*'s New York headquarters began checking the information Robinson filed. But by mid-August 'David phoned back to say he was too frightened to go ahead with the story,' Robinson said.

The photographs which Vanunu had secretly taken inside and outside the nuclear reactor were to be the lynchpin in the *Sunday Times* deciding to publish his allegations. Had there been no photographs, it is extremely doubtful that a news organisation would have been tempted to go through the task of checking Vanunu's allegations. Robin Morgan, editor of the Insight team, sent a reporter, John Swain, to Madrid to check Guerrero's story. Within twenty-four hours he replied, as Tim Brown had: 'The man's very devious, but he does have these photographs. Where did he get them from?' Swain flew Guerrero to London.

The photographs of the inside of the reactor's buildings were shown to a nuclear physicist at London University in order to verify whether the pictures, including one showing control panels, were of the inside of what Guerrero claimed to be a plutonium enrichment plant or, say, the inside of an electricity generating plant. The physicist said that they looked like nuclear devices, models, plant and technical equipment, and control panels lining the wall. Morgan, together with Steven Milligan, the paper's foreign editor, then compared the pictures of the exterior of the Dimona reactor with the ones which the *Sunday Times*'s photo library possessed: the form of the cooling towers, the palm trees, the shape of the buildings. The library's photos had been taken during the period of Dimona's construction in the early 1960s. Morgan and Milligan kept in mind that there were other desert reactors, like Iraq's, but nevertheless 'felt 90 per cent certain' that the buildings in the photographs were the same as in the newspaper library photos but at a later stage of construction.

Guerrero, according to Morgan, told the Insight team that he had managed the escape from Israel of the country's top nuclear scientist, whom he called Professor Mordechai Vanunu. He had taken the man by boat and plane through a series of safe houses to a safe house in Australia. 'It was crazy that Israel's top nuclear scientist should be spirited away by this young man; if he had, we'd all know about it – or that Israel possessed or was producing hundreds of neutron bombs.' Morgan and Milligan thrashed out their dilemma with editor Andrew Neil. 'We've got a guy who looks like a conman,' Morgan told Neil. 'He doesn't know what he's talking about. It could be a hoax. We have one problem. We have these photographs. They are obviously taken inside Dimona and the pictures we've got are not easily come by.'

It wasn't the first time in the *Sunday Times*'s history that the fear of being hoaxed loomed high. The hoax which was at the forefront of everyone's mind was the Hitler Diaries affair in April–May 1983. Murdoch's News International group bought publication rights of what were claimed to be Hitler's Diaries from *Stern* magazine. After the *Sunday Times* trumpeted its acquisition of the historical wonder it was discovered to be a massive forgery.

Stern was very reluctant to allow independent inspection of the diaries, fearing that their contents would be leaked. But at the insistence of the *Sunday Times*, the magazine agreed to let Lord Dacre (formerly Professor Hugh Trevor-Roper), an expert on the Hitler period (and a Times Newspapers director), examine the diaries. In fact, at the Zurich bank vaults, Dacre, surrounded by members of *Stern*, simply handled the volumes and listened to the assurances by *Stern*'s men that the paper had been scientifically tested, and that they knew and could vouch for the identity of the 'Wehrmacht officer' who was supposed to have salvaged Hitler's diaries from the wreckage of a plane in 1945, and kept them hidden since then. Dacre telephoned Charles Douglas-Home, editor of *The Times* (who was appointed to the post after Evans had been fired by Murdoch), and said that on the external evidence he was convinced of the diaries' authenticity. Before Dacre had examined the diaries themselves, *Stern* decided to publish, earlier than originally planned, and the *Sunday Times* announced its outstanding scoop. That Saturday night, as the paper which would announce the find went to press Giles telephoned Dacre to tell him what would be appearing in the paper. The editor's office was full of excited staffers. Then Dacre told Giles of his doubts. "I hope you are not going to make a hundred and eighty degree turn, are you?" asked Giles. His reply made those there realise, to their horror, that he was.

Dacre then travelled to Hamburg to meet Heidemann, the *Stern* journalist who had originally obtained the diaries. Heidemann refused to reveal anything about the Wehrmacht officer whom he claimed had salvaged and hidden the diaries. Dacre then denounced the diaries as forgeries. *Stern* subsequently agreed to hand over two of the sixty volumes for independent examination. A leading chemist and the German Federal Archives at Koblenz said the paper used in the diaries was of post-war manufacture, and a British historian judged that the contents of the two volumes – supposedly containing Hitler's inner thoughts – were quite simply a historical digest.

Giles said of Dacre, 'I had known him well for thirty-five years, respected his scholarship, appreciated his values in general and his unemotional approach to facts. Was it conceivable that the former Regius Professor of History at Oxford, now the Master of Peterhouse Cambridge, could have declared himself so positively had there been even a small risk of being proved wrong?'

The paper printed an apology to its readers. 'Our mistake was to rely on other people's evidence and to be governed by their demands for urgency. *Stern* magazine . . . previously enjoying a reputable standard in world journalism, insisted that it had established the diaries' authenticity. This was confirmed by Hugh Trevor-Roper. We are unreservedly delighted that the proof was made before we had published any portion of the serialisation.' Giles himself had been dubious about the diaries from the start. He felt that Murdoch had placed commercial goals above the editorial standards of a quality newspaper. He was also critical of Dacre for being too hasty in his judgement, and of Charles Douglas-Home for being gullible.[1]

Now Mark Twain once remarked that a cat which touched

a hot stove would never touch one again; the problem was that it would never touch a cold stove either. The *Sunday Times* had been burned. It remained to be seen whether Vanunu was hot or cold and whether the *Sunday Times* would touch him.

In investigating Vanunu's claims Insight had to answer three questions. First, was the man in Sydney actually Mordechai Vanunu? And did such a man work at Dimona? Second, were the processes depicted in the photographs and described by Vanunu technically accurate? And third, were these processes being carried out at Dimona?

While no two investigative assignments are completely alike, most may be said to pass through three phases. First comes a clue that a news story lies hidden somewhere. The tip-off may be a leak or just a reporter's, or editor's, hunch. The second consists of legwork: checking facts, searching through documents, talking to people. If a story is there, this is when it will be unearthed. The last phase is a confrontation with the principals involved, when they get a chance to explain their sides of the story, deny the charges, turn away with a 'no comment', or confess. Given that the *Sunday Times* Insight team could not gain access to Dimona, to the participants, or to witnesses, all that it could do beyond checking the accuracy of Vanunu's personal details was to test the credibility of the information. Most of his personal life story could be checked. But while acquaintances could confirm that he worked at the nuclear research centre there was no way Insight could gain independent confirmation that he was one of the select few who had access to the super-sensitive Machon 2 where Vanunu claimed plutonium was produced. They would also have to take his word as to how he managed to smuggle in a camera and take over fifty photographs inside and outside Machon 2.

Morgan and Neil decided that Peter Hounam, who had a background in physics, should be the reporter to accompany

Guerrero back to Australia to meet the mysterious nuclear professor. Aged forty-three, Hounam had joined the *Sunday Times* some eighteen months earlier from the London *Evening Standard*. He arrived in Sydney at the end of August to meet a frightened Vanunu, who suspected Hounam of being from Israeli intelligence, and only two or three hours later did Vanunu open up.

He quickly corrected the impression promoted by Guerrero that he was a professor, and told Hounam that he had worked as a technician at the Dimona centre for nine years. The reporter asked Vanunu to describe his working shift, day by day, minute by minute, telling him what processes he regulated. Vanunu went on to describe the structure of the nuclear research centre, and in particular Machon 2. He claimed Machon 2 comprised two floors above ground level and a further six floors hidden underneath, where plutonium was separated from uranium and baked into plutonium 'buttons'. Hounam and Vanunu then closed the curtains of the hotel room where they were meeting and placed the roll of transparencies on a projector. Hounam saw picture after picture of dials, controls, so-called flow panels and other gadgets which showed what he deduced to be a plutonium production process. The value of some of the photos was impaired by their poor exposure.

Asked how he was able to get a camera into the reactor, and how he managed to take some fifty-seven photographs, Vanunu explained that he smuggled the camera and film in separately, hidden with his sandwiches and drink. He said perimeter security was relatively lax and that he was free to roam the plant during the long tedious nights. He regularly evaded the endless games of canasta with his workmates, going to the demonstration room on Level 2 where visiting Israeli VIPs – the prime minister, the defence minister, and the top military brass – were briefed.[2] The room had boxed models of atomic devices and a wall-mounted floor plan of Machon 2.[3] Hounam did not send Vanunu's photographs to

London for security reasons but did, surprisingly, send written reports.

He spent a total of fourteen days with Vanunu in Sydney, and had a gut feeling from the start that he was genuine. 'I knew we had a big story,' he said. When not extracting information from Vanunu about his work and life, Hounam spent hours in a Sydney public library undergoing a crash course in nuclear physics and atomic weapons production.

Armed with details of Vanunu's personal history received from Australia, a reporter flew to Israel to verify the information. A couple of people at Beersheba's Ben-Gurion University were able to identify Vanunu from a photograph. Neighbours and others confirmed that he had worked at the Dimona reactor. Vanunu was able to produce his letter of dismissal from Dimona as further proof that he had worked there. Another reporter who went to Israel, Roger Wilsher, tried to get close to the nuclear research centre but was turned back near the periphery fence by landrovers. Satellite photographs were used to verify Vanunu's description of the centre.

In London, the Insight team began the arduous task of checking the technical information which Hounam was sending back from Australia. The team was headed by Robin Morgan, who had joined the paper in 1979 as a general news reporter before a three-year stint as an Insight reporter. He concentrated on defence matters, then became deputy home news editor. In addition to Hounam, the team comprised Max Prangnell, a baker-turned-journalist, Rowena Webster and Roger Wilsher. While Webster and Wilsher had done some investigative reporting – the former with Hounam on the financial situation of the National Theatre and the latter on the Greenpeace affair – only Morgan and Hounam could be said to have had hard investigative reporting experience. In this sense, the Insight team was weaker than it had been ten or twenty years earlier, when all or most of its members had possessed hard experience. The team was joined for this story by Peter Wilsher, an associate editor (and Roger's father) who had been with the *Sunday Times* for over twenty-five years, to act as a devil's advocate and pass a sceptical eye over all the information being checked. In one sense it was an unusual choice because, apart from a period as the paper's foreign editor, most of his experience was in business news. In another sense it was precisely because he brought no preconceived views that his value as a sceptic lay.

It was clear from the first day the newspaper heard about Mordechai Vanunu that outside expertise would have to be consulted. Insight took Vanunu's description of his work plus the photographs to a scientist whom Roger Wilsher knew at Britain's Atomic Energy Authority at Harwell, where plutonium grade material is extracted, to an official at the Ministry of Defence, and to officials who worked in similar government agencies in the United States, to verify whether they were dealing with a technician who said he extracted plutonium. At this stage Insight just wanted to determine the technical aspects of Vanunu's story, and these officials (who were approached in a non-official capacity) were not told from which country the informer came. One of the experts confirmed that the photographs were entirely consistent with what a plutonium separation plant would look like.[4] Each official consulted said that the informer had not learnt in a university chemistry laboratory or from a textbook, but had worked for a long time in plutonium pro-duction. 'It was like a Detroit car worker coming to us, not saying what the product was, just telling you precisely what he did on the production line,' Robin Morgan said.

This warranted bringing Vanunu to London to be debriefed by experts. Given that the newspaper had three years earlier been caught by Professor Trevor-Roper's error of judgement, it was surprising that they were prepared to proceed with the investigation of a story which relied heavily on experts' opinions. But the onus of proof lay with attempting to destroy Vanunu's story; in essence to prove, as one Insight reporter put it, that 'Vanunu was a liar', and this required expertise.

The *Sunday Times*'s choice of Dr Frank Barnaby as chief adviser in the Vanunu investigation was surprising in two respects. First, while Barnaby had worked for six years in the mid-fifties on the British nuclear programme at Aldermaston, he had not actually been working with nuclear weapons for twenty years. Nor was he recognised in the United States as in the top league of nuclear scientists. Second, would the conclusions of an activist in Europe's nuclear freeze movement and outgoing director of SIPRI, Stockholm's International Peace Research Institute, be perceived as objective? Although Barnaby had a political viewpoint, he is very methodical. With regard to his no longer being active in nuclear weapons' production, he had through his work at SIPRI kept abreast of the subject. 'Because Vanunu knew virtually nothing about the design of the weapons themselves, though he had photos of the models, in terms of his information the paper really didn't need much knowledge of anything of actual weapon size,' said Barnaby. There were few other nuclear scientists in Britain whom the newspaper could have turned to with a similar level of nuclear knowledge. Some of these, among them government scientists, would not talk or agree to be quoted by name.

As he was about to leave Australia for London with Hounam, Mordechai Vanunu was still having doubts about whether or not to publish Israel's nuclear secrets. He was to have these doubts all the way to publication. Two days before his departure in the second week of September, he went to see John McKnight in the St John's parish where he was staying to thrash out his dilemma.

'I took a non-directional approach,' McKnight said. 'My role as his parish priest was to help him just think through the issues and I believe he'd already come to a decision, but I think he just needed to talk through the issue and consequences.' Stephen Gray, the associate minister, said, 'Vanunu had reached a stage where he realised there were two kingdoms, of God and man. He had to choose between that which he felt was right under God, and what might have been best for his country.' 'He was a person of integrity and was loyal to his country – perhaps not to its administration but certainly to its people,' McKnight added.

The projector cast the pictures on to the screen. The crucially important pictures for Barnaby were those which appeared to show the lithium separation process. The models showing neutron warheads 'were clearly feasible. But models are models,' he said. The same was true of the control room photograph which the newspaper was to print on its front page. 'All reactors and reprocessing plants have control rooms – although the flow charts added credibility.' For two days Barnaby questioned Vanunu about every detail, dot, dial and control in the pictures. The Insight reporters in the smoke-filled room took copious notes. Language was not a major problem. Although the debriefing took a little longer, there was no need for a Hebrew translator given that the information was of a technical nature. According to Barnaby, Vanunu both had detailed information of the techniques used, and had worked on the processes. Vanunu was honest about his limited areas of knowledge and did not comment beyond these. The photographs strengthened Vanunu's credibility. Barnaby was left in no doubt following the debriefing that Israel had a nuclear capability.[5]

The quantity of information which Vanunu provided to Insight and Barnaby was clearly much more than the three-page exposé eventually published. Insight was planning some follow-up reports, as well as a book, the profits from which the newspaper planned to share with Vanunu, on such aspects as the development of Israel's nuclear programme, the question of nuclear cooperation with South Africa, and the raid on the Iraqi reactor at Osiraq.

The Insight team took the detailed evidence gathered from the two-day debriefing back to the experts earlier consulted. One expert they consulted concluded that Vanunu was a junior technician working at a plutonium processing plant given the detailed knowledge of the processes on which Vanunu worked. Some of the British officials consulted, however, were sceptical that the reactor could have been enlarged six times to 150 megawatts without altering the exterior of the plant.

While the reactions of the experts were being canvassed, Peter Sullivan, a senior graphics artist on the paper, got down to prepare what would be a blown-up diagram of the eight-tier structure of Machon 2, which would run the length of one of the pages of the story. Sullivan sat with Vanunu for ninety minutes to take down his description of the buildings and roads at the research centre. By coincidence the same week that Sullivan was preparing the graphics, a nuclear power station was opened to the public for one day as part of a drive to improve the British public's image of the nuclear energy industry. The technical equipment was useful to Sullivan for gaining an idea of the inside of Machon 2.

By the closing days of September – some two weeks after Vanunu had arrived in London, and a month after Guerrero first contacted the newspaper – Insight had convinced itself of the validity of Vanunu's claims. Reporters noted a change in Vanunu's mood at this point: 'He realised rather slowly that he was a man possessing a unique body of information. But once he had handed that out he was nothing, just another thirty-year-old man in a foreign country, and one who couldn't speak the language very well. He didn't like it when he stopped being the centre of attention. It was really getting to him,' an Insight reporter said.

Andrew Neil read Insight's hard copy and passed it as accurate. An unexpected development then occurred. Guerrero, the man who had introduced the paper to Vanunu, arrived in London to claim payment for his introduction. Dissatisfied, he took the story to the *Sunday Mirror*. Interested to see how the *Mirror* would handle the matter, Neil delayed publishing that Sunday. The *Mirror* cast doubt on the photographs Vanunu had taken. Given that the Vanunu disclosure would make or break his reputation, Neil wanted one additional check, by an internationally-known scientist who would be prepared to subscribe his name to the authenticity of Insight's story. They decided to approach Dr Theodore Taylor, who had been head of the Pentagon's atomic weapons test programme, in which capacity he had designed and tested nuclear weapons and had built plants which produced atomic weapons. Taylor had been taught by the 'father' of the atomic bomb, Robert Oppenheimer. Taylor, after seeing the photos and transcripts, concluded that there could be no doubt that Israel had a nuclear capability. Moreover, Israel's nuclear programme was more advanced, according to Taylor, than earlier estimates.[6]

A different question which Neil had to resolve in dealing with the story was his relationship with proprietor Rupert Murdoch, an admirer of Israel and friend of Ariel Sharon, the hawkish defence minister who masterminded the 1982 Lebanon war. According to Michael Jones, the paper's political editor, 'Mr Murdoch's well-known Israeli sympathies were never a consideration whether the story ran or not,' but clearly Neil had to make doubly sure that the story was correct. 'Neil is aware that if he makes a mistake on a major story concerning Israel it is more serious than with a story not concerning Israel,' an editorial executive remarked. Like many conservative people in Britain today who regard themselves as pro-Israeli, Neil did not see the Vanunu story as anti-Israel. It was a major story which could enhance his reputation as recently appointed editor of the *Sunday Times*.

One 'participant' whom Insight managed to get to was Professor Francis Perrin, who, as head of France's nuclear programme from 1950 to 1971, oversaw the construction by France of the Dimona reactor – for ostensibly peaceful purposes. In the interview, which the paper published the week following the publication of Vanunu's exposé, Perrin revealed that France, in addition to building the reactor itself, had provided technology to build nuclear bombs, built the secret underground plutonium processing plant housed in Machon 2, and supplied some initial uranium fuel. The interview with Perrin confirmed Vanunu's claim that Israel had the technology, the plant and the resources to make atomic bombs. It corrected a 1976 *Time* magazine report – one of the few to have appeared before the *Sunday Times* story – that the plutonium processing plant was not built until the late sixties.[7]

Insight's examination of Vanunu's claims had therefore passed through some five stages. First, the initial reports of Hounam's questioning in Australia were shown to experts. Second, associate editor Peter Wilsher joined the team to pass a sceptic's eye over their findings. Third, Vanunu was debriefed by Barnaby. Fourth, the evidence from this debriefing was referred to the other experts consulted. Fifth, the hard copy was shown to Theodore Taylor. The reporters had, of course, themselves acted as 'gatekeepers' in their interviews with Vanunu, and there was the confirmation that he had been employed at Dimona.

The last stage in many investigative stories consists of confronting the party under investigation. The object of this encounter depends upon the nature of the story and on how much the reporter has already learned. Sometimes the reporter lacks essential material and hopes to fill in the missing pieces. Ideally, as was the case with the Vanunu investigation, the reporter already has enough information to write the whole account and is only giving the other party a chance to give his or her side. Peter Wilsher and Hounam took an eight-page summary of Vanunu's testimony, some of the photographs, Vanunu's passport number and worker's certificate to the Israeli embassy. It gave the Israeli government the opportunity to respond to the investigation either by destroying the credibility of the man or by refuting the allegations about the nuclear arms production process at Dimona.

For a news organisation to approach any foreign government to obtain a reaction is a serious matter. It had added importance in this case because in June 1977 the *Sunday Times* published a four-page Insight report alleging systematic torture of Arab suspects from the West Bank by Israelis during interrogation. That investigation, which took five months, comprised interviews which Insight reporters had with a number of suspects. The editor, Harold Evans, had made a decision not to approach the Israeli embassy for its reaction prior to publication because he feared that the suspects named would be placed in danger. Nor had the reporters spoken to any Israeli officials, such as the police, the Justice Ministry, the army or the prison authorities, while they were carrying out their inquiries in Israel. Subsequently, some of the allegations were shown to be inaccurate.

When the two journalists from the *Sunday Times* telephoned the embassy to seek an appointment, all they told press attaché Eviator Manor was that they wanted to check a story 'about Dimona'. Manor thought they were doing a story about the Black Jews of Dimona, a number of black Jews from the United States living in the town, whose religious status had become controversial. When Wilsher and Hounam left their meeting with Manor, the latter tried to telephone the ambassador, Manchester-born Yehuda Avner, at his residence. He told Avner about the forthcoming Insight exposé but did not refer on the phone to the photographs or to the fact that the reporters wanted a confirmation of the story. Manor said he had to come over to see him, but Avner, who was preparing for a public dinner engagement, said that Manor should repeat the standard

Israeli position, namely that Israel would not be the first to introduce nuclear weapons into the region. Manor said that this was something totally different, and that Israel was past that stage. He had to see him. Manor arrived as Avner was putting on his dinner suit. When Avner's eyes fell upon the photographs he sat down. 'This is really something,' he murmured. The ambassador reported to Jerusalem. Back came the instruction to confirm that Mordechai Vanunu had been a technician at the Dimona reactor from 1976 to 1985, and to state that he was dismissed for unstable behaviour. The ambassador was late for his dinner engagement.

The remaining obstacle to publication was doubt by Neil and Insight regarding Vanunu's motives in divulging the information. Leaks may be the stuff of investigative journalism, but they are fraught with danger. People may leak for altruistic or ideological reasons, but generally motives are less pure. Some of the most talkative sources are people who have been hurt by developments which make up the particular story and have a vendetta against others involved. That Vanunu had been laid off could be important. Vanunu had struck up a warm acquaintance with Insight researcher Wendy Robbins. Noticing her medallion which bore her Hebrew name 'Rebecca', Vanunu asked her, 'Are you Jewish?' Insight staffers encouraged Robbins to try to find out his true motives for his disclosure.

Alternatively, as Neil increasingly asked himself during the investigation, was the paper being used by a foreign government? Barnaby's estimate of the number of Israeli nuclear warheads was much higher than previous estimates. Barnaby thought that Israel would be pleased for its nuclear capability to become known – notably to counter Iraqi and Syrian chemical weaponry. Yet, given the negative reaction in the US Congress, no Israeli government, Barnaby argued, could formally announce that it had nuclear capability.[8] Leonard Spector of the Carnegie Endowment Fund's Nuclear Proliferation Program shared this view. He even went so far as to suggest that Shimon Peres, about to hand over the prime ministership to the Likud Party's Itzhak Shamir under the coalition agreement, might have wanted to impress public opinion at home in order to prepare the ground for making territorial concessions.[9]

There were other theories as well, some attempting to explain how on earth Vanunu could have roamed about so freely and taken so many photographs. A variation to the theory that he was working for the Mossad was that the Israeli authorities simply allowed him to serve their interests. 'Having Vanunu say it, and adding credibility to his story by subsequently kidnapping him and putting him on trial, I think suits the Israeli government very well,' Barnaby speculated.[10] 'My conversations with Vanunu convince me that he was not a willing tool of the Mossad. But it is entirely possible that unwittingly he was allowed to serve a purpose – to tell the world about Israel's nuclear weapon activities.'[11] Though there had been a genuine security breakdown, in the end was Vanunu given just enough rope? A different possibility the newspaper had to weigh was that he was working for an Arab or eastern bloc intelligence service. The motives for Vanunu's disclosure were to concern Neil until the day of publication. 'Governments lie. Middle East governments lie and western governments lie. All governments lie, and it is the job of journalists to try and expose these lies. I take the view that news is telling the people what governments and powerful people don't want the people to know,' Neil said.

The embassy's confirmation that Vanunu had been a technician at Dimona raised the question again of whether the Israelis wanted the story published. Though it was reasonable to assume that the Israeli authorities had not intended Vanunu to tell his story, the Mossad, as is shown later, already knew he was speaking to the paper and were hard on his heels.[12] The Israeli government, therefore, expected the inquiry from the newspaper, but were apparently in the dark about what Vanunu actually knew, what he had told the paper, and whether the paper would publish his testimony, and if so what part of it. The Israeli government followed a classic rule in government public relations by giving a simple confirmation that Vanunu had been a technician at Dimona.

Neil was surprised that the Israeli authorities did not make any attempt to get him to drop the story; he had even lunched recently with the Israeli ambassador. The Israeli embassy in London maintains active ties with the British media to promote its viewpoint on the Arab–Israeli conflict. Describing the nature of the relationship, a former ambassador to London, Michael Comay, said that he 'knew the editor of *The Times* whom he met three or four times a year', and the editors of the *Daily Telegraph* and the *Financial Times*. He met less frequently with the editors of the *Guardian*, the *Sunday Times* and the *Observer*. Comay said, 'any ambassador in London has free access to chief editors – and if I have a complaint they will make a note of it because it is extremely difficult for foreign diplomats to have influence.' Neil asked himself whether the absence of any Israeli pressure was evidence that Vanunu's disclosure was an officially-sponsored leak, but the Israelis had wisely ruled out pressure. Jane Moonman, then director of the British–Israel Public Affairs Committee (she is now married to the present ambassador), argued, 'If you let the person on whom you are applying pressure know that it is extremely important to you, unless he happens to be a committed Zionist you run the risk of him saying "Let's go full steam on the story."'

And what of Rupert Murdoch? Murdoch's predisposition towards Israel was reflected in the pro-Israeli coverage and editorial positions taken by the *New York Post* which he then owned. Denis Herbstein, a former *Sunday Times* reporter, described 'the real Murdoch' as somebody 'who will come into the *Sunday Times* one Saturday night after a spell abroad, take a quick look at the first edition which has a piece on Israeli ill-treatment of Palestinian refugees. He is heard to say "this bloody paper is getting anti-semitic", and the message descends pretty sharply through the ranks. Open debate barely exists.'[13] On the other hand, one of Neil's colleagues characterised Murdoch's approach as 'quite simple: if it's a good story and sells papers, print it.' Murdoch might even have turned around and said 'Why not do ten pages instead of three?'

'The Vanunu story is not an anti-Israeli story – it's a scoop, a revelation, something exciting,' Philip Kleinman, a former contributor to the paper on advertising and the media, remarked. Squashing the story seemed out of the question. Given the struggle between the newspaper management and the unions, it would not have been difficult for a dissenting voice to have come out with the story elsewhere had Murdoch and Neil acceded to an Israeli request not to publish. Former Insight editors Bruce Page, Godfrey Hodgson and Phillip Knightley said that they had never been asked, instructed or hinted at by the editorial management to drop investigation of a story. To have done so would have meant the end of Insight. 'If you are dealing with areas where freedoms are paramount like the media, then you will upset a lot of sensibilities if you start saying "If you don't do what we want there will be repercussions." It's the kind of action that all decent people try to avoid,' Jane Moonman explained.

A turning point for Neil was to occur a couple of days after Wilsher and Hounam's inquiry at the Israeli embassy. Assuming that the *Sunday Times* intended to publish on the following Sunday, Prime Minister Peres convened the Israel Editors' Committee, a group of newspaper editors and broadcasting chiefs who are given briefings on sensitive military and diplomatic matters by senior government ministers. Peres informed the assembled editors of the imminent publication in London and while Israeli censorship regulations do not cover what appears in foreign media he asked them not to engage in any local reporting or comment about the story for forty-eight hours after its appearance in London. The *Sunday Times* learnt about this meeting from an Israeli source; Peter Wilsher knew two of the newspaper editors personally. It convinced Neil that Vanunu was a genuine security leak. Censorship had backfired.

Neil might have published that Sunday had the paper not known that the *Sunday Mirror* was also looking into the story. The date for publication was eventually set for the issue of 5 October.

Yet another clue that the disclosure might be genuine was Vanunu's disappearance. When he disappeared on 30 September, the paper was in a quandary whether to publish or not. A meeting of editors was called on Friday, 3 October, to decide whether to publish or not. In addition to Neil, those attending included deputy editor Ivan Fallon, managing editor (news) Anthony Rennell, news editor Andrew Hogg, foreign editor Stephen Milligan, political columnist Peter Jenkins as well as Morgan, Hounam and some of the reporters who had dealt with Vanunu. Those who opposed publication argued that the paper was at a distinct disadvantage in being unable to produce its key witness. The strength of the story depended on an insider confirming the existence of Dimona. Even if the paper was satisfied with the story's veracity, it had to convince the rest of the world. Some remained sceptical about Vanunu, saying that the story would be Andrew Neil's 'Hitler's Diaries'. Robin Morgan argued that Vanunu's disappearance was an additional reason to publish because 'if we didn't publish, and there wasn't any witness, the Mossad would quietly put him away somewhere. We had to publish to protect him – an annex to his existence.' The meeting divided fairly evenly among those who favoured publishing and those opposed, and Neil disbanded it, closeting himself with Fallon and Milligan, who were both in favour of publishing. Neil was still undecided:

'Andrew was terribly anxious about it. If we had run the story and it had been wrong, the editor would probably not have survived,' said an executive. In deciding to go ahead, Neil was influenced by the news about the Editors' Committee meeting in Israel: 'It was a powerful confirmation of something which was causing Peres anxiety.' He was also persuaded by the Israeli government confirmation that Vanunu was a former employee at Dimona. Leaving Neil's room, Fallon flashed a thumbs up to those outside. As he made his way towards the newsroom, a number of staffers approached him saying, 'I want you to know that I regard this as Neil's "Hitler's Diaries".'

During the five weeks when Insight was checking the story thought was given to the possibility that intelligence services, British or foreign, might try to obtain the evidence Vanunu had given. Insight had several thousand words on computer discs, most of which had been transcribed and photocopied. During their investigation into the murder in Egypt in December 1977 of David Holden, the paper's chief foreign correspondent, material which Insight had collected about his murder suddenly vanished. Afterwards Paul Eddie, the Insight editor, installed a safe: 'It is generally accepted that what is going on in all the main newspapers is known to the security services, either by reading outgoing telex messages or because they have somebody in the office,' Phillip Knightley, a former Insight editor remarked. A number of *Sunday Times* journalists possessed intelligence backgrounds, and after his death Holden was suspected of also having worked for a western intelligence service. A BBC *Panorama* programme by Tom Mangold on the security services uncovered an intelligence man in the BBC personnel department. In the first weeks of the Vanunu investigation its details were restricted to a handful of Insight reporters.

The entire top half of the front page of the *Sunday Times* of 5 October carried Vanunu's story under the headline:

'Revealed: Israel's Nuclear Arsenal'. The report summarised the longer article which took up two pages inside. After setting out the details of the structure of the nuclear research centre, the article described Vanunu's background and employment at Dimona, and then gave a brief history of the plant. It continued with a survey of the regional balance of power and the abortive attempts at inspection by the United States.

The article then gave a detailed description of Machon 2, where it said plutonium was separated from uranium, and plutonium buttons for the warheads 'baked'. It calculated the number of warheads which Israel had produced over the years, based on the quantity of plutonium which could be separated during the time the reactor had existed and on known arrivals in Israel of yellowcake, from which uranium is extracted.

At the foot of one of the two pages, under the caption 'How the experts were convinced', were the different examinations which Barnaby and Insight had put Vanunu through. The article ended by noting that ten scientists approached by the paper said that Vanunu's testimony could not be faulted. A comparison between the first and subsequent editions shows that this sentence was omitted from the first edition. 'We were trying to fit this story on the page and we were short of space, so I cut the paragraph at the end,' Morgan said. 'Neil was on the printing stone when he spotted this missing crucial paragraph. It's a reaffirmation that ten experts we approached saw Vanunu's testimony and could not fault it.' To make room for the sentence, another one was dropped which explained the absence of workers in Vanunu's photographs of Dimona. 'Vanunu has a simple answer: "I wasn't going to take pictures in front of my colleagues".' Of all sections of the Vanunu exposé in the 5 October issue, it was the side-bar article, 'How the experts were convinced', which showed most changes from edition to edition. Certain explanations by the scientists were excluded or altered. In the first edition the paper included the qualification by Dr Theodore Taylor, that Vanunu's description of the Dimona infrastructure, and his description of materials corresponding to the models of weapons components seemed accurate on the assumption that the photographs were taken at Dimona. But by the paper's final edition this had been dropped. In its place was Taylor's conclusion, which had already appeared on the paper's front page, that Israel had had nuclear weapons for at least a decade, and that, Taylor added, the Israeli programme was more developed than earlier estimates had suggested.

These edition changes reflected the anxiety running through the *Sunday Times* newsroom on the night of 4–5 October not only to get the story right but to be seen to do so.

In its front page article the paper wrote that 'nuclear scientists consulted by the *Sunday Times* calculate that at least 100 and as many as 200 nuclear weapons have been assembled.' This has been used as evidence that Israel has up to 200 nuclear weapons, but Barnaby's estimate, in fact, was 150 weapons. 'Two hundred would be an absolute upper limit. It assumes the same output from the reprocessing plant for the entire period of operations,' he said. Apart from this, he could not fault the way the paper had written its report 'given the nature of newspaper articles. I was pleasantly surprised that they'd put so much in. It was a good précis of Vanunu's knowledge.' Barnaby included a lot of what had been left out in a book he subsequently wrote. Of the paper's journalists he thought that only Hounam 'understood totally what was going on – he's prepared to read text books to learn about the subject.' He didn't think there was much in the exposé of specific interest to the physics community, 'but then that's not their readership'.

The account ran to a little over 6,000 words. Some

previous *Sunday Times* Insight investigations have run to 10,000 or even 15,000 words, one-sixth of the size of an average book. The paper was planning to run further articles about other aspects of Israel's nuclear programme and to write a book in collaboration with Vanunu, but his disappearance made it impossible to proceed. The exposé published on 5 October covered only about 10 per cent of the information Vanunu disclosed.

The investigation cost the paper £40–50,000. It involved five to six reporters working on the story for five weeks, with visits to Australia, the United States, and so on. By past standards this was not expensive: the Philby and thalidomide investigations, for example, involved fifteen or twenty reporters working for up to three months, and they were estimated to have incurred expenses into six figures. The *Sunday Times* expected to recover the Vanunu expenses through contracts which it had signed with the foreign newspapers and magazines prior to its publication of the story. But Vanunu's disappearance put paid to that also. Moreover, the paper's later contribution to Vanunu's defence put the story in the debit column of News International's balance sheet.

The publicity which the *Sunday Times* earned has unexpectedly been much more than originally envisaged owing to Vanunu's disappearance, abduction and trial in Israel. The exposé also helped to crown Neil's three-year editorship of the *Sunday Times,* and showed his mettle as an editor. 'It was the most important story that the paper ran since Neil took over as editor. It was the one with the biggest international implications,' an Insight staffer said. Neil hoped that it would contribute to stopping the paper's sagging circulation, which had dropped some 200,000 in the two previous years, to its lowest figure for some twenty years. Even though the revelation of a friendly western government's nuclear secrets did not precisely fit the conservative values of Neil and the newspaper's owner (it was a story more typical of the socialist-libertarian values which underlay the Insight reporting during Harold Evans's editorship) Neil had gone ahead.

4. A TALE OF TWO PAPERS

One week before the *Sunday Times* published Vanunu's story, the *Sunday Mirror* came out on 28 September with a centrefold spread which raised questions about the authenticity of claims made to the paper that Israel had manufactured the neutron bomb. The same day that the *Sunday Times*'s debriefing of Vanunu by Dr Frank Barnaby began, Oscar Guerrero, Vanunu's ostensible agent, had walked into the offices of the *Sunday Mirror* to offer them the story.

The circumstances which led Guerrero to a rival newspaper were a matter of dispute. A relationship of mutual suspicion existed between Guerrero and the *Sunday Times* from the beginning because of Guerrero's claim that 'Professor' Mordechai Vanunu was Israel's top atomic scientist. Peter Hounam did not have an easy time interviewing Vanunu in Australia because, he said, Guerrero was frustrating to deal with.[1] In an attempt to pacify him prior to his return trip to London with Vanunu, Hounam agreed a deal under which Guerrero was to receive the first US $25,000 from any earnings by Vanunu, such as syndication rights to his story and a planned book. No formal written agreement between the *Sunday Times* and Vanunu existed in Australia because it involved discussion in London with a prospective book publisher. An agreement was due to be signed on the day Vanunu disappeared. Guerrero claimed that Hounam had left Sydney with Vanunu in the middle of the night, cutting him out of the deal. He flew to London in hot pursuit,

87

and offered the story to the *Observer*. Given the rivalry between the *Sunday Times* and the *Observer* it was a clever move. But the *Observer* turned him away. His next stop was the *Sunday Mirror*. Cheque book journalism seemed to loom large in Guerrero's considerations; he was concerned that he should receive proper payment.

The *Sunday Times* denied that it broke its agreement with Guerrero. According to Hounam, 'there was never a question of cutting him out of the deal. It's outrageous to suggest that we would do that. We just simply don't do that sort of thing.' John McKnight rejected Guerrero's claim that Hounam and Vanunu had slipped away in the middle of the night: Guerrero, he said, had accompanied Vanunu, Hounam and McKnight to Sydney airport. Moreover, Guerrero was in possession of a letter guaranteeing him the first payment from Vanunu's earnings. Yet, according to the Israeli paper *Maariv*, drawing on an interview with Hounam a month after the Vanunu exposé, in Australia Hounam distanced himself from Guerrero whom he saw as an exploiter, and, at Hounam's insistence, Vanunu met him without Guerrero's knowledge.[2] According to the Israel Supreme Court ruling in May 1990 on Vanunu's appeal '. . . Hounam distanced Guerrero from contact between the paper and Vanunu, and flew together with Vanunu to London . . . Guerrero, whose requests for a significant payment from the *Sunday Times* were rejected, telephoned in the meantime to another paper, the *Sunday Mirror*.'[3]

When Guerrero arrived in London he contacted the *Sunday Times* and spoke to Robin Morgan; Hounam was busy checking Vanunu's story. Morgan tried to reassure. 'We said "Wait, be patient. We will come back to you. When we've proved the story, that is the time to talk."' But Wendy Robbins, who worked as a researcher on the story, says, 'Guerrero kept ringing, and kept wanting to speak to Robin [Morgan]. He then asked to speak to me' (Robbins had met him on his previous trip to London from Madrid). 'I said

"You'll have to speak to Robin". He said "But I never get through to him".' Then Guerrero said that he wanted to meet her in a park at 8pm as he had something 'hot' to tell her. Morgan initially agreed, but according to her, later cancelled it saying it was too dangerous. According to Hounam, however, Guerrero telephoned Morgan 'insisting that he had decided not to pursue his agreement with us. He told Robin that he thought that by now the story was worth a million dollars and he was taking it elsewhere.'

When Guerrero contacted the *Sunday Mirror* he said, according to Tony Frost, then the news editor, that he had the greatest story since Watergate, and that he was looking for a lot of money. 'It's a million dollar story,' he told Frost, who replied that he had 'been watching too many films. We have never paid a million dollars for a story.' Later they renegotiated and Guerrero went down to half a million dollars. But Frost refused. Frost then asked him about the *Sunday Times*. 'He claimed to have been double-crossed by the *Sunday Times*, that he had introduced Hounam to Vanunu, and one morning they upped and left, leaving him asleep in the hotel bedroom.' According to another *Sunday Mirror* journalist, Mark Souster, who had spent considerable time with Guerrero, the *Sunday Times* said that it would honour their agreement with him if he went back to them but he declined. In the Vanunu exposé itself, on 5 October 1986, the paper's first edition said that after his arrival in London, Guerrero telephoned the *Sunday Times* demanding $300,000 threatening that he would sell the story to another paper otherwise. Guerrero, according to the paper, did not keep appointments to meet its staff and subsequently telephoned to inform them that he had taken the story to the *Sunday Mirror*. But by the paper's final edition, this version had been altered to say that after he arrived in London, Guerrero took his account to the *Sunday Mirror*. The main witness to what happened in the crucial period in Australia, Mordechai Vanunu, is unable to give his version of events.

The two versions of events came up in March 1992 in the London High Court when Guerrero sued the *Sunday Times*. The court rejected Guerrero's legal action, as well as ordering him to pay the newspaper's legal costs.

In popular journalism, news is only one ingredient. Success depends as much on the sports section, features and competitions like bingo. The Vanunu story was not one which a popular tabloid paper would normally be interested in. 'Foreign affairs are box office poison. Nobody wants to know about them,' remarked Joe Grizzard, a former *Mirror* executive. According to Souster, 'We were asking ourselves "What do we do with it?" The fact that Israel has a nuclear bomb makes no odds to our readership.' Frost's scoops in the *Sunday Mirror*, for example, included pictures of the Duchess of Windsor lying on her deathbed, which he obtained from a member of her staff, and the life story of the man who had been Princess Diana's hairdresser for seven years. 'In tabloid terms this was a much more important story than Vanunu,' Frost remarked. But Mike Molloy, the paper's editor, felt Vanunu was of certain relevance: 'You're dealing with readers who essentially don't want demanding papers – otherwise they'd buy the broadsheet ones. But popular entertainment is only part of the paper. All the balancing elements are important. If you give someone a mass of sugary content, ultimately, after a few years, you begin to suffer.' 'The big stories all have a place in newspapers, be they tabloid or broadsheet,' according to one executive. 'The only difference is how large the headline is and how it is written. The Vanunu story had a spy element. There was a James Bond feel to it – there was subterfuge, nuclear bombs, snatched photos. The story could have a format which would be totally understood and valued by *Sunday Mirror* readers,' he added.

The *Sunday Mirror* and its daily sister were struggling to contain and reverse a declining circulation. In the mid-sixties the *Daily Mirror* had enjoyed an unrivalled circulation of more than five million copies. In the year after Robert Maxwell purchased the *Sunday Mirror* in July 1984 its circulation declined by 450,000 from 3.6m to 3.15m. Sales of the *Daily Mirror* also declined in the same period by 19 per cent. The *News of the World*, by contrast, increased its sales in the same period by nearly half a million to almost 5m copies. The *Mirror* papers used to include serious, campaigning articles. But the rise of the daily *Sun*, and fierce competition among the popular Sunday paper readership, forced them to go downmarket. An important factor in the *Sunday Mirror*'s decision to go for the Vanunu story was the knowledge that the *Sunday Times* was on to it. 'The *Sunday Times* may not be in direct competition with the *Sunday Mirror*, but it's still a Sunday paper. Because we knew that the *Sunday Times* were chasing it, it forced our hand and we were keen to get in first,' a reporter said.

Tony Frost was an obvious choice; he had built a solid reputation as an investigative reporter. Starting his career in journalism on his local paper in Cambridgeshire, he moved, after a stint on a suburban news agency, to the defunct London *Evening News*. In 1976 he began a fifteen year career on the *Sunday Mirror*, from staff reporter to chief reporter to deputy news editor and news editor. Later he was to be appointed deputy editor. 'Frost was best at investigative journalism. It was felt that Vanunu was the sort of story that only he could handle sensibly and get together,' said one of the paper's executives.

The strategy which the *Sunday Mirror* adopted in approaching the story was similar to the *Sunday Times*'s – to check the information and the person bringing it by trying to disprove the authenticity. If Guerrero were proved genuine, the paper would move on to the story itself. Guerrero described himself as an international journalist who had interviewed world leaders. He showed Frost six photos which appeared to show him standing with politicians like

Lech Walesa, Argentine President Alfonso, Shimon Peres and the PLO's Issam Sartawi. But something seemed wrong with some of the pictures; Guerrero appeared to be as prominent as his subjects, in some cases more so. Tempers began to fray. Frost did not believe Guerrero's claims about his journalistic background. Guerrero repeatedly said: 'I've got the proof that Professor Vanunu is right . . . that Israel has been making neutron bombs.' Then he said, 'I have the same pictures which Vanunu had passed to the *Sunday Times*. I was his agent. I got the pictures copied.' The photos were in a bag Guerrero had been clutching assiduously. But without a contract Guerrero said that he would not show them the photos. Peter Miller, the assistant editor for news and Frost were hesitant given the question-mark over Guerrero's background. Eventually a contract was drawn up, but it included a clause that he would be paid fourteen days after exclusive publication of the story. An additional clause required that the information and the photos be found genuine. Guerrero then opened his bag and produced two pictures of what he said was Dimona. He added that it might be possible to get more – but it would cost money.

'You said that you had the evidence,' Frost countered. 'Yes, yes, but they're not here. They're in . . . a luggage lock-up.' When Guerrero gave them the two pictures, Frost had seen that there were more photos in the bag. A cup of coffee was ordered for Guerrero. According to Frost, 'as the secretary offered him the cup, Guerrero relaxed his hold on the bag. I grabbed it.'[4] That Guerrero had been unwilling to part with these pictures – in contrast to those of him appearing in the company of international politicians – added to the genuineness of the Dimona photos. 'Although we doubted and were unsure of his motives, we became more and more convinced about what he was selling,' said one of the journalists. They took the material to John Parker, the paper's deputy editor. Given the other dubious pictures, who's going to back these up, Parker asked rhetorically. They had to be shown to experts. Molloy took a cursory but genuine interest and okayed showing the pictures to outside experts, asking that he be kept posted on progress.

It was Thursday, 18 September. Through a 'mole' on the *Sunday Times* staff, the *Sunday Mirror* was able to follow the other paper's progress with the story. 'One of our reporters heard from his contacts at the *Sunday Times* that there was something very big, secretive, going on,' said Frost. According to the reporter, 'I had a friend working in the *Sunday Times* who while not actively involved with the story was able to tell me how far advanced they were in their investigation and when they were intending to publish – which obviously determined when we would.' Not all the intelligence fed proved correct; in that third week of September the contact reported at one stage that the *Sunday Times* did not even have Vanunu. Now that the *Sunday Mirror* had some solid material the race was on. Would a tabloid scoop one of the 'heavies' on a story which the latter would usually cover? According to Frost, 'we were terrified that the *Sunday Times* might publish that weekend (21 September), but the word on the jungle drum was that they were having huge difficulties and that they would not be publishing that weekend.' Had the *Sunday Mirror* gotten its 28 September story right – namely that Vanunu and his pictures were genuine – the disloyalty by the mole would have cost the paper its most important foreign story of the year.

The *Sunday Mirror* showed the photos to some five experts, among them a man who had worked at Aldermaston, a Royal Air Force officer with knowledge of nuclear arms, and a Leeds University scientist. The paper's Paris correspondent consulted a French expert. The photos – black and white reproductions from the copies Guerrero had shown them – were of four types: exteriors of what appeared to be a nuclear reactor, scenic views of the nuclear research complex, photos showing spherical figures described as bomb components, and components of the Domesday device. The experts, on being shown the photos, were not asked 'Is this a nuclear installation?', but 'What do you believe this is?'. If they failed to identify them as connected to nuclear weapons production, then, the experts were told, 'Look, we understand this to be . . . Do you agree?' Some of the experts did not want to put their reputations on the line for the paper. Others were non-committal. While Souster and Geoff Garvey were meeting experts, Richard Brecker was preparing a dossier on nuclear arms and the neutron bomb, including drawing on published sources.

Other aspects of the story were being checked. Theodore Levite, the *Mirror*'s veteran correspondent in Tel Aviv, had been instructed to gather any information about Professor Vanunu. Without any spokesman at Dimona to turn to, and with the Israel Atomic Energy Commission having 'a spokesman who doesn't speak', as one reporter put it, Levite contacted the Defence Minister's Media Adviser, a close friend. 'The reply was that there was no Professor Vanunu. But one official source said that there had been a low-ranking technician with that name,' Levite said. He checked with contacts in Beersheba and Dimona and found that there had been a person of that name, that he was eccentric and had participated in a pro-Arab demonstration. In Australia the information that Guerrero had met Vanunu at King's Cross was confirmed by McKnight, who also said that Guerrero had been there but was 'cagey, protective' about Vanunu.

The key proof the *Sunday Mirror* wanted was to meet Vanunu. Given that he was with the *Sunday Times*, the only way they could reach him was via Guerrero. Throughout the ten days Guerrero was dealing with the *Sunday Mirror* he made a number of attempts to reach Vanunu at the *Sunday Times*, as an inspection of the logs of telephone calls at the hotels where he stayed showed. The *Sunday Times* had put up Guerrero at the Tower Thistles Hotel during his first visit to London from Madrid, so Guerrero, not knowing that Vanunu was at a country lodge, where he was being debriefed, thought that he might also be at the Tower Thistles. Brecker was sent to the hotel in the vain hope of locating Vanunu, who was only moved to the hotel from 19–23 September, by which time the *Mirror* had decided that he was staying at a guesthouse. Those in Bloomsbury, Paddington and Victoria were checked out, hotel staff being shown a photo of Vanunu. Guerrero then claimed that Vanunu was staying in a warehouse in St Katherine's Dock with two *Sunday Times* minders, sleeping in sleeping bags. He said that it would be possible to meet Vanunu but only with the minders being present. According to Hounam, a request by Guerrero was passed on to Vanunu who refused to meet him. Finally on Wednesday, 24 September, Guerrero said that he could arrange a meeting with Vanunu at Leicester Square men's toilets at 7.30 p.m. Frost positioned himself across the entrance on a corner outside a cinema. Miller was on another corner, and McGarvey on a third. Guerrero was at the main entrance to the toilets. They waited for an hour, but Vanunu failed to show up.

It was the last they saw of Guerrero. In addition to the dubious pictures of him, the experts consulted failed to give a non-conditional okay, and the final proof – a meeting with Vanunu – failed to get off the ground. Guerrero took a cross-channel ferry to Amsterdam and from there via Bangladesh Airlines back to Australia. He was apparently afraid lest the story on him which the paper was left with would lead him into the hands of the Israelis.

The following day, Thursday, the twenty-fifth, *Mirror* reporters on the story, and Frost and Miller, met to draw together the various strands of their investigation. Until then the story had no specific line. Their draft was pegged to the Guerrero aspect but allowed that the photos might well be of Israel's nuclear programme. Miller and Frost met with

John Parker, and were joined by the editor. 'Right boys, are we going with the story or not?', asked Molloy. Miller and Frost went quickly through the various aspects. Question: Had we proved conclusively from our experts that the pictures were of the inside of Dimona? Answer: No. Had we proved conclusively from our experts that Israel was manufacturing neutron bombs? No. Molloy became more and more sceptical as reporters ran through their material. Molloy instructed Frost to take all the material to the Israel embassy in the hope of shedding more light on the matter. The embassy confirmed – as Levite had been informed by officials in Israel – that there was no Professor Vanunu but that there was a technician of that name who, according to the embassy's spokesman, had been fired from his work because of unstable behaviour.

On Molloy's instructions, the underlying line of the draft was altered from its 'maybe – maybe not' stance to being a hoax. The article which was published raised the question of whether the story was intended to discredit Israel. A side-bar article quoted two scientists as raising serious doubts about the photos' authenticity. One of these, Dr John Baruch of Leeds University, was reported as saying that the pictures could be of any laboratory – even a food sterilisation plant or car wash. Baruch had, in fact, told McGarvey that it might be a nuclear manufacturing facility but that there was insufficient evidence to state it with certainty. *If*, however, the story was a hoax, it was a highly sophisticated one. Frost, who sometimes clashed with Molloy on editorial policy, says that he complained to him over the projection of the article. His apparent reservations notwithstanding, it is noteworthy that Frost told *Haaretz* newspaper after the *Sunday Mirror*'s story appeared, 'if the *Sunday Times* go after the story, on the basis of the information we have, they will commit a terrible error. This will be Hitler Diaries Mark II.' 'Mike Molloy was obsessed with showing the *Sunday Times* were being hoaxed and I believe this cost us a fantastic story,' remarked Peter Miller. When the following week the *Sunday Times* reported that Vanunu's allegations were true, the *Sunday Mirror* was not only left with egg on its face but it had lost an international scoop. 'Such a story would have given the paper, Tony Frost and, to a lesser extent myself, a lot of kudos,' said Miller. 'Tony Frost and I felt there was a way of giving more weight to Guerrero's claims without stating positively that they were true. We wanted to be first with the story and even a watered down version would have taken the sting out of the *Sunday Times*,' he added.

Where did the *Sunday Mirror* err when the *Sunday Times* got it right? Both applied similar rules of investigative journalism to the Vanunu story. Both went through rigours of checking the information and its source. Both were suspicious of Guerrero. And both differentiated between him and the pictures of Dimona. The *Sunday Times* stood at an overwhelming advantage because they had Mordechai Vanunu. Had the *Sunday Mirror* met him, let alone debriefed him, this would have given greater credence to the photographs and to Vanunu's story. It is surprising that while the ten experts consulted by the *Sunday Times* said, according to the paper, 'that Vanunu's testimony cannot be faulted,' none of the five consulted by the *Sunday Mirror* said so. The *Sunday Mirror*, in its report, claimed to have thirty-seven of the fifty-seven photographs which Vanunu had taken of the nuclear research centre. But only a selection appears to have been shown to their experts. 'If they had been shown the entire set of photos, they would not have known what they were talking about. I guess they had no experience of nuclear weapons,' Dr Barnaby remarked. More experts should have been shown the material given that none of the experts which the *Sunday Mirror* did consult gave a completely negative evaluation, and given the Israeli authorities' confirmation that Vanunu had worked at Dimona. 'The question of the experts was the one big mistake I made on the whole thing,' Tony Frost admitted. 'I should have sent the material to our US correspondent to show it to an American expert – that's what the *Sunday Times* did.'

Organisationally, the *Sunday Times* also had the advantage, with five times the number of journalists the *Sunday Mirror* has. It could call on a network of intelligence contacts in the CIA, British intelligence, French intelligence and Israeli intelligence.

'We didn't have resources, the time, the manpower, or the contacts with the experts,' the *Mirror*'s Souster remarked. Had Vanunu turned up at the *Sunday Mirror* instead of the *Sunday Times* it is most unlikely that *Mirror* reporters would have carried out the rigorous checks, including an intensive two-day debriefing, which the *Sunday Times* did, or have spent three pages on Vanunu's detailed description of the separation of plutonium and uranium which even by Insight standards was intricate. It would be wrong to conclude that if, say, Vanunu had been a curvaceous blonde instead of an oriental Jew the tabloid would have given the story a warmer embrace. The *Mirror* had a number of reporters dealing with it for ten days. But ten days was not enough.

It also seems that Molloy, the editor, misjudged the story's news value. According to Molloy, 'the deputy editor told me that Frost and Miller had been offered a story that Israel had the atomic bomb. Everybody knows it, so I wasn't taken with it. Frankly, I thought it was a huge confidence trick – they were talking about huge sums of money. There was somebody who had taken a lot of newspapers for rides. One's always susceptible to those sort of things and the paper being made a fool of.'[5] Molloy seemed not to distinguish between the dubious Guerrero and the pictures of Dimona, despite the fact that he knew that the *Sunday Times* were seriously investigating the story and that they had the man from Dimona. He appears not to have appreciated the significance of Vanunu being the first person with direct knowledge of Dimona to speak about his work, while the *Sunday Times* masterfully reconstructed from Vanunu's description of the flow processes an estimate of how many warheads Israel had produced. And Molloy erred when he claimed 'that if Israel would have a bomb factory they would hardly have it in Tel Aviv. They would have it somewhere secret, wouldn't they?!' Neither Guerrero nor Vanunu claimed there was a bomb factory in Tel Aviv; they claimed it was in Dimona, in the isolated Negev region in the south.

At heart an artist, Molloy, a graduate of Ealing College of Art, joined the *Sunday Pictorial* as a cartoonist, moving to the *Daily Sketch*. He worked with the Mirror Group for twenty-eight years including as editor of the *Mirror Magazine*, and for ten years was editor of the *Daily Mirror*. He was a respected expert in design, often drawing the page plan for the front page. Notwithstanding that he had been an editor of 'Mirrorscope', the section in the daily paper which provided background and light analysis of the news, and that he belonged to the old school of *Mirror* editors who recognised that there was a place in the popular tabloid for serious reporting, his handling of this story suggests that he was unable to evaluate the complex story in its many aspects. Frost said of him that 'it was no good giving Molloy too much minutiae.'

Alternatively, the line that Molloy took with the article may have been due less to an erroneous news judgement than to not wishing to upset proprietor Robert Maxwell. One interesting point was that after the raw copy had been sub-edited, Frost 'complained at least twice, possibly three times, about the projection and the handling of the story' – including how the noncommittal reactions of the scientists had been changed. Molloy, according to Frost, replied 'Well, there's no more space. It's too late.' But it wasn't too late because it was still Friday night, twenty-four hours before edition time.

A year earlier Molloy had been eased out of the editorship

of the daily paper by Maxwell into the Sunday paper. 'Molloy knew how to handle Maxwell, and he knew it was a story he had to cover his back on,' said Miller. Said one staffer: 'The question is whether Molloy genuinely had doubts about the story or was only second guessing Maxwell's wishes when he told us how he wanted the story treated or even carrying out Maxwell's specific instructions.'

The way the *Sunday Mirror* handled the story lacked interest in contrast to the *Sunday Times* which basked in the glory of getting it right. The fact that the *Sunday Mirror* got it wrong posed for American journalist Seymour Hersh the additional question of whether the paper got it wrong deliberately. According to Hersh, Nicholas Davies, the foreign editor of the *Daily Mirror*, heard that Guerrero was offering the Sunday paper the pictures of Dimona and tipped off a business partner, Ari Ben Menashe (one of Hersh's sources) who worked in Israel military intelligence. Ben Menashe immediately flew to London, Hersh says, where Davies had arranged a meeting with Guerrero.[6] The latter was persuaded to part with a couple of photos – because before offering payment it would be necessary to verify them. The photos, Hersh says, were taken to Israel where it was realised that it was necessary to discredit the whole story. Davies set up a meeting for Ben Menashe with Robert Maxwell who said that he had already spoken to 'Ben Menashe's bosses' and knew what had to happen.[7] According to Hersh, this explains the treatment which the story received. A clue to this was contained in one italicised paragraph in the paper's report which asked rhetorically whether the story was a hoax or, worse, a campaign to discredit Israel.

Arguably more significant was Hersh's claim that Davies, at Ben Menashe's request, located the place where Vanunu was staying. The allegations about Davies were strengthened in Hersh's eyes because the former and Ben Menashe had a business arranging arms shipments to foreign governments. One question arising from the allegations concerned a clash of interests between arranging international arms deliveries and being a foreign editor. A separate question concerns Maxwell's alleged relationship with the Mossad.[8]

These allegations were included in *The Samson Option* published in autumn 1991. Subtitled *Israel's Nuclear Arsenal and American Foreign Policy*, Hersh described the role of the Israeli nuclear capability in US–Israeli relations and how the US turns a blind eye to Israel's nuclear programme. Hersh's original manuscript submitted to his American publishers, Random House, did not include his allegations about Vanunu and the *Sunday Mirror*. When Random House sent the manuscript to the book's British publishers, Faber & Faber, they liked it but asked Hersh if there was something he could add with an explicitly British angle. Chapter 22, the last chapter of the book, was drafted. The book was published in Britain amid great secrecy. The title did not appear in the publisher's catalogue, and copies were hand-delivered to bookshops on the weekend prior to publication because the publisher feared that Maxwell might attempt to seek a High Court injunction to prevent the book's distribution.

A press release failed to excite news organisations, but copies of the book were in the hands of the two MPs, Rupert Allason, a Conservative, who under the name of Nigel West has written books on espionage, and George Galloway, Labour for Dundee. An ardent campaigner for Palestinian rights, Galloway was instrumental in the twinning of Dundee with the West Bank town of Nablus. The two MPs tabled motions calling for an inquiry into the claim that Davies had passed information to the Israelis about Vanunu's location, and expressed concern that the *Daily Mirror* and Maxwell had maintained ties with the Mossad. They called for an independent tribunal to determine 'the extent of foreign intelligence penetration of Mirror Group Newspapers'. In an editorial comment covering its entire front page (a space normally reserved for news), the *Daily Mirror* accused the MPs of exploiting parliamentary privilege which allows an MP to speak without fear of being sued. Maxwell denounced Hersh's claims as 'ludicrous and a total invention', and Davies said they were a complete and total lie. Davies said that he had never met Vanunu, adding that Maxwell 'knew that it was laughable that he himself was involved in the Mossad and he didn't believe for a second that I was.' Fourteen libel writs were exchanged between Maxwell, Davies, Mirror Group Newspapers and Hersh, Faber & Faber, and the two MPs. At the time of the Hersh book Maxwell, who could claim to have been the most litigious newspaper proprietor in Britain, was estimated to have about a hundred legal actions going against journalists and news organisations.

Nick Davies had been the *Daily Mirror*'s foreign editor for fifteen years. He was from a middle-class family and educated at a British public school. His father wanted him to go into the legal profession, but Davies was more interested in journalism, and began his career on the *Birmingham Post*. He moved to the *Daily Mirror* after impressing them by bicycling ten miles to a story they had asked him to cover. As a foreign correspondent, and later foreign editor, Davies visited many of the world's trouble spots, and in the 1980s he travelled frequently to Israel. He succeeded in edging himself into Maxwell's inner circle of advisers, often accompanying his boss on foreign trips, and sometimes helping to arrange meetings with foreign leaders and officials through the contacts he had acquired over the years. Hersh's allegations were to cause an unplanned interruption in his journalistic career. Denying in public, and to his editor, other allegations made by Hersh that he was involved in arms sales, he was dismissed after the *Daily Mail* published a picture of Davies in Ohio where he had visited an arms dealer. An internal inquiry failed, however, to find any evidence regarding Hersh's allegations that Davies was a Mossad 'asset' or had betrayed Mordechai Vanunu.

The impact of Hersh's allegations came to a crescendo with the death of Robert Maxwell some two weeks after publication of the book. His body was found at sea after he disappeared from his yacht near the Canary Islands. One possibility was that Maxwell had been a victim of foul play by an Arab hitman or by somebody he had crossed in a business deal. Ben Menashe, today no longer part of the Israeli intelligence community, went so far as to claim that 'elements within the Israeli government in particular had an interest in shutting Maxwell up. Just as Maxwell had to separate himself from Nick Davies – whom I was running – so his own mentors had to separate him from themselves.'

Another theory was suicide. Maxwell was clearly angry at the Hersh allegations; he was forced to dismiss Davies. Moreover, three days before his death he became aware of fresh charges Hersh was about to make to back up his earlier ones about Vanunu's abduction. These concerned a video-tape and still photographs allegedly showing Davies meeting Mossad agents in Geneva to arrange wire tapping the telephone of the *Sunday Times*'s Peter Hounam in the hope of discovering Vanunu's location. On the night before Maxwell's death, Richard Stott, *Daily Mirror* editor, had spoken to him on his yacht, but Maxwell did not seem depressed, rather 'very angry' about the Hersh allegations. And, his associates said that he was an unlikely figure to commit suicide. With the subsequent revelation of the collapse of the Maxwell empire, however – including the disappearance of £42m of company pensions funds in the two months before his death – the suicide theory gains significance. Mike Molloy argued that when he saw his corporation crumbling Maxwell realised that it was only a matter of time. While he could bear hatred, insults and scorn he could not take being ridiculed. If suicide was the cause of the death, the collapse of his empire was the trigger.

*

Two points support Hersh's theory of a disinformation plot. First, the manner in which the slant of the article was changed from its neutral stance – that the pictures might be of Dimona – to its being a hoax story; the second, the protestations by Frost about the line Molloy took, ignoring the official confirmation that Vanunu had worked at Dimona, and the view of the experts consulted that the pictures might be genuine.

A third point concerns the instruction for the material to be taken to the Israeli embassy. The reporters questioned the wisdom of the decision since it might be tipping off the Israelis about Vanunu. Molloy was genuinely suspicious from the beginning. John Parker, deputy editor, claimed that 'Molloy was suspicious from the outset not so much about the Vanunu claim but by the man Guerrero who produced a set of photos which appeared to me, and certainly to Molloy, to have been suspect.' In the hope that an embassy reaction might shed light on whether the paper was being hoaxed, or provide other information, the step (also taken by the *Sunday Times*) was justified. That the paper had already received an official reaction via its Tel Aviv correspondent was irrelevant since there is always the chance of getting more, or different, information from another official source. Surprising was Molloy's instruction to take all the material instead of, as in the *Sunday Times* case, a summary of Insight's findings, a couple of photos and Vanunu's passport number.

Molloy denies the Hersh allegation that Maxwell was involved in the decision to go to the embassy. 'The decision was made by me alone,' he said in an interview after Maxwell's death. He acknowledges that he mentioned the article to Maxwell given the proprietor's interest. It is something which the editor of a newspaper owned by an interventionist proprietor would do. 'I spoke to him about the story because I kept him informed of all big stories that were going on.' He went on to explain that he had told him, 'I've got an extraordinary story that somebody thinks that there is an Israeli secret atomic factory. I don't like the look of things but I'm going to have it checked out. Maxwell said "Oh really. That's good." And then we talked about something else.'[9] In an interview with the *Sunday Mirror* after the publication of the book, Molloy again said that he had told the publisher beforehand of his decision to take the material to the Israeli embassy. Maxwell, Molloy said, neither reacted nor paid any special interest. Yet in the same interview Molloy said that the decision to take the material to the embassy had never been referred to Maxwell. Molloy denies having actually shown Maxwell the material. He didn't see the pictures, nor did they actually have a conversation with him face to face.[10] There remains no evidence that Maxwell took the decision that it was anything more than seeking an embassy reaction or possible lead to solve what appeared to Molloy to be a hoax. Molloy also denied that the hoax theme which he gave the article was part of an Israeli disinformation effort. 'There was no question of Robert Maxwell giving instructions to the *Sunday Mirror* how the story should be handled. He didn't say "I want this story handled in this particular way." It just wasn't so.'

There is no evidence that Vanunu's location in London was given to the Israeli authorities by Davies or Maxwell. It is true that Davies acted as an eyes and ears for Maxwell in the *Daily Mirror* newsroom. 'He was the sort of journalist who was always sidling up to you to find out what you were doing. But he never came near to us in connection with the Vanunu story, and I'm convinced he had nothing to do with its treatment by the *Sunday Mirror*,' said Miller. Davies was then the foreign editor of the *Daily Mirror* only. The *Sunday Mirror* had its own. 'If Nick Davies had come any where near the story I would have strangled him,' remarked Tony Frost. 'We are very protective.' It is true that Maxwell was able to eavesdrop on the telephones of Mirror Group executives. But there was nothing to learn since the *Mirror* journalists failed to make contact with Mordechai Vanunu and did not know his location.

After Hersh made his allegations Yael Lotan, an Israeli journalist and campaigner on Vanunu's behalf, claimed that Shimon Peres, the Israeli prime minister, had told Israeli editors when briefing them about the *Sunday Times*'s planned report that Maxwell had agreed to discredit the Vanunu claims. Lotan, literary editor of the Israeli left-wing daily *Al Hamishmar*, said that she learnt of this from the paper's editor, the late Mark Geffen, who participated in the briefing. But according to another participant, Ari Rath, editor of the *Jerusalem Post*, who made detailed notes of the briefing, 'There was absolutely no mention by Peres either to the *Sunday Mirror* or to Maxwell at that meeting. There was no mention of anybody or anything beginning with "M".'

The question of whether the *Sunday Mirror* article was part of an Israeli-sponsored disinformation effort to discredit Vanunu needs to be seen against the wider perspective of the parallel activities of the *Sunday Times*. As noted earlier, its editor, Andrew Neil, was not approached by the Israeli ambassador, despite their good ties. When Frost and Souster took the material to the Israeli embassy they received the same reaction as the *Sunday Times* had: that Vanunu had been a technician at Dimona who had been laid off. When the *Mirror* journalists contacted the embassy's press attaché, Eviator Manor, and showed him the material, Manor proposed to Jerusalem that the portrayal of Guerrero in derogatory terms placed a definite shadow over Vanunu and provided an opportunity to discredit the whole Vanunu story. But, Manor said, this was just his view, and all the decisions were being made in Israel. The official reaction which Manor was instructed to convey was similar to that which had been given to the *Sunday Times* – noting that Vanunu had been fired from his work at Dimona because of 'unstable behaviour'.

106

If the *Sunday Mirror* was used in an Israeli disinformation effort it had not been pre-selected for the purpose because Guerrero turned to the paper only after unsuccessfully offering the story to the *Observer*. Any conspiracy could have been hatched only subsequently. True, there was a question mark over Guerrero. He moved to the Eccleston Hotel a day after the Mossad's Cindy had moved out. Mark Souster, who spent a number of days with Guerrero, believes that he saw Guerrero have breakfast at the hotel with a lady subsequently identified as Cindy.[11] That Guerrero has since claimed in press interviews that Vanunu was not abducted to Israel via Rome and that Cindy did not exist, might appear to add credibility to a Mossad connection. But, if such a connection existed, why back in Australia, when at one stage Vanunu was having second thoughts about going ahead with the whole thing and wanted to destroy the photographs, was it Guerrero who persisted and refused to let the story die. Moreover, according to McKnight, Guerrero never went to King's Cross, Sydney, of his own accord. He was sent there by the local employment office to paint a fence as part of a government-sponsored employment scheme. His lack of credibility would have made him a most unsuitable and unreliable intelligence link, and if, initially acting as Vanunu's agent, he was subsequently 'turned' and became an Israeli asset, when did this occur? Given the manner in which he refused to hand over the pictures of Dimona to Frost and his colleagues – indeed, Frost had to use a trick against Guerrero to get the photos – he could not have been working for the Israelis at that stage. That Guerrero offered the story for a fraction of what the *Sunday Times* had offered might be explained by the fact that the US $25,000-payment the *Sunday Times* discussed was to be taken from any future payment made to Vanunu, but in the end, Guerrero did not even attempt to collect payment from the *Mirror*. According to his agreement, the information had to be correct and the story was to be exclusive to the *Sunday Mirror*. Guerrero probably assumed that since the *Sunday Mirror* presented his story as a hoax and the *Sunday Times* also had the story, the chances were slim that the *Sunday Mirror* would pay him.

To sum up, the sensational allegation that Davies provided information to the Israelis about Vanunu's location in London appears baseless. Concerning the allegation of disinformation, 'with hindsight,' according to Parker, 'the *Sunday Mirror* report appeared as a classic exercise by the Israelis in disinformation.' The question remains whether this is true or whether other reasons explain Molloy's line on the article – such as an editor's editorial misjudgement or a desire not to run an article which could arouse the ire of the publisher. If he truly thought the story to be a hoax, his motive in running the story may even have been a desire to rubbish the *Sunday Times*.

There is also no direct evidence that Maxwell was asked by the Israelis to knock down the story. Unless Molloy changes his version of events or an Israeli official discloses any contacts with Maxwell, the verification of which version is correct will remain buried together with Maxwell on the Mount of Olives overlooking the Old City of Jerusalem.

It was a state funeral in all but name. The attendance of President Chaim Herzog, Prime Minister Shamir and Shimon Peres at Maxwell's burial strengthened for some the allegations made by Hersh. That Herzog was there ostensibly in a private capacity – he and Maxwell had served together in the Second World War in British intelligence – is little excuse because his very presence, let alone giving the funeral eulogy, is enough. Shamir praised Maxwell for putting his worldwide connections at Israel's service, describing him as 'a passionate friend of Israel.' In what an editorial in *The Times* described as 'an extraordinary graveside eulogy', Herzog said: 'We in Israel have been deeply moved by his feeling for this land and our cause; the feeling that led him to profound concern and commitment, expressed in significant involvement in many facets of our struggle for economic independence, for the absorption of the Russian immigration, for the security of the country and for the achievement of peace.' Very few non-Israeli individuals have been accorded such an honour. That Maxwell married out of the religion, and only became interested in Jewish and Israeli affairs in his final years, added to the mystery. Cynics suggested that Israeli officials – unaware of the state of the Maxwell empire – hoped that Maxwell's children would continue their father's investments in Israel.

By the end of the 1980s Robert Maxwell was Israel's single biggest foreign investor. His investments, estimated to be worth £250m, included a computer imaging enterprise, Scitex, a pharmaceutical company, Teva; a controlling interest in the second largest afternoon newspaper, *Maariv*; and the 'Keter' publishing firm. His business interest began after a trip to Israel in 1987 (he bought 27 per cent of the highly-rated but financially ailing Scitex firm at US $39m and sold it a couple of months later for well over US $200m). When Maxwell got involved in something he did it in spades. He became a friend of Shamir, broadly supporting Likud policies, and opposed the establishment of a Palestinian state on the West Bank and Gaza. He placed his wide contacts in eastern Europe at the disposal of Israel, which had been seeking to reopen diplomatic ties cut in the aftermath of the 1967 Six-Day War. He used his influence to improve the exit of Soviet Jews. In one instance he used his personal jet to facilitate the flight to Israel of stranded Jewish children from Chernobyl. In another instance he helped the Lubavitch Hasidic community to rescue Lubavitch manuscripts in Russia. He raised £3.6m in a week during the Gulf War selling State of Israel bonds.

His new-found energies on Israel's behalf also gained expression in the news media. The editorial columns of newspapers in the Mirror group became decidedly pro-Israel during his proprietorship. For example, in the outrage after the killings of Arabs at the Temple Mount in Jerusalem in October 1990, a *Daily Mirror* editorial attacked those who failed to express criticism of those who provoked the riot. Another instance occurred when the foreign secretary, Douglas Hurd, wrote in the *Sunday Express* arguing that Israel has yet to talk realistically about peace. The *Daily Mirror* carried an editorial signed by Maxwell himself castigating Hurd for failing to discuss the need for Arab states to accept Israel's right to exist. In Israel Maxwell publicly criticised his own paper, *Maariv*, for publishing leaks from a secret intelligence report.

The media was a medium of personal publicity. If political benefit could be gained from ingratiating himself by revealing information, or having something positive written about somebody, he would. Nick Davies claimed 'there was never a case' of Maxwell's changing something. 'I cannot recall at any time that he interfered with the news columns as distinct from the editorials.' Others, however, have painted a portrait of an interventionist press proprietor: he was in the office most evenings, checking editions. Publicity for individual foreign leaders appeared; news reports were altered. It would need a strong editor to resist pressures from the boss. Richard Stott, *Daily Mirror* editor, knew how to handle Maxwell, by ostensibly agreeing with him, and then doing things his own way. This general picture lends circumstantial support to Hersh's claims.

However, the Robert Maxwell of 1991 was different from the Robert Maxwell of 1986. In 1986 he was ambivalent in his attitude to the British Jewish community and to Israel. Born into an impoverished religious Jewish family in Czechoslovakia – his father was a farmhand – Maxwell, or Jan Ludwig Hoch, had an upbringing (not very different from Mordechai Vanunu's) involving Jewish elementary school and *yeshivah* or religious high school where the focus was on religious study. His mother wanted him to be a rabbi.

110

When he settled in England, after marrying a French Prot-
estant, he recognised that social acceptability in the Britain
of the fifties entailed being more English than the English
and not identifying too closely with the Jewish community.
After he was elected Member of Parliament for Buckingham
in 1968 he declined to be interviewed for the *Jewish Year-
book* and told the *Jewish Chronicle* that he had joined the
Church of England. (In 1988 his wife, Betty Maxwell, wrote
to the *Jewish Chronicle* dismissing this as 'a prankish telephone call to your paper twenty-five years ago.') Slowly,
after the 1967 war Maxwell became a little more familiar as
a figure at Jewish or Israeli fund-raising events. During a
visit to London in 1984 President Herzog remarked that 'the
man is moving, coming closer to us.' In 1986, in an interview
with the *Jewish Chronicle Magazine* Maxwell observed:

> . . . I ceased to be a practising Jew just before the war
> when I left home. I still believe in God and Judaism's
> moral education which teaches the difference between
> right and wrong . . . I don't believe in any church, just
> God. I certainly do consider myself Jewish. I was born
> Jewish and I shall die Jewish.

As a clue to his identification with Judaism, this should not
be exaggerated. Maxwell was no more than an assimilated
Jew in British public life. The interview itself – which happened to appear nine days before the *Sunday Mirror* report
on Vanunu – had taken fifteen months for the *Jewish Chronicle* to obtain. And, according to the reporter, Jenni Frazer,
'Maxwell looked far from pleased to see us.' At the end of
the interview, Frazer wrote, 'Peter Jay (Maxwell's aide) is
ushered in. The *Mirror* boss sways ponderously towards him.
"I", he intones, "have been interviewed by the *Jewish
Chronicle*".'[12] It would be irrelevant – were it not for the
claim by Hersh that the same person collaborated with the
Israeli Mossad – to note that Maxwell took the opportunity
to reassure everybody, including himself, where his loyalties

111

remained. Yes, he shared the aspirations of the Jewish Community 'unless they conflict with those of the United Kingdom; then I shall opt for the UK'.

But the mid-eighties were the beginning of a turning point. He had achieved political status and was a newspaper publisher, but he failed to get a ministerial appointment. More so, the warm but ebullient European-born Jew had failed to be truly accepted by the British establishment in spite of, or because of, his wealth and prominence. This gradual realisation was helping Maxwell to come to terms with his Jewish origins. The memory of the Holocaust was to be the catalyst. Nearly all his family had been murdered by the Nazis, with his mother, three of his five sisters, a brother and his grandfather killed in Auschwitz. In 1985 Maxwell attended a Holocaust survivors' conference in Jerusalem, the first time he spoke in public about the fate of his family. Ironically, Betty Maxwell was instrumental in her husband giving expression to this. In 1988 she organised a conference for Holocaust scholars in Oxford 'Remembering the Future'. At the opening ceremony he broke down, as he did at the annual Jewish exservicemen's parade in Whitehall in 1989, and when he visited Yad Vashem, an Israeli museum commemorating the six million victims of the Holocaust, weeks before he died. What Maxwell might well have done if the Vanunu story had occurred in 1991 would have been most unlikely in 1986. If, as Hersh claims, in 1986 Maxwell discredited Vanunu either on his own initiative or that of Israeli officials, it seems inconceivable that he would have involved himself in the man's abduction.

Seymour Hersh, a history graduate from Chicago University, began his career in American journalism when he joined the Associated Press news agency in 1963. Two years later, he was appointed its Pentagon correspondent, and is an internationally recognised investigative journalist.

Born in 1937, Hersh declined the wishes of his parents,

immigrants from eastern Europe, to become a lawyer. He worked for a period as press secretary and speechwriter to Senator Eugene McCarthy, but rose to national prominence through his account of the My Lai massacre of villagers by American troops in the Vietnam War. It took him more than eighteen months to establish the first clear account and he subsequently wrote two books about the massacre. The hidden arsenal thesis which underlies *The Samson Option* also came up in the first book he wrote, *Chemical and Biological Warfare*, which had limited impact.

He later joined the *New York Times*, concentrating on investigative reporting. Subjects he covered included connections between President Manuel Noriega of Panama and drug trafficking in Latin America, and the involvement of former CIA agents in arms sales to Libya. He wrote a critique of Henry Kissinger's foreign policy, *The Price of Power*; and *The Target is Destroyed*, an account of the shooting down of Korean Airlines Flight 007 by a Soviet missile. He has won a Pulitzer prize, four George Polk awards, and more than fifty other journalistic prizes.

Hersh has built up a wide network of contacts in Washington and elsewhere. The US Freedom of Information Act is a valuable tool for penetrating bastions of secrecy like the CIA and the Pentagon. Much of the information in *The Samson Option* was drawn from American intelligence sources. He reads retirement notices in the newsletters of the State Department, the CIA and the National Security Agency, and invites those leaving out to lunch in the hope of gathering information. It is said that after a lunch date with Hersh interviewees have to rest for an hour. Hersh was also helped by Israelis who had worked at the nuclear research centre in Dimona and who, according to him, are critical of Likud policies. Some of these also provided US officials with detailed information, in the hope, Hersh said, that 'they would receive a green card.'

The author's source for his material about Vanunu and

the *Sunday Mirror* was an Iranian-born Jew, Ari Ben Menashe, who had been the head of the translation unit in the external relations department of Israeli military intelligence. Fluent in Hebrew, Farsi, English and Arabic, Ben Menashe's work entailed translating documents provided under exchange agreements to foreign armies and intelligence agencies. He claimed to have carried out operations abroad, and to have risen to an intelligence adviser to Prime Minister Shamir. Initially, Israeli officials denied any knowledge of Ben Menashe. Later, it was confirmed that he had been a translator and subsequently, it was acknowledged that he was a middle-ranking intelligence officer. Some of Ben Menashe's claims have been questioned when examined by major news organisations. A lie detector test conducted by the US network, ABC, found that on a reliability scale from zero to minus eight Ben Menashe recorded either minus seven or minus eight. But some of his claims have aroused interest: when he claimed that George Bush intentionally delayed the release of the US embassy hostages in Tehran until after the US elections which President Carter lost, he was invited to testify before a congressional committee.

Ben Menashe's allegations about Nick Davies and the *Sunday Mirror* seem to have been drawn from his former business relationship with Davies. In 1983 the two men formed a company named Ora, after Ben Menashe's wife. Operating from Davies's London home, it arranged arms shipments on behalf of the Israeli defence ministry. In 1988 Ben Menashe met Maxwell at a meeting arranged by Davies, where he unsuccessfully tried to interest the publisher in a book he was writing on Irangate. The *Sunday Times* had toyed with the idea of serialising Hersh's book, but an examination of Ben Menashe by Peter Hounam found, the paper said, that none of his information coincided with the large quantity of information which the paper itself had on Vanunu. Particularly damning was Ben Menashe's boast that a photograph of Vanunu that appeared in the *Sunday Mirror* had been especially flown from Israel to Davies. In fact, the photograph had been taken by Hounam himself and given to Guerrero. Ben Menashe claimed that his evidence about the *Mirror* was twelve sworn affidavits from Mirror newspaper executives. In fact, the publishers reportedly had only letters from three former *Sunday Mirror* executives.[13] One of these, Tony Frost, denied that Davies had any involvement in the Vanunu story. It was the depth of Ben Menashe's knowledge of certain operations which persuaded Hersh to believe him. But was Hersh a victim of his own technique – of believing him about one subject, Vanunu, because he had been correct on other subjects?

A closer reading of Hersh's section on Vanunu and the *Sunday Mirror* suggests that the author appears to prove something by stringing together facts. The allegations regarding Hersh and Maxwell are not written in plain prose. Furthermore, the allegations about Nick Davies's involvement are attributed to Ben Menashe. There is a great deal of innuendo in his treatment of Maxwell. The lack of distinction between hard evidence and the allegations of others is confusing. Given the questions prompted by the author's allegations – which gained wide currency – the lack of apparent evidence he attributes to the original allegations is confusing.

Apart from Ben Menashe, Hersh's sources for his section on Vanunu and the *Sunday Mirror* are journalists who were on the paper dealing with the story at the reporter and editor levels. Hersh's interviews with them cast suspicion on his allegations and the lack of hard evidence to support these. Mark Souster, asked by Hersh, 'Will Nick Davies have been involved in the Vanunu story?' replied 'No, categorically. The *Daily Mirror* and *Sunday Mirror* were separate entities.' Hersh countered: 'Would it surprise you if I told you that Nick Davies was a Mossad agent and that he and Maxwell were involved in it all, and they knew where Vanunu was . . .' Souster replied: 'Nobody knew where Vanunu was, Guerrero didn't know where Vanunu was, so

115

I can't believe that Nick Davies knew where Vanunu was.'[14] According to a memorandum by Tony Frost, Frost told Hersh that Nick Davies had not been involved in the paper's Vanunu report. Moreover, according to Frost, Hersh confused the editor of the *Sunday Mirror* with another leading British journalist. Hersh, according to Frost, told him that this theory was drawn from his source to which Frost replied that if so it made a nonsense of the information. Hersh said that he would check it with his source.[15]

The Hersh book quotes deputy editor John Parker as saying that '. . . It was a classic exercise by the Israelis in disinformation'. Parker claims that he told Hersh that 'it appeared, in hindsight, to have been a classic exercise in disinformation'. 'It was easy after publication of the *Sunday Mirror* report,' said Parker, 'to have come to that conclusion because it was such an odd way to present a story like that. There would seem to be no logical explanation for it.' When the publishers sent Parker the quotation, which they planned to use, Parker wrote to the publishers' lawyer with the corrected version 'but', he said, 'they chose not to do anything about it.'

The controversy over his book days old, Hersh flew to London to defend himself against criticism and counter-claims. Journalists filled a press conference at London's Imperial Hotel – among them a brace of *Daily Mirror* journalists including its deputy editor and news editor. By British standards it was less a press conference and more a kangaroo court as Hersh fielded question after question. Hersh was unmoved. He berated his British colleagues: 'In the United States this would already be a war zone'. Much of the press conference concerned the allegations about Davies's involvement in arms shipments. He spoke of the central allegations in such detail that after three-quarters of an hour a BBC journalist remarked that there was nothing he could legally broadcast. Asked about the allegation that Davies was involved in disclosing Vanunu's whereabouts, Hersh

116

replied, 'I have Ben Menashe's account that he asked Nick Davies to help him find Vanunu in two calls.' The man from the *Financial Times* asked if Ben Menashe was the only source for this allegation. 'Yes', replied Hersh.

If the allegation about a disinformation effort had, with hindsight, some circumstantial support, the more serious one about the revealing of Vanunu's location – which took up a single paragraph at the very end of Hersh's chapter – went unsubstantiated. Three weeks after *The Samson Option* was published Hersh introduced new 'evidence' to support his claim about Davies disclosing Vanunu's location. These involved the wire-tapping by a private detective of Peter Hounam's telephone hoping it would lead to information about Vanunu's location. Meeting in a Geneva hotel to discuss this were, Hersh said, two men who described themselves as *Daily Mirror* reporters, one Frank Thorne, an Israeli security official, and the other, calling himself Nigel Dennis, was Nick Davies. A second meeting was attended by the detective and three people thought to be Israelis. Telephone calls were made from the hotel to the Israeli embassy in Paris, a Mossad operations centre, and the Tel Aviv residence of Samuel Nahmias, a former Israel police intelligence chief, now private security consultant. Hersh's disclosure had been preceded by an announcement by Matthew Evans, Faber & Faber's chairman, that the book contained only 20 per cent of the story relating to Maxwell. However, the new revelations provided no direct link between Israeli intelligence and Maxwell himself.

The 'evidence' came from Joe Flynn. Days after the publication of *The Samson Option*, Matthew Evans was contacted by somebody who introduced himself as 'Mr Begg, a private detective'. He claimed to know about Maxwell's and Davies's activities with Vanunu. He would talk to Evans and Hersh for a price. Evans flew to Amsterdam to meet the 'private detective'. Evans was reportedly promised documents, including a videotape of the meetings in Geneva and records of telephone calls from the hotel. In three instalments Evans reportedly paid £1290.

But Flynn's story was littered with factual errors. A reporter named Frank Thorne was not working on the *Daily Mirror* at the time of the Geneva meetings, 25 September 1986; Cindy had already met Vanunu in London. Nahmias lived in Jerusalem not Tel Aviv, and the hotel in Geneva, the Cornavin, was not equipped to monitor outgoing telephone calls. According to *Sunday Times* editor Andrew Neil, only two journalists knew where Vanunu was being kept by the paper, and Hounam, Neil said, was not one of these. But Wendy Robbins, who was a researcher with Insight, claimed that Hounam collected Vanunu each day from his secret location. Moreover, Hounam told Australian Television in August 1987 that on the night before Vanunu left London with Cindy for Rome – against the newspaper's advice – Hounam telephoned Vanunu and 'suggested that he didn't tell the rest of the office just me where he was going so that I knew if he disappeared, we could trace him'. (Vanunu did not do so.)

Flynn managed to persuade Hersh about the truth of the Geneva meetings by producing for Evans the home telephone number of Peter Hounam and the business card of the *Daily Mirror* reporter Frank Thorne. Because Hounam's home number is ex-directory and matched Hersh's own number for Hounam, Hersh took it as proof that the private detective was genuine. In fact, Flynn had lured Hounam to Naples in 1987 saying that he could assist him in the Vanunu story, and in the process had obtained Hounam's telephone number. Thorne had given Flynn his business card nearly three years earlier, in Portugal, when he interviewed Flynn for a story he promised about arms dealing. Flynn had passed Thorne's business card to Evans and Hersh as proof that he had met Thorne in Geneva. Prior to Hersh's announcement of Mr Begg's evidence of the Geneva meetings, the author said that 'I feel I have now defended my book and will not go any further.' With this 'evidence' being unacceptable, Hersh was back to square one with unsubstantiated allegations about Maxwell and Davies.

5. THE MOSSAD V THE SUNDAY TIMES

One of the Mossad's first clues that a former employee of Dimona was offering secret information to the media about the nuclear research centre came inadvertently from the *Sunday Times* itself. One of its reporters arrived in Israel on 2 September 1986 to check Vanunu's personal details: that he had worked at Dimona, had studied at Beersheba's Ben-Gurion University, and that he was who he said he was. The reporter talked to a girl whom Vanunu had mentioned, and who was a military reservist. Anxious, she told him that she would have to speak to her boss.[1]

But another theory is that the Mossad heard earlier when Vanunu was still in Australia. Vanunu recalls that while waiting in the bar of Sydney's Hilton Hotel for a meeting with Peter Hounam, he became aware of two Israelis sitting beside him. They tried to engage him in conversation with comments he might find politically sympathetic. He immediately suspected them as Mossad agents and left, frightened and suspicious.[2]

The Mossad also approached one of his brothers. On 7 September, two men from Shin Bet, the internal intelligence agency, waited for Albert Vanunu at his carpentry workshop in one of Beersheba's industrial areas, and said they needed his help to get Mordechai back from Europe.

The Mossad may also have been tipped off later either directly from Australian external intelligence, AS-10, or indirectly via MI6, Britain's external intelligence service.[3]

After Oscar Guerrero saw Vanunu off with Peter Hounam from Sydney airport on 11 September, he bragged to somebody who had been staying at King's Cross rectory about the great story, showing some of the photographs which Vanunu had taken of the Dimona reactor. This person happened to be a former communications officer with AS-10, who remained in touch with his ex-employers. After an hour's thought he telephoned Special Branch telling them that Vanunu and Hounam were en route to London, where the Israeli planned to hand over complete details of, and photographic evidence concerning, Dimona. According to the *Sunday Times*, a telex was immediately sent off to MI6. But the Mossad had already known a week earlier.[4]

Australian and British intelligence have developed close ties since the 1950s at all levels including exchange of intelligence reports, assistance in training, and some joint covert operations. So close is the relationship that AS-10's London base is MI6's headquarters at Century House. The scale of exchange of information may be seen from the fact that between 1950 and 1974, British intelligence received some 10,000 reports from their Australian counterparts, while transmitting 44,000 in return. MI6 has provided AS-10 with a copy of its Far East Personality Index. In areas where both AS-10 and MI6 are represented, field officers keep in touch with one another, making it possible to share and analyse intelligence regarding local developments. In places where only one of the services is represented, it can serve as the point of liason for the other service. In giving the information about Vanunu to MI6 there can be little reason to doubt that the Australians did not inform their Israeli counterparts.[5]

When Vanunu, accompanied by Hounam, arrived at London's Heathrow Airport the following day, entering under an assumed name, two British Special Branch men saw him pass through passport control, and the news of his arrival was passed by MI6 to the Mossad. On 21 September, following a meeting between Prime Minister Peres, Foreign Minister Shamir and Defence Minister Itzhak Rabin, where the Vanunu leak was discussed. Peres – anxious that Vanunu be brought to Israel – reportedly telephoned Mrs Thatcher to discuss possible implications of the information Vanunu was giving the media.[6]

Over more than thirty years, MI6 and the Mossad have developed operational ties.[7] For example, in the 1970s, Mossad investigators on the Boeings of Ugandan Airlines flying between Stansted and Entebbe spied on Libya's military airfield at Benghazi, where the planes refuelled en route to England, and the results were passed to MI6 and the CIA. The Mossad accurately forecast the downfall of the Shah of Iran in contrast to MI6 and the CIA: information on the role played by Libyan and Palestinian organisations in supporting the Shah's opponents indicated to the Mossad the inner developments of the Iranian revolution. Following the practice of not stationing covert agents in friendly countries, Britain had relied almost wholly on information from Iran's external intelligence agency, Savak, regarding the strength of the opposition.

Britain and Israel share a common threat of terrorism; Britain and Israel are both members of Kilowatt, established in the mid-seventies by Western countries to deal with Arab terrorism. Other members include West Germany, Italy, France, Belgium, the Netherlands, Switzerland, Denmark, Sweden, Norway, Luxembourg, Ireland and Canada. In the aftermath of the abortive assassination attempt on Israeli ambassador Shlomo Argov in London in June 1982, the Mossad's freedom of movement increased.[8] By the time of the Vanunu abduction the Mossad was one of five services in Britain with friendly intelligence status, the others being the United States, Canada, Australia and West Germany.[9] These countries are able to run their intelligence operations from their embassies. The Mossad has taken a leading role in providing intelligence regarding the fate of Western hostages in Lebanon:[10] other key agencies involved were the CIA, MI6 and French and West German intelligence. British intelligence, in an eavesdropping operation targeted at the Syrian embassy in London, produced evidence of Syrian involvement in the attempt in April 1986 to place a bomb on board an El Al jumbo jet en route to Israel. The National Security Agency intercepted a message sent from the embassy to Damascus asking for further help for Nazar Hindawi in carrying out the bomb attack. Hindawi was then put under continuous surveillance by MI5, and permission was granted to bug rooms and telephone lines from outside the embassy.

The Israeli–British connection had not been without friction, however. Wary of the preponderance of Arabists in the Foreign Office which has increasingly influenced MI6 matters, as well as Britain's pro-Arab posture, the Mossad has been cautious in the information it has given lest it reach undesirable hands. The discovery in 1982 that a British diplomat at its Tel Aviv embassy, Rhona Ritchie, was passing sensitive information (including plans for the multinational force in Sinai) to an Egyptian diplomat with whom she was having an affair strengthened these fears. The Israelis did not make a public issue over Ritchie, who was subsequently given a nine-month suspended sentence. Suspicions have not been one-way. Despite Israeli denials, MI6 believes that an abortive attempt to smuggle a former Nigerian government minister Umaru Dikko back to Lagos in a crate, following which three Israelis were involved and imprisoned, was a Mossad operation. Britain also suspected Israeli involvement in the attempted coup in Cyprus in 1974 by Nikko Gigadis, otherwise known as Sampson.

Part of the credit for Israel's wide network of ties with foreign intelligence services went to the then head of the Mossad, Nahum Admoni. After studying international relations at the University of Berkeley in California,

Admoni became an instructor in the secret service's school of international relations. He then transferred to the Mossad's department of external relations, responsible for ties with foreign intelligence agencies. Information exchanged covered the breadth of military-related matters, including nuclear arms developments.[11] For example, information received from Dutch intelligence regarding a message intercepted between Italy and Iraq determined the timing of Israel's air raid on the Iraqi nuclear reactor at Osiraq in June 1981. And Israel has received information from India regarding Pakistani attempts to make a nuclear bomb.[12]

The Vanunu abduction was one of the very many covert operations which the Mossad have carried out over the years.[13] The organisation traces its roots to the Palestine Mandate period, when Haganah, the main Zionist underground army, maintained an intelligence department called Shai (an abbreviation of Sherut Yediot). Its functions included infiltrating British Mandate officers in order to inform the Jewish–Zionist leadership about British strategy, penetrating Arab factions in Palestine, and providing security for the arms smuggling and illegal immigration programmes of Haganah. The Shai managed to penetrate British customs, police, postal services and offices dealing with transport. A separate body, Mossad le Aliya Bet, was established to bring into Palestine the many Jews who were not able to enter under the British restrictions on immigration. Some ten Mossad agents in Europe arranged forged papers, travel routes, hideouts, and chartered ships to take the Jewish immigrants to Palestine. Another body, Rekhesh, was responsible for acquiring arms from overseas for the Jewish underground forces.

In recent years, a major area of action has been Palestinian terrorism: the Mossad is proud that all those responsible for the 1972 Munich Olympics massacre of Israeli athletes have been hunted and killed. Yet their major activity remains in the sphere of information gathering and evaluation. Another important function is the maintenance of ties with states which do not have formal diplomatic relations with Jerusalem.[14]

There has been a need to obtain raw materials for the development of Israel's nuclear programme.[15] With Dimona not open to international inspection, agencies such as the International Atomic Energy Authority and the European agency Euratom prohibit the supply of nuclear materials to Israel, and covert means have to be used.[16] 'Operation Plumbat', in which a West German chemical firm, Asmara Chemie, was used as a front to buy 200 tons of uranium oxide from the Société Générale de Belgique, the parent company of Belgonucléaire, is one of the Mossad's more celebrated operations. The task of transporting the uranium was assigned to a Turkish-born shipowner who had worked with the Israelis since 1947. In Antwerp, the *Scheersberg* took on 560 specially-sealed oil drums marked Plumbat.[17] But instead of heading for Genoa, and then on to a paint and chemical company in Milan, the *Scheersberg* turned towards the east Mediterranean where, between Cyprus and Turkey, the uranium cargo was transferred to an Israeli freighter.[18] An early assignment concerning arms production was the assassination of German scientists in Egypt in the early 1960s. In June 1980 the head of Iraq's Atomic Energy Agency, Egyptian-born Dr Yihye el-Mashad, was assassinated in a Paris hotel by the Mossad.[19] A year earlier the core of a nuclear reactor and other reactor parts housed at a warehouse at Seyne-sur-Mer awaiting shipment to Iraq were blown up, which increased tension between French intelligence and the Mossad.[20] In July 1980 bombs wrecked the Rome offices of SNIA Techint, the Italian nuclear company working in Iraq, and the same day there was an abortive attempt to assassinate a French scientist working on the Iraqi nuclear project at Osiraq. In September 1988 an Italian–Palestinian nuclear scientist, Omar Abu Khadir, was killed in Florida; in the Arab world speculation lighted on the

Mossad. The mysterious killing in March 1990 in Brussels of Dr Gerald Bull, an internationally acclaimed expert in artillery, who was advising the Iraqis on delivery systems for non-conventional warheads, was attributed by many in the west to the Mossad.

There was also the disappearance near Marseilles of a former construction worker at Dimona, Meir Zohar, and his son. In May 1974 Zohar's brother in Israel, Yosef, received a telephone call that Meir and his nephew had died in a car accident, and that he should travel to France to collect the corpses. When Yosef arrived, nobody, including the Israeli consul, the local rabbi or the burial society, knew about any corpses. One person hinted that his brother may have tried to sell Dimona's secrets, another that the two were alive but could not be reached. Some months later, after returning to Israel, Yosef received in the mail a picture in a newspaper showing a car crash. But years later the family discovered that Meir Zohar's entry in police records was updated in 1978 – four years after he had died. Persistent inquiries to the Israeli foreign and defence ministries, and to Interpol, failed to reveal any information. The family's belief that Zohar and his son were alive was strengthened by their receipt in 1989, after sixteen years, of the death certificate which began: 'On 29 May 1973, 1 p.m. the corpse of Meir Zohar was brought to Darom Hospital . . .' Their suspicions were not helped by the fact that they received letters from Meir for a year after this date.[21]

When Vanunu arrived in Britain on 12 September, both he and the *Sunday Times* were concerned that the Mossad might be tailing him. He was taken first to Heath Lodge, a country hotel in Welwyn, thirty miles outside London, and it was here that Dr Frank Barnaby's debriefing took place. At the different places he stayed, Vanunu refused to sleep on the ground floor, insisting on an upper floor. But he also declined Insight's suggestion that one of their reporters sleep in the same room as him. Vanunu wanted his solitude, although he did agree to a reporter staying in a nearby room.

After a couple of days at Heath Lodge, Vanunu wanted to see the lights of London. There, he was moved from hotel to hotel. The paper's journalists accompanied him everywhere; when not debriefing him further, they entertained him in a bar, in a restaurant or in Vanunu's room. Notwithstanding the linguistic barrier, subject matter in conversation was often of a philosophical nature. Hounam developed the warmest friendship with him given his physics background. On one of the weekends the paper arranged a one-day tour outside London to relieve Vanunu's boredom while Insight checked the details of his story.

The Mossad were not far behind Vanunu and the *Sunday Times*; overseeing the operation was one of the deputy chiefs, who had based himself in a European capital.[22] Just two days after Vanunu arrived in England and was walking down Regent Street in London's West End he was amazed to see Yoram Bazak, whom he knew from Ben-Gurion University, walking towards him.[23] It was not the first time that Yoram Bazak's name had come up in the Vanunu Affair. Bazak was one of the names given by Vanunu to Peter Hounam in Australia when he asked for people in Israel who could verify that Vanunu had worked at Dimona. (When a reporter tried to reach Bazak in Israel he was away.) Vanunu's first instinct on seeing Bazak was to duck into a side street to avoid him. Bazak, who was accompanied by a girlfriend, Dorit, said they had arrived in London at the end of a European tour. This offered a clue to the Mossad's tactics. Bazak invited Vanunu to dinner on Wednesday, 17 September.[24] Accompanied by his *Sunday Times* escort, researcher Wendy Robbins, he went to Bazak's hotel room, where Bazak tried to get more information about Vanunu's plans.

Vanunu stayed at a number of addresses in London. At one stage he was so frightened that he was being followed that he stayed with one of the Insight reporters. It was therefore surprising that when Bazak asked where he was staying, Vanunu volunteered the information: the Tower Thistle Hotel, by St Katherine's Dock, not far from the *Sunday Times*'s offices near Tower Bridge. Later, on 23 September, he was moved to the Mountbatten Hotel, room 105, registered under the name of Mr John Forsty. This was also the day when two *Sunday Times* staffers took a summary of their investigation to the Israeli embassy for its reaction, and a succession of two-man film crews stood opposite the entrance of the newspaper offices, ostensibly photographing the picket lines of workers protesting against the introduction of new print technology. The first crew said they were from a students' union; they were tall and sporting stubble. By the time the two journalists returned to the paper at 4 p.m. there was a second crew, wearing suits and with a tripod. While having no proof, the newspaper thought that these men whom British police described as having a Middle East appearance and were not television crews, might have followed Vanunu when he left Wapping to go to his hotel.

Cheryl Bentov, born in 1960 in Orlando, Florida, whom the *Sunday Times* alleged abducted Vanunu, seemed on the surface an unlikely person to lure him to Israel.[25] Because Peres ordered that no British laws be broken in the process of abducting Vanunu, the strategy adopted was to lure him out of British territory, and only then to take him back forcibly to Israel.[26] According to H. H. A. Cooper and Lawrence Redlinger, authors of *Making Spies: A Talent Spotter's Handbook*, the cravings and longings which the human sex drive generates cannot be disciplined or denied, and the quest for their satisfaction leads to behaviour which is often imprudent to the point of being dangerous, and sometimes irrational in the extreme. Cheryl was the perfect bait.[27] Her looks and figure were good without being conspicuous, and a woman and man are less noticeable than two men together. Of course, it didn't always work. In 1988 there was an attempt to kill the PLO representative in Greece, Izmat Sabri; Greek police arrested Menahem Rom, whom they named as a Mossad agent, together with his girl accomplice Daliah Eyal, after they caught the authorities' attention when they photographed Sabri. And the young and pretty Nura Eldat, a senior Mossad operative, was sent in 1960 to kill Dr Joseph Mengele, the infamous Nazi doctor who performed experiments on Jewish twins.[28] But after she was murdered Mossad chief Isser Harel abandoned the plan to kill Mengele. A Mossad operative named Salima reportedly had a romantic relationship with the head of Iraqi intelligence in London, which subsequently resulted in the disclosure in 1990 of the trafficking of nuclear weaponry parts to Iraq.[29] There was an obvious need in the Vanunu case to use a non-Israeli so that Vanunu's suspicions would not be roused.[30]

Cheryl Hanin's first contact with Israel was in the late seventies when she went to the country for a three-month intensive course on Jewish history and Hebrew. Later, after high school, she returned to Israel, joining a Nahal unit (Pioneering Fighting Youth) for protecting new border settlements. In March 1985 she married Ofer Bentov, a major in Israeli military intelligence, who comes from a military family; his father is a retired army general.[31] A right-wing anti-Israeli American magazine *Spotlight*, which was the first to reveal Cheryl Bentov's Florida origins and which has good CIA sources, alleged that after moving to Israel she went to work for the CIA as a covert operative. If true, her marriage to a major in Israeli military intelligence would mean that the CIA had successfully infiltrated an agent into the military intelligence apparatus. *Spotlight* also reported that Mr Peres, in a secure phone call to the White House, personally asked the US for help to 'plug the leak'. But the Americans appear to have been as surprised as others about Cheryl's American past because the principal and assistant principal in Cheryl's school, Edgewater High, were subsequently contacted by both the CIA and the FBI asking to examine her school records.

Arriving in London from Israel on 20 September, the agent booked into the Eccleston Hotel at Victoria. Four days later Mordechai Vanunu happened to be strolling near Leicester Square when a lonely-looking woman who seemed to be looking at him caught his eye.[32] Loneliness, the need for human companionship and an understanding human ear in a large, strange city attracted the seemingly like-minded. Although she seemed shy, they started talking over a cup of coffee. Vanunu was totally unsuspecting because he thought he'd made the first move. Her name, she said, was Cindy. She declined to give her full name and address, but she managed to get from Vanunu the name of his hotel.[33] Cindy had tried to attract Vanunu's attention for three days as he walked round the sights of London. Lest she failed, the Mossad had devised an alternative strategy involving a former student acquaintance of Vanunu's at Ben-Gurion University, Ofer Keren, who would try to persuade him to return to Israel. Keren, an MA economics student, was active in a right-wing political group on the campus called Metzada at the same time that Vanunu was active on the Left.[34]

Cindy declined Vanunu's suggestion that she come back to his hotel. The two went to see the film *Snow White and the Seven Dwarfs*. By Friday Insight reporters chanced on the liaison when Vanunu chose to meet the girl rather than attend one of the debriefing sessions with Insight. They immediately suspected she was a Mossad plant.[35] Max Prangnell managed to catch a glimpse of Bentov from a taxi while waiting for Vanunu. 'She was about five foot eight, she had blonde dyed hair, she was wearing a brown kind of raincoat, and she looked quite stocky. She had a very full face as well,' he said, and added that she was 'probably Jewish'.[36] In fact, Bentov is brunette. The paper warned Vanunu but, upset at what he thought an unnecessary delay in publication while

130

the paper checked the story, he failed to heed their warnings.

On that Sunday the *Sunday Mirror* came out with its double-page centre-fold raising grave doubts about Vanunu's claim. Frustrated, not knowing that the *Sunday Mirror* was a paper not taken seriously, Vanunu feared that the *Sunday Times* would now not publish, given the doubts expressed about his allegations and about Guerrero's integrity. Moreover, with his photograph splashed in the paper, he had to get rid of the *Sunday Times*'s protection and disappear. Cindy popped the suggestion of the day. 'You can be recognised all over the country. It's better if you go abroad somewhere,' she said, adding, according to Mordechai's brother, Meir, that she had contacts in the Italian press.

The following day Robin Morgan of Insight vainly attempted to persuade Vanunu not to go away, but he said he would be back in three days. On Thursday, 2 October, Vanunu was due to sign a contract with the paper for a book on his work at the Israeli nuclear programme, for which he would be paid an advance of £100,000 plus royalties. Morgan accepted Vanunu's argument that somebody might be tailing *Sunday Times* reporters to locate where Vanunu was, but warned him not to leave British territory, to travel on bus and train only and not to hire a car because he would then have to produce his passport and give his true identity. Morgan also advised Vanunu to stay at small bed-and-breakfast establishments, again not to have to show his passport. He did not know that Vanunu had already given his true name to Cindy. Then Peter Hounam tried to dissuade him from going. 'You must realise that it's quite possible that Cindy is a "plant". Can we arrange to meet her?' Hounam asked. 'Vanunu said that evening (Monday) would not be good. I suggested that we should have dinner with my wife and Cindy the following evening, the Tuesday. Vanunu replied, "Fine yeah, let's do that. Let's all go out together,"' Hounam said.[37]

But Vanunu never made dinner. Cindy decided to bring things to a head and she purchased a £426 business-class ticket to Rome from the Thomas Cook travel agency in Berkeley Street in London's West End. A flight on British Airways would be least likely to arouse Vanunu's suspicions. Showing the ticket to Vanunu, she explained that she would be leaving the next day, Tuesday, and would be staying at her sister's apartment in Rome.[38] Did he want to go? Romance is used in espionage not only for attraction but to cause pain, and apparent romantic attachment can be withdrawn, causing extreme reactions of disappointment and loss. The entrapment was complete.

Hounam did not give up, and reached him at 11.30 at night. 'I'm sorry, I am going out of the city. I am not going very far,' Vanunu told Hounam. 'I won't be able to make dinner tomorrow evening.' Hounam warned him not to use a credit card, although he doubted that he had one. He warned that it would be a terrible mistake if he set foot abroad because he would be easily picked up. 'Indeed, it would be better if he didn't go anywhere, or if he did I suggested that he didn't tell the rest of the office, but just told me where he was going so that I knew if he disappeared, we could trace him. But he wouldn't do that,' Hounam said. He did promise to telephone three times a day.[39]

Vanunu then made a long-distance call to St John's rectory in Sydney. During his stay in London he had been telephoning John McKnight every five or six days, talking about what he was seeing during his stay. As time dragged on, and as Vanunu grew increasingly tense at the delay caused by the paper's checking his testimony, these conversations had an important cathartic effect. Before Vanunu left Australia, McKnight had given him letters of introduction to a friend of his, the rector of St Helen's Bishopsgate, and another addressed to any Anglican clergyman asking for assistance should Vanunu be in danger and need refuge. In his last call to McKnight, at one o'clock on the morning of Tuesday, 30

September, McKnight was out and the assistant minister, Stephen Gray, took it. 'He seemed alone, worried, disturbed, disillusioned. And he spoke about the damage that Oscar [Guerrero] had done – not in detail, but just that Oscar had done them a great deal of damage and that he didn't feel safe any more, that he was feeling very alone, and that he wanted to be back here at St John's with us. He didn't say that he was going abroad,' Gray said.

At 10.30 the following morning Vanunu left the Mountbatten Hotel with two small bags to join Cindy for the flight to Rome. Unable to bring Vanunu directly from England to Israel, the Mossad had two strategies available: to woo him to international waters and take him forcibly from there to Israel, or to woo him to another country and, again forcibly, take him from there to Israel.[40] Given the danger of arousing his suspicions by wooing him to international waters, such as on to a yacht, the second strategy was more appropriate.[41]

That other country, Vanunu later revealed, was to be Italy. The whole apparatus of law and order in Italy had been weakened over the years through the challenges to the authorities from the Red Brigade and from right-wing fascist groups, through Rome being a base for an estimated 2,000 foreign spies and their 12,000 informers, and through the very instability of Italy's coalition government. With its central location in the Mediterranean and long coast-line it was not surprising that Rome had become a centre of the internecine Arab–Israeli conflict.

Vanunu was only one of a long series of incidents which have occurred in the city and been linked to the Mossad.[42] In November 1964 Rome airport was a bizarre scene when Italian police stopped porters from loading a trunk marked 'diplomatic baggage' on to a Cairo-bound Egyptian airliner after hearing a call for help from inside it. They opened the trunk to find a half-conscious man later identified as Mordechai Lok, an Israeli national who had deserted from the Israeli army to Egypt where he was pressed into service by Egyptian intelligence. But while on a mission in Italy he had argued with his superiors, who kidnapped him in a Rome street and tried to send him back to Egypt. Rome police were tipped off by Israeli agents, and he was handed over to them and sent to Israel, where he was sentenced to ten years' imprisonment for assisting the enemy.[43] In 1973 the Mossad were linked to the destruction of an Italian military helicopter in which its crew of four died.[44] The operation was carried out by Italy's external intelligence agency, Servizio Informazione Difesa which was then split between a pro-American pro-Israeli faction and a pro-PLO pro-Libyan faction. The crew had flown to Libya five Palestinian terrorists arrested at Rome airport in possession of land-to-air missiles and intending to destroy an Israeli jet. There was speculation that the terrorists had been freed after Palestinian groups reached an agreement with Italian officials under which Italy would not be the target of terrorist operations. An official report in 1973 claimed that the helicopter crashed through technical failure, but after an intelligence head General Ambrogio Viviani charged the Mossad with responsibility for the helicopter crash, a judicial inquiry was opened. In another instance, Italian President Sandro Pertrini and a magistrate Ferdinando Imposimáto claimed in the seventies that the Mossad had infiltrated Italian subversive groups including the Red Brigade and offered them weapons, money and information. These groups had been the target of infiltration by Nazis, Libyan agents and Palestinian groups. Israeli officials dismissed the claim as ridiculous. In December 1979 three Italian Leftists and a Jordanian were arrested on Italy's Adriatic coast in possession of two surface-to-air missiles. They were transporting them back to Lebanon, they said, under the Italian–Palestinian agreement. But the pro-Israeli faction of Italian military intelligence, Informazione Sicurezza Militare (SISMI) got wind of the operation and sent the police to arrest those responsible. And months prior to the Vanunu operation, two hydrofoils

134

belonging to a Palestinian group were sunk at anchor in an Italian port.

The Vanunu abduction occurred at a time of considerable criticism of the Italian authorities for releasing Abu Abbas, who had masterminded the hijacking of the Italian liner *Achille Lauro*, during which an elderly American passenger, Leon Klinghoffer, had been murdered. Vanunu was abducted just when Italy and Israel were negotiating an anti-terrorism agreement involving the exchange of information about terrorist groups. In the belief that European terrorists had links with Arab terrorists, the Italian intelligence services were trying to tighten their links with Israel as well as with Morocco.[45] 'Italy had decided to sign a separate anti-terror agreement with Israel because the efforts of EEC countries to combat terror were ineffective,' Italian Interior Minister Luigo Scalfaro said. It was perhaps because Italy felt that she had more to gain than Israel from such an agreement that the abduction went ahead.

The London–Rome flight took two and a half hours, arriving at 6.28 p.m. at Leonardo da Vinci airport at Fiumicino. Cindy hailed what Vanunu thought was a taxi. The car sped off on the *autostrada* to Rome, and Vanunu suddenly started to feel afraid. He realised he was in a dangerous position but convinced himself that it was all in his mind.[46] Twenty or thirty minutes later the car drew up at an apartment block in a working-class neighbourhood of the city. Cindy took him to a third-floor flat. The two men appeared and he was held down and injected with a drug which knocked him out. Mossad had finally seized him.[47]

Italian officials believe that a van took a drugged Vanunu the 425-kilometre journey to the southern port of La Spezia where he was taken on board an Israeli cargo vessel, the *Tappuz*.[48] The ship had sailed from Barcelona, putting into La Spezia for only four hours.[49] It is part-owned by Zim, Israel's national shipping fleet, and according to a 1976 CIA report on Israel's intelligence services, Zim is sometimes used by the Mossad during covert operations. The maritime agency handling Zim's freight at La Spezia, Lardon, remarked that it would be very easy to smuggle a person on a ship, given the lack of security typical of harbours. Yet the *Sunday Times*, which first published the story of the *Tappuz* and how Vanunu left Italy, now has some reservations about its accuracy, although the paper still believes that he was taken to Israel by sea.

When Vanunu eventually recovered consciousness, he found that he was held captive by the two men who had grabbed him and was in a small room with no porthole and confined by chains.[50] The ship arrived in Israel on 7 October. In less than four weeks from when the Mossad apparently traced Vanunu, he was en route to Israel. It was relatively easy to locate him: just follow Peter Hounam and his associates in the Insight team. Yet for the *Sunday Times* reporters and Barnaby the whole affair had smacked of over-efficiency. And Prime Minister Peres, despite his instructions not to infringe British territoriality, apparently failed to consider the fall-out which would be caused by kidnapping a key informer of an internationally respected newspaper.

6. THINGS FALL APART

Despite the operational success of the mission, it caused fall-out in a number of spheres: in London, in Rome and at home in Israel. But the first 'fall-out' was the publication of Vanunu's disclosures. The Israelis did not know about the second thoughts editor Andrew Neil was having, suspecting that the whole thing was an Israeli disinformation effort to boost its nuclear posture. But the possibility was not entirely absent from their considerations, as was shown by the fact that no Israeli official approached Neil to dissuade him from publishing; such an action would simply confirm the genuineness of the revelations.

One clue to the editor's reservations which ought to have given the Israelis food for thought was the fact that the *Sunday Times* failed to publish on the Sunday after two of its journalists had taken an eight-page summary to the embassy for a reaction. Vanunu's disappearance on 30 September divided the paper's editorial staff for and against publication. Insight editor Robin Morgan argued that failure to publish would endanger Vanunu, because then the Israelis would be able to try him secretly and put him away without anybody knowing about it. Given rigorous Israeli censorship, if Vanunu's story had not been published, the whole affair would never have seen the light of day.

After Vanunu's disappearance it was six weeks before the Israeli government surrendered to pressure and confirmed

137

that he was back in Israel and under arrest. Spokesmen engaged in a disinformation effort to explain how Vanunu was taken from Britain to Israel, and ironically they leaked to the foreign media – the very crime which Vanunu committed. The appetite of the media for stories about spies and espionage gives those in power many opportunities to manipulate public channels of information. At first, an impression was created that Vanunu had been enticed out of British territory to international waters, where he was arrested, and that no state's sovereignty had been infringed.

Milan Kubic, Jerusalem correspondent of *Newsweek*, which had missed the disclosure after Guerrero and Vanunu broke off their contact with its Sydney correspondent, quoted 'sources close to the intelligence community' that the Mossad had run a sophisticated land and sea operation to get him. A glamorous story was invented about a woman luring him on to a yacht in the Mediterranean. Once in international waters the crew of Mossad agents arrested him and took him back to Israel.[1]

The yacht theory sent the *Sunday Times* and other papers after information about the possibility of Israeli ships being in the region at the time of Vanunu's disappearance. The *Sunday Times* discovered that three Israeli ships were sailing at the time of the abduction of Vanunu in northern European seas.

Andrew Whitley of the London *Financial Times* was also a victim of the disinformation effort. Whitley, whose network of sources in Israel's defence establishment have sometimes put him in trouble with Israel's censorship authorities,[2] reported that Vanunu was kidnapped by Mossad agents while travelling between London and Paris and taken back to Israel aboard an El Al flight from Paris.

'Accompanied by two Israeli agents, a drugged Mr Vanunu boarded El Al's flight LY324 from Paris's Charles de Gaulle airport on 2 October, some forty-eight hours after he checked out of his London hotel. Intelligence sources say that to avoid arousing the suspicion of other passengers, he was put on the Tel Aviv-bound aircraft minutes before it took off. Mr Vanunu sat in first class with his captors. Only the El Al security guards aboard the plane knew who their special passenger was, though Israel's ground security must also have cooperated in bypassing French immigration controls and smuggling him aboard,' Whitley reported. He was correct in dismissing the yacht theory. 'The tale about a lengthy sea journey back to Israel is a red herring designed to cover up the length of time Mr Vanunu was back on Israeli soil before he was brought before a judge.' But flight of fancy got the better of Whitley, who then suggested, 'if the stories about being lured aboard a boat in the Mediterranean are untrue, doubt must also be cast on the widely publicised account of the blonde woman friend "Cindy" said to have duped the nervous Israeli out of Britain.' Moreover, explaining the choice of France, Whitley wrote: 'Few scruples were displayed over the sensibilities of the government of M. Jacques Chirac in France, regarded as being less well-disposed than that of Mrs Thatcher towards Israel. At some stage in the proceedings, French law was undoubtedly broken.'

The British authorities were keen to dispel any notion that Vanunu was abducted from British territory. 'Israel,' Whitehall sources told the *Jerusalem Post* London reporter, 'would not have been so stupid as to abduct Vanunu from British territory, particularly since Britain has emerged, since the Hindawi trial [of an Arab backed by Syria arrested for attempting to smuggle a bomb on to an El Al plane at London airport] last month, as Israel's staunchest ally in Western Europe.' And a Foreign Office spokesman told the *Sunday Times*, that while the government would take an extremely serious view of kidnapping from British soil they could not justify intervention if UK laws were not broken.

The cover-up went a stage further when *The Economist* –

which Andrew Neil had left to become editor of the *Sunday Times*, without any great love lost on either side – suggested that Vanunu had been unwittingly manipulated by the Mossad or that he was even a Mossad agent, and that the *Sunday Times* had been the victim of a gigantic public relations exercise to boost Israel's nuclear posture.

For the first three weeks after Vanunu's disappearance, Israeli officials from the prime minister's spokesman downwards claimed not to know anything about his whereabouts, even though he was in Israel and was undergoing interrogation. They broke the basic rule of spokesmanship: credibility hangs on his or her not stating an untruth. For the spokesman of the prison services, though, it was not a total lie to say that 'the Vanunu affair is not the concern of the police and we know nothing of his whereabouts', because at that time he was being held in a section of Gedera prison under the control of the Shin Bet.

There is no obligation on the Israeli authorities to confirm that somebody is under arrest. The Emergency Powers (Detention) Law, the essence of which was inherited from the British Mandate, empowers the authorities to detain a person for six months 'for reasons of state security and public security', and as long as the detention order is approved by a district court judge, it can be extended again and again. In cases of security sensitivity like Vanunu's, this process is completed behind closed doors; sometimes only the defendant's lawyer knows the full reasons for the indictment. And the appointment by Vanunu of Dr Amnon Zichroni, a veteran civil rights lawyer, was not made public. Zichroni adhered to the rules of the game. To announce that he was representing Vanunu would be tantamount to a confirmation that Vanunu was back in Israel, which in turn would raise questions regarding how he got there and how he left Britain.

Eight days after Vanunu vanished, and three days after the publication of their exposé, the *Sunday Times* reported his disappearance to the British authorities. The British police visited the room at the Mountbatten Hotel where he had last stayed, but failed to uncover any evidence that the law had been broken. Nor was there a record of his departure from any British airport or seaport. Israeli officials hoped that media curiosity would die away.

Military censorship in the Vanunu affair could be summed up in two words: damage control. When the *Sunday Mirror* came out with its hoax story about a nuclear conman, a week before the *Sunday Times* disclosures, the Israeli censor initially banned Israeli media from publishing reports from London despite both the convention that military censorship in Israel does not suppress quotes from the foreign media and the meeting of the Editors' Committee a day earlier at which Peres confirmed that foreign sources could be quoted. A few hours later on the Saturday night the censor finally passed the reports quoting the *Sunday Mirror*. Apart from his appointment by the Minister of Defence, the military censor draws his powers from the statute book, and is supposed to be free from ministerial and chief-of-staff pressures. But this is not always the case. At one point during the Vanunu Affair, the military censor had to persuade Defence Minister Itzhak Rabin of the illogicality of the censorship policy. He succeeded.

Vanunu's disappearance was a difficult story for Israeli reporters to cover. Information they gleaned came from Vanunu's family and later from his lawyer, as well as from the prison service, the Shin Bet, and the Cabinet. Israeli reporters with contacts in the intelligence establishment tend to use these sparingly. In this case, officers were tight-lipped. A key source was the Justice Ministry, which would normally have been very reticent. But the Shin Bet affair months earlier, when the Attorney General, Professor Itzhak Zamir, resisted government pressure to cover up the deaths of two Arab terrorists arrested in the 1984 Tel Aviv-Ashkelon bus hijacking, and which resulted in Zamir's dismissal, turned the press and the Justice Ministry into unlikely bedfellows. 'The Ministry of Justice had used the press in order to combat what it felt was the politicians' destruction of justice. To the extent that reporters got Justice Ministry officials to speak about Vanunu it was because they felt they owed us something,' Menachem Shalev, then the *Jerusalem Post*'s justice affairs reporter said. 'Yet it was a futile attempt to get anything past censorship which had not already appeared in the foreign media,' he added. 'The *Sunday Times* was made into the Bible,' remarked Mark Geffen, former editor of *Al Hamishmar*.

Things began to fall apart with the bizarre arrival in Israel of Reverend John McKnight of St John's rectory. He had been in London for two weeks helping the *Sunday Times* try to discover Vanunu's whereabouts. When he arrived in Israel, he turned first to the Anglican Church. While the canon of St George's Cathedral was initially sympathetic to McKnight's cause, the dean and other Anglican leaders, given the Church's sensitive position in Israel, distanced themselves from McKnight. He turned to the Prime Minister's Office, which has formal responsibility for the security services, but was given the runaround, with one official suggesting he try another, and with phone calls unreturned. 'McKnight has no standing, and we see no reason to meet him,' an official said. McKnight said, however, that he managed 'to speak to somebody who had seen somebody who had seen Vanunu and was able to confirm that Vanunu was being held in gaol' – a reference to a member of the Vanunu family who had been in touch with the lawyer representing Mordechai. In front of some one hundred foreign newsmen McKnight, speaking in the elegant surroundings of the American Colony Hotel, which is situated on the green line which once separated Israeli-controlled West Jerusalem from Jordanian East Jerusalem, the Australian parson brought to the world the news that Vanunu was alive and well, albeit in an Israeli prison.

Initially, Israel's military censor told newsmen that they would be unable to report McKnight's news conference but later retracted this. Thomas Friedman, the *New York Times* Jerusalem correspondent, suspected that the Israeli authorities subsequently realised that it was an opportunity for them to let it be known that Vanunu, as everybody suspected, was indeed back in Israel without formally acknowledging it. 'The Israeli intelligence services would seem to have an interest in letting both Israelis and foreigners know that anyone who tries to sell Israeli state secrets abroad will be hunted down and brought back to face an Israeli trial,' Friedman opined. But this Machiavellian view is hardly plausible given the desperate attempts of Israeli officials to put a damper on an embarrassing episode in Israel's relations with London. Rather, the authorities realised it was difficult to stop one hundred newsmen from reporting a news conference they had attended. It showed the vulnerability of the open society.

The officially-inspired leaks that Vanunu had been lured on to a yacht or to France, together with the McKnight episode, had the ricochet effect in Israel of raising questions among left-wing politicians regarding his fate. Mordechai Vershubski of the Party for Change told the Israeli Parliament's Law and Constitution Subcommittee that the people have a right to know. But Prime Minister Shamir said, 'Israel has its own considerations in avoiding a public comment on the case of Mordechai Vanunu. The government will say what it finds fit to say, and it will fulfil its duty to its citizens.' Were it not for two separate developments, 'nothing', claimed *Yediot Aharonot*, the country's largest-selling afternoon newspaper, 'would have been disclosed. Shamir, Peres and Rabin haven't given a fig for Israeli media and national opinion.'

The first development was that the *Sunday Times* turned to Vanunu's lawyer, Amnon Zichroni and asked him to petition the High Court of Justice to ascertain Vanunu's whereabouts. Since the paper had no legal standing in Israel, the petition had to come formally from Vanunu's family. It wasn't easy to get the family to agree, since they had been warned by the Shin Bet not to discuss the affair. Once they did, Zichroni wrote to the prime minister saying that unless the government formally confirmed Vanunu was back in Israel he would petition the High Court which, if successful, would be tantamount to such a confirmation. The game was up, Attorney General Yosef Harish argued.

The second development which forced the Israel government's hand was an orchestrated campaign of questions in the British Parliament to Mrs Thatcher regarding how Vanunu left Britain. Conservative MP Denis Walters asked the foreign secretary to 'press the Israeli government for clarification about the involvement of the Israeli intelligence service in the alleged kidnapping of Mr Vanunu in London and his subsequent illegal removal from Britain.' So did other MPs. Comparing Vanunu to the case of the former Nigerian minister, Umaru Dikko, discovered drugged in the hold of an aircraft, Anthony Beaumont-Dark asked how Mr Vanunu 'could vanish from a London hotel and, like a rabbit out of a hat, had appeared in Israel.' British officials privately pressed Israeli officials for more information about how he had disappeared.

The foreign press corps in Israel – the tenth largest in the world – followed the story aggressively, particularly the contingent of correspondents representing the British media. Shamir blamed the fact that the affair had come to light 'on the media, on all kinds of people, on this terrible curiosity. But', he told Israel Television, 'let us leave this, we shall overcome it despite this exposure.' Asked about the attacks it provoked on Israel, Shamir replied, 'Israel is not being attacked, and I do not feel attacked.' In an abortive attempt to stop the Thatcher government from ceding to British MPs' demands for clarification from Israel, officials in Jerusalem told specific British correspondents about the Peres telephone call to Mrs Thatcher prior to the abduction in which he told her of the need to bring Vanunu home and that no British laws would be broken in the process. Israeli officials were careful not to say what Mrs Thatcher's reply had been. The message was clear: if more information was divulged the British government would implicate itself in his abduction. One MP, Dale Campbell-Savours asked Thatcher in Parliament whether she had had any discussions with Mr Peres or with any other member of the Israeli government regarding Mr Vanunu prior to his departure from Britain. 'No' was the reply: 'prior' could be interpreted as just before as opposed to nine days, as was the case. Asked by Campbell-Savours, 'whether any member or official of the Israeli government communicated to the prime minister or her office to procure the return of Vanunu from the UK,' the prime minister's reply again was 'No'. He was not 'returned' to Israel from Britain; he was returned from another country.

On 9 November the Israeli government broke its silence and confirmed that Vanunu was in Israel, under arrest, and the subject of judicial proceedings: 'The government of Israel announces that Mordechai Vanunu is legally under arrest in Israel, in accordance with a court order following a hearing in which a lawyer of his election was present. All the rumours to the effect that Vanunu was "kidnapped" on English soil are without foundation. Moreover, there is no basis for the report that Mr Peres contacted Mrs Thatcher in order to tell her something that did not happen.'

In addition to Attorney General Harish's argument that the appeal to the Supreme Court meant that the government had to make a statement, the prime mover was Peres, who wanted to relieve the pressure on Mrs Thatcher. Just a month earlier Britain had severed diplomatic ties with Syria over that country's involvement in the Hindawi affair. Shamir opposed the statement, arguing that the British, who were not pushing the issue, had said there was no evidence

145

of a crime being committed on British soil. Nor was there evidence that Vanunu had even entered or exited from London airport's immigration controls. To say anything would – and did – stimulate more questions. Most Israelis agreed with Shamir: 53.8 per cent questioned by the poll company Modiin Ezrachi thought that the Israeli government need not have published the fact of Vanunu's arrest as opposed to 36.8 per cent who were inclined to support it.

The statement itself explicitly denied that a kidnapping had occurred on British soil and implicitly repudiated one report that Vanunu was conveyed from Britain to Israel in a crate as diplomatic mail. But it left open the possibility that the technician was somehow enticed by Israeli agents to leave Britain and was only subsequently kidnapped and brought to Israel aboard an Israeli naval vessel. Asked if the statement meant that Vanunu had not been taken from Britain, Mr Shamir replied, 'I didn't say anything about that. I said British laws were not broken.' Nor did the statement repudiate the notion that Peres had telephoned Mrs Thatcher. The call, it was now explained, was to tell Thatcher that the *Sunday Mirror* story was incorrect and based on somebody who was unstable and bore a grudge. Politicians do not telephone foreign leaders about reports in the news media, either as a matter of course or out of self-respect.

While the Vanunu affair simmered, President Chaim Herzog was on a state visit to Australia, New Zealand and Fiji. The fact that Vanunu had stayed in Australia before going to Britain, and that in both Australia and New Zealand the nuclear arms issue is controversial, ensured that the question of his abduction would come up in journalists' questions to Herzog. But the Office of the Cabinet Secretary overlooked informing the travelling president when the Israeli government made its announcement, resulting in Herzog continuing to deny knowledge of Vanunu's where-

Mordechai Vanunu

Uzi Hasson, prosecution
lawyer

The nuclear research centre at Dimona. This photograph, shot by *Time* photographer David Rubinger during its construction in 1960, is the only one passed by Israeli military censorship

Peter Hounam, *Sunday Times* reporter

Nahum Admoni, then head of the Mossad

Avigdor Feldman, Vanunu's defence lawyer

Meir Vanunu, campaigning
brother

Vanunu's hand signal from
a police van, which
disclosed that he was
abducted to Israel via
Rome

abouts when Jerusalem had already officially confirmed that he was being held in gaol awaiting formal charges.

The British ambassador to Israel, Clifford Squire, in the face of growing criticism at home, including a full-scale debate scheduled in the House of Commons about Vanunu's disappearance, was instructed to seek further information about how he had reached Israel. Curiously, rather than do so at the levels of either the Foreign Ministry's director-general, or the assistant director-general for Europe, Squire approached the political director-general, Yossi Beilin, Foreign Secretary Peres's right-hand man. But he was told that Israel had nothing to add to its statement that no crime had been committed on British soil. The ambassador turned to Vanunu's lawyer but Zichroni directed him back to the Israeli authorities. There were vague hints, attributed to 'Whitehall sources', about British–Israeli diplomatic ties being lowered in status. A few days before the House of Commons debate Peres, who was visiting the United States at the same time as Mrs Thatcher, spoke to her by telephone: 'It was a very friendly conversation and I think that our misunderstanding has been cleared up,' he said.

The debate attracted some fifty MPs, a larger number than might have been expected. Most were seated in the chamber, but a few hung around out of sight of the public – among them the chief whip, John Wakeham, and Thatcher's parliamentary private secretary, Michael Alison. Denis Walters called for an official government inquiry into Vanunu's disappearance. There were several ways in which Vanunu could have found himself in an Israeli prison but one that could be ruled out was that he reached there 'of his own free will'. Logically, it followed that he must have been abducted 'almost without doubt, by Israeli agents', he said. Anthony Beaumont-Dark, who initiated the debate, said that an international jurist should be allowed to interview Vanunu, thereby 'allaying our fears'. Opposition foreign affairs spokesman Donald Woods said that 'the British government

147

cannot expect to get away with their current line, particularly in the light of allegations that the prime minister herself was consulted.' In reply, the Home Office minister, David Waddington, said that an official inquiry was impractical since Britain had no power to ascertain from Israel, in the absence of any evidence that a crime had been committed, how Vanunu got there. However, given the concern in Britain, Waddington, going further than his Foreign Office colleagues, urged Israel to explain how Vanunu reached Israel. As regards the lack of evidence of Vanunu's entry and exit at London airport's immigration control, the minister explained that with thirty-five million passing through passport controls yearly only limited records were kept.

The British press also remained unconvinced by the Israeli statement. The *Daily Mail* considered that if Jerusalem could not come up with an account of how Vanunu was brought back to Israel without breaking UK law, they should be condemned by the British Foreign Office. The *Daily Telegraph*, which, like the *Daily Mail*, is generally regarded as pro-Israeli, also was concerned about the circumstances in which Vanunu left Britain. Yet, within two weeks of the Israeli statement and the House of Commons debate, feelings died down. But the matter would be revived when the truth about how Vanunu reached Israel did come to light.

Britain's low-key reaction contrasted with that when Farzad Bazoft, a journalist on the *Observer*, was arrested and charged with espionage in 1990 and later executed in Iraq while gathering information on Iraq's nuclear development. More than fifty separate representations were made by Britain to Baghdad on behalf of Bazoft, who was not a British citizen but was travelling on British papers. These included a request (turned down) for Foreign Secretary Douglas Hurd to visit Baghdad. In this case the pressure which the British government applied may have hardened Iraq's determination to show its hand. The difference in the levels of response by Britain in this and the Vanunu abduction reflected the differences in the seriousness of the crimes committed by Vanunu and Bazoft as well as the punishments imposed on them. It also reflected the different styles of government in Israel and Iraq which in turn are reflected, in Israel's case, in its warm ties with London.

Britain's reaction also contrasted with another case involving the murder, by people working for Taiwanese military intelligence, of a Chinese-American author, Henry Liu, in California in January 1985 after he published a critical biography of Taiwan President Chiang Ching-kuo. There was a certain hesitancy by the United States to push the matter; US Congressman Norman Mineta wrote to the Attorney General protesting the 'apparent lack of interest and activity by the Justice Department in pursuing the killers of Henry Liu'. Although the US and Taiwan have not had formal diplomatic ties since 1979, when the US recognised Communist China, some Congressmen talked about cutting off arms sales to Taiwan, about $750m a year, in retaliation. The US did not expel any Taiwanese (non-diplomatic) representative in the US, but the FBI sent officers to Taiwan to seek more information about the killing. They wanted the extradition of a leader of Taiwan's underworld gang, the Bamboo Union, whom the FBI believed had masterminded the killing, but in the absence of an extradition agreement between the US and Taiwan nothing came of it.

The operation apparently did not have the consent of President Ching-kuo, who had earlier embarked upon a path of strengthening US–Taiwan informal ties. He ordered the arrest of the head of the intelligence bureau of Taiwan's Defence Ministry, Vice-Admiral Wang His-ling, and two deputies. Taiwan's parliament, the Yuan, met in emergency session to discuss the case, which had tarnished Taiwan's image.

The seeds of a crisis between Britain and Israel had been sown earlier, in the summer of 1986, with the discovery in a telephone booth in West Germany of a bag containing eight forged British passports, a genuine Israeli passport and envelopes linking the documents with the Israeli embassy. The incredible claim has been made in West Germany that the passports were to be used to kidnap West German nuclear scientists engaged on constructing an Islamic nuclear bomb.

It was not the first time that the Mossad used forged British passports.[3] In the killing by the Mossad in 1979 of Abu Hassan Salameh, who masterminded the 1972 massacre at the Munich Olympics of eleven Israeli athletes, the woman agent who detonated the bomb used a British passport with the name of Erika Mary Chambers.[4] British passports were also used during an Israeli operation in Beirut in 1973 in which three senior officials of the Palestine Liberation Organisation were killed. In both cases the British Foreign Office complained but did not receive assurances that forged British passports would not be used again. In the case of the passports found in a West German telephone booth, the Foreign Office got a formal apology from the Israeli ambassador to London, Yehuda Avner, but only after the matter was raised some seven times.[5] In a meeting with Foreign Secretary Sir Geoffrey Howe in January 1987, Mr Peres gave assurances that it would not happen again.

But the straw that broke the camel's back was the discovery by British police in August 1987 of an Arab terrorist arms arsenal in a Hull flat. In the late seventies, Ismael Sowan, still in his teens, left his village in the south of Jerusalem to study engineering at Beirut University. Before he left, the Shin Bet recruited him to inform on the activities at the university of Fatah, the Palestinian organisation.[6] Either at the prompting of his Israeli masters or quite by chance, Sowan rented a Beirut flat belonging to Abder Rahman Mustapha, who was in charge of Commando 18, a section of Force 17 which had responsibility for the PLO's special operations abroad. In 1982 Ismael went to Paris to continue his studies, which were financed by the Mossad,[7] and during his stay he followed local Palestinians. But in 1984, unsuccessful in his exams, he moved to London to continue his studies – only to find his old landlord Mustapha in charge of security at the PLO office.

On the orders of Albert, his Mossad handler at the Israeli embassy, Sowan renewed his friendship with Mustapha, regularly visiting him at the PLO's London office.[8] The Israelis suspected that Mustapha was holding an arsenal of PLO arms and ammunition smuggled into Britain in the early 1970s and already much depleted.[9]

After his marriage in 1986 to an English girl, Sowan told Albert that he would have to stop spying as he now had a wife. He had moved to Hull where he worked as a research assistant at a local college. But cutting himself off from Mustapha abruptly would have alerted the PLO man's suspicions, so Sowan kept up the relationship, including visiting him at his Romford home for dinner. Mustapha seized the opportunity to ask Sowan to store a few suitcases for him since, he said, he was selling his house. In the six cases were four rapid-fire assault rifles, seven fragmentation grenades, nearly seventy pounds of plastic explosives, detonators, timing devices and 300 rounds of ammunition.

In April 1987 Mustapha was expelled from Britain on suspicion of involvement in the killing of three Israelis on a yacht at Larnaca in 1986. On 14 July Sowan went to Israel with his bride. Just before that, on 6 July, Mustapha secretly returned to London, and eight days later Al Al-Adhami, an Arab cartoonist, known for his anti-Arafat cartoons, was shot and killed on Arafat's orders. Mustapha left London the next day, and police suspected him of the killing. News of it reached Sowan in Israel. With Mustapha being sought by British police, it would be only a matter of time before British detectives closed in on his Hull flat. He had to tell the Israelis about the suitcases. He renewed contact with the Shin Bet, and met 'David' in Israel. Yes, David agreed, the matter of the suitcases was very serious indeed, but Sowan need not worry. Somebody would be in touch with him when he got back to Hull, and the whole matter would be sorted out. Sowan flew back to Britain on 5 August; the days passed but there was no word from the Israelis. Finally, on 12 August there was a knock on the door. Two Hull policemen stood outside. Sowan bowed to the inevitable and invited the detectives in. On 16 June 1988 Sowan was sentenced at London's Old Bailey to eleven years' imprisonment for possessing explosives and firearms.

The court case showed once again how British streets had become a hunting-ground for Israelis and Palestinians squaring off in their internecine war. Moreover, it shed public light for the first time on the Israeli government's involvement. The verdict was promptly followed by the British government's expulsion of a 'diplomat', Arie Regev, Mossad's liaison with MI6 and MI5.[10] The decision was initiated by the Foreign Office and by MI5, Britain's domestic intelligence agency responsible for counter-espionage. It had been opposed by MI6, which was well aware of the value of the Mossad as a source of information to Britain.[11] Earlier, when Sowan was arrested, another 'diplomat', Jacob Barad, who had been one of Sowan's handlers and who had returned to Israel 'for holiday leave', was informed that he was undesirable and would not be allowed back. The British authorities said that they had been informed neither about the arms cache which the Israelis knew of in March 1987, nor of Mustapha's return to London under an assumed identity.[12] The Mossad had broken the basic rule that foreign intelligence services are supposed to keep the host country's intelligence service aware of what they are doing. After all, had the British been informed the cartoonist might still be alive. When the arms cache was discovered, a horrendous dispute erupted between MI5 and the Mossad.[13] In an unusual step Mrs Thatcher wrote to Mr Shamir after Sowan's arrest, saying that the British would have no alternative but to limit Mossad activities if it did not fall into line.[14] But the Mossad still did not inform MI5 about what they were doing, so the same message was given to Mr Peres by Sir Geoffrey Howe.[15] While diplomats from the Soviet Union, Syria, Libya and Cuba had been expelled from Britain, it was the first expulsion of someone with diplomatic status from a friendly country.

A question which needs to be asked is why Sowan was brought to trial in the first place. After all, in 1972 when British police were about to issue an arrest warrant against an Israeli who had attempted to break into an Arab embassy, the home secretary instructed that instead the man be put on a plane bound for Israel. Sowan's imprisonment reveals the seriousness with which the British took the whole matter. Also expelled was the PLO's press officer in London, Zahi Al-Awa. Although not involved in the affair he was expelled, the Foreign Office statement said, so that 'the PLO would understand that the use of violence on British territory by groups within the PLO would not be acceptable to the British authorities.' Thatcher was anxious that not only the terrorist hunters should be punished, but the Israelis protested, arguing that this equated terrorist hunters with terrorists.

Weeks after Sowan's sentence and Regev's expulsion, Peres, with Shamir's approval, asked Abba Eban, the chairman of the Knesset's Defence and Foreign Affairs Committee, to pay a secret visit to London. There, Israel's elder diplomat-statesman had a forty-five-minute meeting with Mrs Thatcher in an attempt to calm the stormy waters in London–Jerusalem relations and to avoid any further steps against Israel. The affair would have ended there, but Israeli officials, including Shamir, went out of their way to criticise the announcement of a British arms deal with Saudi Arabia which included planes, minesweepers and support facilities. They described it as 'an irresponsible pursuit of economic interests at the expense of principles'. Outraged British

153

ministers called for a report from MI5 on Israeli clandestine activities in London.[16] It revealed that under cover of a private business five men attached to the Israeli embassy were still running secret operations.[17] MI5, ordered to act, met their Israeli colleagues, and asked them formally what they were doing.[18] When the Israelis replied with their cover occupations, the British, referring to the Thatcher letter warning that Israeli intelligence officers would only be tolerated if they kept the British authorities informed of their actions, told them to leave.[19] In all, two senior diplomatic-status agents and five others were expelled, and Sowan was serving an eleven-year prison sentence.[20] In addition, Bashar Samar, a Golan Druse, who, like Sowan, had worked himself into Mustapha's inner circle, had been expelled the previous year.

There may well not have been the crisis between the two countries without the Sowan trial. But it is equally clear that it required the earlier cases – most notably the Vanunu disappearance and the parliamentary and media criticism – to provoke the diplomatic repercussions which followed Sowan's sentencing.

The expulsions, and the collapse of the Mossad unit in Britain, resulted, according to a British intelligence officer, in 'almost no intelligence of any great worth from the Mossad – and none was passed from us to the Israelis.'[21] The freeze lasted five months until December 1988, by which time both MI6 and the Mossad pushed for a restoration recognising, as a Mossad officer said, that the 'no-contact approach is not serving either side well. The British need us and we need them.'[22] Israel broke the deadlock by providing MI6 with crucial information about British hostages held in Lebanon and other intelligence from the Middle East.[23] The end of the freeze had also eased tension between MI6 and MI5, whose counter-espionage officers had originally ordered the expulsion. In March 1989 it was to the Mossad that MI6 turned after the discovery of an IRA death list with the names of some 200 MPs and information regarding arms arriving from Libya for the IRA.[24] But if links were to be restored, British controls on Mossad activities meant that the agency had to move its main base for West European activities out of Britain, reportedly to West Germany.[25]

The Italian connection in the Vanunu abduction seemed safely concealed. The *Tappuz*, the cargo boat involved in the operation, had given a false destination when it sailed from La Spezia.[26] The harbour authorities were told that the ship was bound for Marseilles, having come from Israel's northern port of Haifa.[27] It had in fact sailed from Barcelona, and, after calling at La Spezia, was next seen when it put into Ashdod, a southern Israeli port, on 9 October, having taken five days to make a crossing that should have taken three.[28] On the day that Vanunu vanished, a member of the Israeli embassy in Rome hired a van.[29] When the van was returned to the hire company, it had covered 900km. The trip from Rome to La Spezia and back is 850km. To prevent Vanunu himself from knowing how he reached Israel, Mossad agents spoke to him in English.[30]

The Italian connection came to light when on arrival at the Jerusalem District Court on 21 December, 1986, where his remand was extended, Vanunu outwitted his guards by flattening one of his palms against the window of the police van. On it was written

> Vanunu M
> was HIJACKEN
> IN ROME ITL
> Came to Rome
> BY BA FLY 504

The police officers accompanying Vanunu initially did not understand the message; when they did – after press photographers had snapped the outstretched arm – they forced his hand away from the window of the van. Inside the courthouse Vanunu's hand was washed. However, on his way out from the court, an Israeli reporter fired questions at Vanunu in Hebrew asking him where he had been kidnapped. Vanunu shouted back 'Rome', before a police guard clamped his hand over his mouth.

Vanunu was proving the man Israel could not gag. Israeli censorship attempted to close the security leak by banning publication of the message written on Vanunu's palm. Israeli newspapers appeared with pictures of his hand with the message blacked out. But it had been seen by many journalists and photographers as well as bystanders. Damage control failed again: in a report under the byline of its London-based defence reporter, Frank Draper, the London *Evening Standard* revealed the news of how Vanunu reached Israel from Britain. The ban on the media was lifted. But the paper's Jerusalem correspondent, Bernard Josephs, had his accreditation as a foreign correspondent suspended. 'It will not be possible for somebody to take the law into his own hands and decide to publish something even though its publication has been prohibited,' the military censor, Brigadier-General Itzhak Shani, said. 'In order to defend the censorship law, local media and other foreign correspondents, I didn't see any other alternative but to take the step,' he added. But Josephs claimed that he 'didn't mention Rome or any other word on Vanunu's palm. I showed police officers investigating the matter a copy of the fax of the report I wrote, and there was no mention of the words that Vanunu wrote.' *Evening Standard* editor John Leese said that Vanunu's message 'came from an entirely different source and our story was compiled in London'.

It was not the first time in the Vanunu Affair that censorship had failed to stop sensitive information being published. The *Financial Times*'s Andrew Whitley had reported that the Mossad held the Shin Bet responsible for Vanunu's leaking Israel's nuclear secrets and the taking of fifty-seven photographs inside the research centre. And before the Israeli authorities formally announced that Vanunu was back in Israel under detention, a newsagency reporter went to his editors saying that Vanunu was back in the country. 'I thought we should run the story and break censorship and prepare to be kicked out of the country. But they said put it to the censor. I was staggered,' he said. There is no formal obligation upon foreign correspondents in Israel to submit all their reports to censorship for prior clearance. Prohibited from publishing information damaging state security, individual journalists use their discretion in deciding what to submit. Nor is the issue of press credentials conditional upon signing a declaration of adherence to censorship regulations. To be honest, there are a number of ways of avoiding censorship, including using a public telephone to send a report instead of a correspondent's own phone or fax machine which might be subject to eavesdropping by the authorities. Other means include publishing the story under a name other than the reporter's or with a two capital byline. 'The Vanunu story has two ends, one here and one in London,' said Robin Lustig, then Middle East correspondent of the *Observer*. 'If I have a lead on a story but I have only one source, I will call London and ask them to try to confirm it. Once confirmed, the story becomes a London-based report and is transmitted from there, and there is no need to involve the censor.'

It is often possible to gain the cooperation of the foreign media in not publishing sensitive information of a strictly military nature. But where political factors are involved this is more difficult. Any damage in the Vanunu Affair to Israel's national security could have been with the original *Sunday Times* disclosure. Censorship of information about his arrest, abduction and trial was mostly to avoid political embarrassment. Even the Israeli media were critical of censorship behaviour. 'Those responsible for the "palm" debacle were those who brought Vanunu to court. The censor should be confined to security matters,' *Maariv*, a mass circulation afternoon newspaper, wrote. 'There was absolutely no security reason to block publication of Vanunu's words.' However, some foreign correspondents, particularly Israeli nationals who are more likely to be subject to prosecution, are critical of the way in which some of their colleagues get away with avoiding the censor.

'It is not popular among journalists to express support for the censor when he brings a police action against a correspondent,' wrote Yeshayahu Ben Porat, a *Yediot Aharonot* journalist, who is also the Israel correspondent of Radio Europe 1, and the West German magazine *Quick*, 'but in the case of Bernard Josephs we unreservedly support the censor because this is self-defeating, and always at the expense of the local media.' Mr Shamir said, 'the problem of our censorship is one which needs a corrective, but perhaps our media people should be more responsible. After all, each of us is not just a journalist or an editor or a correspondent: we are all citizens of Israel, and we have to be concerned about Israel.'

In the wake of censorship lapses with Vanunu, and earlier matters, an inter-departmental inquiry was launched in November 1986 to find ways of stopping foreign correspondents from avoiding censorship. The issue came up again in August 1989 when the *Sunday Times* published claims that two Israeli soldiers being held hostage by the Hizbollah had died, a story put out during the interrogation of a Shi'ite cleric abducted by the Israelis from South Lebanon. Only a couple of foreign correspondents have had their accreditation withheld in the history of the Jewish state, partly due to an awareness that such steps create a negative image abroad. Comfort may be drawn by officials from the belief that substantial damage to the country's security has not apparently been caused by foreign correspondents breaching censorship.

The palm message had all the promise of a diplomatic crisis in Israeli–Italian relations, with a replay, or even

158

worse, of the mini-crisis with London which had just settled. And while in the British case Peres had prepared the ground by speaking to Mrs Thatcher before Vanunu's disappearance, no such contacts appear to have been made with Rome.

The abduction once again confirmed how foreign intelligence services used Rome as a staging-ground for their operations. Italy had, up to then, been the scene of settling of accounts between Arabs and Israel, Arabs and Arabs – and now Israel and its own people, commented Rizzo of *La Stampa*.

The Vanunu abduction occurred against the background of a number of sensational earlier disappearances in the city. In addition to the case of Mordechai Lok, the spy found drugged in diplomatic luggage bound for Egypt, there was the mysterious case of Vitali Yurcenko, Number Five in the KGB hierarchy who disappeared while touring the Vatican in July 1985, and who turned up months later at the Soviet embassy in Washington where he claimed he had been kidnapped by the CIA to its headquarters at Langley, Virginia, and debriefed. The Americans initially claimed Yurcenko sought to defect to the West, but later backtracked. Yet he returned to the USSR, where he is reported to have been shot.

Two years earlier Soviet journalist Oleg Bitov disappeared while travelling from Rome to a film festival at Venice, only to turn up in London as the 'guest' of the British and American intelligence services. The following year he appeared in Moscow claiming that he had been kidnapped by British intelligence. And in summer 1986 another Soviet journalist, Yuri Varechtchaguine, disappeared in Rome. There was also the mysterious case of the spiritual leader of Lebanon's Shi'ite Muslims, Musa Sadr, who flew from Tripoli to Rome in 1978 but disappeared. The Italian authorities claimed that Sadr never left Tripoli and that his flight was invented by the Libyan authorities to disguise his captivity in Libya. Shortly before Vanunu's palm message, the Italian government had become embroiled in a domestic crisis after it became known that Italy had allowed the US to use the Tuscan port of Talamone for clandestine supplies of arms to Tehran, partly to obtain the release of Italian hostages held in Iran.

Partico Liberate Italiano, Italy's liberal party, which formed part of the government coalition, raised in Parliament 'the freedom of movement of the Israeli and US intelligence services on Italian soil' as well as the question of possible links between these services and Italian intelligence. 'It is intolerable that Italy should take on a colony status,' a member said. The small Proletarian Democratic Party asked how a kidnap could occur at an airport under the intensive surveillance of the police's anti-terror squad. The only explanation, the party said, was 'that the kidnap was the product of cooperation between Italian security and Israel's secret service'. The question of connivance by the Italian intelligence services in Vanunu's abduction focused attention on its ties and dependence. Despite the restructuring of the intelligence services in 1977 there still seemed a need to invest the Italian Parliament's committee for the security services with adequate powers to know in advance about intelligence actions which could be illegal or detrimental to national interests.

The question also came up later in 1987 when an Italian judge investigated the crash in 1973 of the helicopter which had carried to freedom Palestinians arrested on Italian soil in possession of a surface-to-air missile. In 1989 the judge issued a summons against the then head of the Mossad, Zvi Zamir. The Vanunu abduction aroused interest about Israel's nuclear development in the country's peace movement and scientific community. 'When the Vanunu case began we wondered why. It was so strong a reaction from Israel against Vanunu that there is a suspicion that there is something to hide,' said Marino Seerino of the peace organisation Associazione par da Pace. The association later succeeded in getting thirty senators of the Italian Parliament to put their names to an appeal for Vanunu to be awarded the Nobel Prize.

Israeli officials had to play out the criticism resulting from Vanunu's palm message. Ambassador Mordechai Drory said he had no information about the case. Italian Prime Minister Bettino Craxi said that he awaited a satisfactory reply from Israel: the Israeli authorities' 'no comment' was significant. Craxi saw no reason why Vanunu should lie, but Ambassador Drory claimed that Vanunu was 'desperate' to stir up publicity about his case. He hoped that Italy 'won't pay attention to any desperate attempt by a person detained under serious charges and awaiting judgement to draw attention and world public opinion with these types of statements'. 'Vanunu's claim sounds as if it came from a cinema movie,' Foreign Ministry spokesman Ehud Gol said, and political director Yossi Beilin said, 'Tomorrow Vanunu might say he came via Tanganyika.' While Israeli officials denied that any Italian law had been broken, they did not explain how Vanunu got to Israel. When asked what action Italy would take if it was true that he had been kidnapped on Italian soil, Craxi replied, 'Protest would be the minimum'. He paused and then added, 'But it would also be the maximum because we could do no more.'

The tone was set. Italy would go through the motions of protesting infringement of Italian territoriality, and Jerusalem would dutifully reassure her, as it had the British government beforehand, that her territoriality had not been infringed. However, in a cable to the Israeli Foreign Ministry a week after the affair began, the Israeli embassy in Rome said the Italians were not entirely satisfied with Israeli explanations, revising its earlier optimistic assessment. There was to be a judicial enquiry by the deputy Rome prosecutor, Dr Domenico Sica, into whether Italian territoriality had been infringed and whether charges should be brought against anybody. The Italian judiciary has been in the vanguard against the lawlessness affecting the country, and it has taken on the task at no small risk: a Genoa prosecutor investigating the Red Brigade was one of the first victims of the group's campaign of assassination in 1976.

The palm incident did not extend to the two countries' diplomatic relationship, and the subject was reportedly not raised during a trip to Italy by Mr Peres in early January. Italy's deputy prime minister, Arnaldo Forlani, visiting Israel at the same time, said that the affair would have no impact on Italian–Israeli relations. 'We've asked for clarification and the Israeli government has given us adequate assurances.'

Judge Domenico Sica sought answers to two questions: what was Vanunu's reason for coming to Rome, and how did he continue en route to Tel Aviv? The task facing Sica was arduous, if not impossible, from the outset. A man in a foreign country on his way to court held up his hand with the scrawled message that he had been kidnapped on Italian soil. An investigation was being opened of an incident learnt from the media. There were no eyewitnesses in Italy to Vanunu's disappearance. The only facts were the writing on the palm, and the list of passengers on British Airways Flight 504 from London to Rome on 30 September 1986, which included the name of Mordechai Vanunu. *Notitia criminis*, it was enough information for the Italian judiciary to have to open a formal investigation.

Sica had conducted many investigations into terrorist crimes, including the murder of President Aldo Moro by the Red Brigade. Italian magistrates have broad powers of investigation and arrest. In addition to spending a couple of hours at Rome's Fiumicino Airport to see whether Vanunu could have been kidnapped inside the airport itself, Sica turned to the Italian police's anti-terrorist squad and to the domestic intelligence agency, SISDE (Servizio Informazione Sicurezza Democratica). In turning to the police and internal intelligence agencies, Sica was faced with the fact that the intelligence community is riven with pro-Israeli and pro-

Arab factions, the former having close ties with their Israeli colleagues. That Vanunu appeared on the British Airways' passenger list, had purchased a ticket and checked in a piece of luggage at London airport, were quickly verified. But for Sica there remained the nagging doubt of whether Vanunu had actually come to Rome or whether it was all a piece of disinformation by Israel to create an impression that he was abducted from Italy and disguise the real manner in which he reached Israel.

In addition to there being no hard evidence of an abduction, there was no flight continuing to Israel until the following day. By the end of the first week of investigations, Sica's attention turned to the possibility of Vanunu's having been taken to Israel by boat. Italian officials investigated which Israeli ships arrived at Italian ports around the time Vanunu was supposed to have reached Rome and found that the *Tappuz* had been the sole one.[31] Moreover, they discovered the false destination the ship had given, claiming it was bound for Marseilles, having sailed from Barcelona and was heading for Israel.[32] When the *Tappuz* called at La Spezia in August 1987 Sica ordered a surveillance operation to be carried out. The van which the Israeli embassy hired on the day Vanunu reached Rome, and which had the return journey distance to La Spezia on its odometer, was also discovered.[33]

Some of Sica's information came from Mordechai Vanunu's brother, Meir, who twice visited Sica, in the spring and July of 1987, and from *Sunday Times* reporter Peter Hounam, whose paper published details which Meir gave it about Vanunu's abduction. Meir obtained the information by talking in Moroccan dialect to his gaoled brother. The Insight team located a couple of the passengers on Vanunu's flight, but none recalled seeing him. The woman who sat in the seat next to Cindy could not remember Vanunu.

Mordechai himself has said that the *Sunday Times* reports on how he was brought to Israel are missing many details.

Although Meir had to sign a declaration that he would not reveal anything his brother divulged to him, he failed to keep this, and, after the *Sunday Times* reported Meir's testimony in August 1987, an Israeli court issued a warrant for his arrest. Meir said that he did 'not want to set foot in Israel for many, many years'. But his parents and family had opposed his action, arguing that it wasn't enough that they would not see one son; now they wouldn't see two. An application to the British government for political asylum on the grounds that he faced persecution for revealing information in the legitimate public interest was turned down. The Home Office replied that Meir Vanunu faced prosecution not persecution.

On the eve of a Jerusalem district court handing down its guilty verdict on Vanunu, in March 1988, Sica said that he planned to visit Israel to interview Vanunu in gaol to find out what had happened to him after he arrived at Rome airport. 'I am not concerned with whether or not Vanunu has been found guilty. What has to be cleared up is how he ended up in Israel,' the judge said. An Israeli Foreign Ministry official said that since Sica had no jurisdiction in Israel, he would almost certainly not be allowed to see Vanunu. 'If Dr Sica comes it would be very, very embarrassing for our government,' he said. Sica did not – the embarrassment was spared.

Sica completed his inquiry in June 1988, reaching a sensational conclusion: Vanunu was working in liaison with he Mossad to publicise deliberately Israel's nuclear capability. The whole affair had been a disinformation exercise. Sica dismissed as romance Meir Vanunu's account of how his brother had been taken to Israel. The judge's arguments were four-fold:

●Despite wide investigation, Sica found no one who could confirm that Vanunu had arrived in Rome. That Mordechai Vanunu used his real name on the flight was proof to Sica that 'Cindy' wanted to leave evidence behind.

•He dismissed Meir Vanunu's claim that his brother had been taken to a third-floor flat in a densely populated area of Rome where he was drugged and spirited off to Israel. 'This was the most unsuitable and dangerous place from which to carry an unconscious body. It is obvious that a group of specialists would never have committed such an error,' Sica said.

•Sica was unimpressed by Vanunu's message on the palm. Since Vanunu had himself admitted that he did not know English well, how could he have written that message, Sica asked? Vanunu's other writings in English show 'elementary mistakes', he said, somebody else must have written it.

•Sica had seen fifty-two photographs which Vanunu took, and which the *Sunday Times* had passed on to the judge with copies to the Italian atomic energy authority, ENEA. These dispelled his last doubts. They showed in perfect chronological order the various stages in the making of a nuclear warhead. No people appear in any of the photographs, even those showing instruments which would normally be watched constantly. Sica wondered how Vanunu was able to make this 'tourist's presentation' of such a top secret operation, given the security measures in effect at Dimona. He concluded that the photographer was acting with the 'full consent of those in charge.'[34]

The judge did not suggest what the operation was for – or who was behind it – but said, 'It would not take much imagination to link it to the Israelis' desire to frighten their neighbours with their nuclear achievements without having to answer to the Americans for their boasts.'[35] Meir Vanunu said: 'If this is a disinformation exercise, release my brother. If the Italian judge is correct, my brother should be sitting on the seashore, and not in an isolated prison cell while all his family suffer.' Once Vanunu had completed his mission he ought to have been on a first-class El Al flight to Israel to receive a hero's welcome at Mossad headquarters.

165

Each of the arguments presented by Sica may be questioned:

1. Sica claimed that despite 'wide inquiries' he failed to find one person who saw Vanunu reach Rome. It is unclear from the term 'wide inquiries' whether Sica contacted the 130-odd passengers plus flight crew. All the passengers could have been traced since the airline had names and addresses.

2. Sica claimed that the usage of Vanunu's real name on his air ticket is proof of his wanting to record the impression that he had gone to Rome. The first lesson any spy learns – including Vanunu, if Sica is correct that he was working for the Israelis – is not to use his or her own name. Was the small credibility to be gained from the use of his real name worth the Italian public, political and diplomatic fall-out which could – and, indeed, did – result? And why did 'Cindy' travel under her alias, 'Cindy Hanin', instead of her real name? No, Vanunu used his own because that was the name on his passport and, not being a spy, he had no forged passport. (It is true that in London he used a pseudonym at the hotels where he stayed but he did not have to show his passport.)

3. Sica argued that a professional intelligence service would not have taken Vanunu to a densely-populated place in Rome lest it arouse suspicions. On the contrary, it may be argued that it is much easier to conceal a person in an anonymous-looking block of flats. Vanunu travelled to, and entered, the flat at his own volition, accompanied by Cindy. Only once inside, Meir Vanunu claims, was he drugged. The unconscious man could have been taken out to a waiting van during the hours of darkness when there was little chance of being noticed.

4. If Sica is correct that Vanunu's English was inadequate to write the palm message, and that somebody else did, why did the Israeli censor ban its publication? And, why was a criminal investigation begun against the correspondent of the news organisation which broke censorship and published

166

the palm message? If it was written by somebody else why did it contain three errors: (i) 'hijacken' instead of hijacked; (ii) usage of hijacked instead of a more suitable word, kidnapped; (iii) 'Fly' instead of Flight. Indeed, these errors are proof that though Vanunu's English was by no means perfect it was enough to get by. Meir Vanunu agrees that his brother did not know English well but like any serious university student he had picked it up in the course of his studies. 'I myself bought him an English dictionary,' he said. Vanunu's English competency was adequate for him to debriefed by Dr Frank Barnaby without the *Sunday Times* requiring an interpreter.

5. With regard to Sica's statement that the fifty-two photographs which Vanunu had taken were all in chronological order and therefore had to have been taken with official sanction, a 'chronological order' is a subjective not an objective sequence. A chronological order may be made out of any number of photographs. In fact, Vanunu had taken fifty-seven, not fifty-two; the others had been damaged by sunlight, according to the *Sunday Times*. Would an officially sanctioned PR job include spoilt photos? Sica would perhaps answer that these were included to give the others a degree of genuineness. He also argued that the absence of any people in the photographs is evidence of official collusion and that if Vanunu was acting on his own there would have to be people there. But, of course, Vanunu could not have taken the photographs with people present. The absence of people is perhaps the best proof that it was a genuine security leak. If it was a disinformation effort, the government would have ensured that people would have been seen, to add to the credibility of the scenes. And how many people would Sica expect to be working and seen in those parts of the nuclear research centre? Finally, Mr Shamir referred on several occasions to the security fiasco of Vanunu's disclosure and that lessons had been learnt.

The biggest weakness is Sica's conclusion that the Vanunu

disclosure was a disinformation effort was the eighteen-year sentence handed down. Also, what need was there for Cindy's role if it was a disinformation exercise? (The *Sunday Times* saw Cindy in London and subsequently spoke to her in Israel.) And why did Shin Bet contact Mordechai's brother Albert on 7 September to verify Mordechai's whereabouts, telling him that his brother was about to reveal secret information to the press?

Avigdor Feldman, Vanunu's defence lawyer – with whom Sica failed to make any contact – was as dismissive as Vanunu's brother had been. 'We are dealing with a serious judge who investigated Aldo Moro's murder as well as other incidents, but this investigation was not serious. He did not turn to me or to Vanunu or request any information, even published, from the trial,' Feldman said. 'It looks like an attempt to erase the Vanunu Affair and to give it the appearance of a sub-standard detective story.'

To be fair, Sica had turned to Amnon Zichroni. Zichroni told Sica that he would need permission from the Israeli authorities before he could speak to Sica about the matter.

Andrew Hogg of the *Sunday Times* Insight team said that Sica's conclusion shows that Italy was trying to avoid political embarrassment: 'It's unbelievable. It appears as an excuse not to investigate it in depth.' Meir Vanunu did not have a great deal of hope. In October 1987 he said that he was 'increasingly convinced that the Italian authorities had agreed to Israeli requests not to investigate the affair'. Given all this, it seems that rather than draw conclusions which produce as many questions as answers, Sica ought to have returned the file to Italy's state prosecutor as lacking adequate evidence for a final conclusion. Sica did have circumstantial evidence: the false destination of the *Tappuz* cargo boat and the van hired by the Israeli embassy, to name but two. The final impression, whether by design or consequence, is of a cover-up useful both for calming the domestic embarrassment over yet another foreign national disappearing on Italian soil and for maintaining good Italian–Israeli relations.

It would by no means be the first cover-up in Italian political life. In June 1980 a plane carrying eighty-one people, owned by the defunct Italian company Itavia, crashed off Ustica, an island north of Sicily. An investigation by Italian officials concluded that the crash was due either to structural failure or that a bomb had been placed on board by terrorists. An inquiry by the US National Transportation Safety Board which examined the radar recordings of the last minutes of the flight showed that before the crash a fighter aircraft appeared to the west of the Italian airliner. The fighter made a turn to the east as if to intercept, and when it was about two miles from the Itavia plane radar screens recorded the disappearance of the airliner. Italian authorities did not take the American report into consideration. Later, when Italian TV ran a 'Telaphono Giallo' (Yellow Telephone) for unsolved cases, one of the military air controllers on duty that night at Ciampino air control tower telephoned the programme, alleging that he had been ordered to keep silent about what he had seen on the radar screen. There is a four-minute gap in the tape at the military radar centre at precisely the time when the Itavia plane disappeared. The personal records of the fourteen people who staffed the radar centre on the night concerned are missing, making their giving evidence impossible.

A number of explanations were given for the crash. The plane, which was two hours behind schedule, could have strayed into the path of a military exercise and become the unwitting target of a missile aimed at a drone. Or a runaway Libyan jet which was being chased at about the same time as the Itavia plane crashed, and was subsequently shot down by other Libyan fighters, may have tried to shield itself behind the Itavia plane. Or it could have been a NATO accident, covered up to preclude grave political embarrassment. After five years of political indifference and casual investigation Italian public interest in the matter revived in summer 1986 with a meeting between President Francesco Cossiga and families of some of the victims of the crash. Cossiga urged Prime Minister Craxi to reopen inquiries. As a result, a French company was hired to raise a large amount of wreckage from the plane, including the flight recorder, from the seabed.

Sica's verdict is not the end of the Italian connection to the Vanunu Affair. Various interest groups, among them the peace movement, some 800 Italian scientists, the Italian Federation of Democratic Lawyers, as well as individual parliamentary senators and journalists, protested against the verdict. Although Sica, in reaching his conclusion, recommended that the file be closed, the country's state prosecutor made no decision on this. Meir Vanunu, threatening to take legal action against the Italian authorities for failing to investigate his brother's abduction, appointed an Italian lawyer, Romeo Ferrucci, to take up the matter. It was Ferrucci, one of the secretaries of the Democratic Lawyers' Federation, who got the Italian president to order the judiciary to reopen its inquiries into the Ustica affair. While he did not expect Israel to release Mordechai Vanunu from prison, 'the process of justice has to go on,' Ferrucci said.

Yet another consequence of the Vanunu Affair was the revelation of the true identity of 'Cindy', who lured Vanunu from Britain. In July 1987 Insight reporter Peter Hounam walked up the path of Number 5 Strauma Street in Netanya, a seaside residential town midway between Tel Aviv and Haifa, and rang the doorbell. A woman named by Hounam as Cheryl Bentov answered the door. Hounam introduced himself as a reporter from the *Sunday Times* and said he wanted to discuss a certain matter with her. She kept her cool and took him into the lounge. Hounam was accompanied by another reporter, David Connett, who had seen her twice in London in Vanunu's presence and whose function was to positively identify her. While Connett himself had not been one of the reporters working on the Insight investigation of Vanunu's claims, he had seen him in the office. Some days later Connett was near Leicester Square with his girlfriend when he saw Vanunu at a distance in the company of Cindy. 'Connett did the sensible thing as a journalist: not knowing who Vanunu was except that we had this informant telling us secret things, he followed them for half an hour and got quite a good impression of her,' Hounam said. Hounam told her that according to the paper's evidence she was the person who lured Vanunu from London. According to the reporters, she did not deny it. Her sole reaction was 'Are you going to publish this?' Then suddenly she got up and almost screaming said: 'I deny this, I deny everything.' One of the reporters photographed her at that moment, but they never published the photo. Then she ran into the bedroom. Her mother, who was visiting her daughter at the time, came into the lounge on hearing Cheryl's screech and suggested that they return later when Ofer, Cheryl's husband, would be back.

Hounam later telephoned Ofer Bentov, telling him about the evidence, as well as evidence that he himself worked in Israeli military intelligence. Bentov denied that he was in military intelligence; he was a fibreglass salesman and did his national service as a driver, he said.

When Cheryl's father, Stanley Hanin, who lives in Orlando, Florida, where he owns a chain of perfumeries, first heard about his daughter's involvement in the affair, he said that he 'found it totally unbelievable'. He was divorced and had not heard from his daughter for some time but he thought there was not 'a speck of truth in the story'.

Practitioners of espionage are notorious for expending tremendous resources on devising clever ruses and subterfuges. Fake identities throw a cloak of impenetrability over an intelligence service's operations and enable it to undertake operations which political leaders would otherwise not approve, operations for which agents themselves are not accountable. When 'Cindy' met Vanunu for the first time, she described herself as an American trainee beautician. In covert special operations which may last for months or even years the Mossad selects a real life person who remains totally unaware that his or her identity has been usurped.[36] This is designed to withstand limited investigation by police authorities or rival agencies. The person is chosen because age group and general physical characteristics correspond roughly to those of an Israeli agent. For instance, Sylvia Raphael, a talented and attractive South African who participated in the ill-fated Lillehammer affair, in which an innocent man was mistakenly identified by the Mossad as being an Arab terrorist chief and killed in that Norwegian town, operated under the identity of a Canadian photographer named Patricia Roxburgh.[37]

'Cindy Hanin' did not exist on 30 September 1986, the day Vanunu was abducted. By 2 November she did exist. On that day Cynthia Morris, from Orlando, married high school friend Randy Hanin. Age was about similar: Cheryl was twenty-six, Cynthia, known to her friends as Cindy, was twenty-two. Cynthia was a trainee beautician. Bentov's choice was to be her undoing: Cheryl Bentov was Randy Hanin's sister. A trail of clues which Cindy left led to her exposure. Although she gave Vanunu only her first 'cover' name, Cindy, when she purchased her air ticket to Rome she used the cover surname 'Hanin'.[38] The paper employed the services of a private detective agency who located somebody in Orlando, Florida, with the name Hanin. The agency subsequently found her school, the Edgewater High, where they spoke to the principal and deputy principal, and obtained a school picture of her. Hounam then flew to Florida and discovered from her father, Stanley Hanin, that his daughter had moved to Israel in her late teens. The local rabbi, Dov Kentof, added more details about Cheryl and the family. Obtaining her address in Israel from her father,

Hounam was led to Kibbutz Bet Alpha. But the couple had moved to Netanya. The *Sunday Times* was going to carry a 6,000 word article in the colour magazine about how they succeeded in tracking her down, and the subsequent encounter in her flat in Netanya. But after Insight found the crucial piece of information that in London she had booked into the Eccleston Hotel in Victoria, giving as her address her father's address, the paper ran it as a straight news story.[39]

Normally, allegations by a newspaper about an agent of a friendly country might raise certain ethical questions. When the *Sunday Times* prepared an article in 1967 on its investigation about Kim Philby as the third man in the Burgess-Maclean spy ring, Insight editor Bruce Page wanted to print the name of an active MI6 agent in Hong Kong, Ian Milne, who, while himself patriotic, had been recruited to wartime intelligence by Philby. He also wanted to print the name of the head of MI6. Page was not impressed by the argument that to print Milne's name might expose a British agent to danger. Editor Harold Evans, however, was, but he agreed that Dick White's name as MI6 chief could be printed. Editor-in-chief Denis Hamilton opposed publication of both names. Evans consulted Lord Radcliffe, who had chaired a number of official inquiries on the security services. Radcliffe did not think it would be a serious matter to name intelligence chiefs but he questioned the wisdom of naming an active MI6 agent. Milne's name was excluded. But such considerations were irrelevant in the Vanunu case given that the intelligence agency suspected had kidnapped the paper's informer.

Though safely back in Israel, the naming of Cheryl Bentov as Vanunu's abductor was a further chapter in an affair which had caused no small embarrassment to Israel's friends. Though the fall-out in Britain and Italy should have been envisaged by those planning the abduction, the disclosure of Cindy's identity was due to carelessness and could easily have been avoided. 'By assuming the identity of a close, living relative,' wrote Hirsh Goodman, then the *Jerusalem*

Post military correspondent, 'Cindy (or rather her masters) left herself open to exposure, and Israel's secret service open to ridicule.' The day Hounam stepped into the Bentov bungalow in Netanya was the last the couple stayed there.

Bentov was not the only person exposed by the newspaper. A reporter in Israel located Yoram Bazak and his girlfriend Dorit. Bazak initially denied that he had been in London, although Dorit who was asked separately confirmed this. Bazak also denied being a friend of Vanunu or having an argument with him. But when asked directly whether he worked for Israel military intelligence he would not reply.[40]

It would be wrong to overemphasise the diplomatic costs of the operation. Peres rightly gauged that Western leaders would 'understand' the need to abduct Vanunu. Yet the abduction cannot be considered an entire success. Public and parliamentary reaction in Britain and Italy, as well as in Australia, was considerable. If there was broad understanding among western governments in 1986, there were also the Sica judicial inquiry and the expulsions from Britain.[41] These reactions raise questions regarding the political expediency of the decision to bring Vanunu home for trial.

'If a traitor is under the hand of the state you can give him a summons,' said Isser Harel, the legendary head of the Mossad during most of Ben-Gurion's premiership, and author of a study on intelligence services and democracy. 'In some cases, a democratic state has no choice than to bring a traitor who threatens the existence of the state to trial or to kill him even if this causes diplomatic problems. The latter is easier and avoids the dangers to Israel at the political, security and diplomatic levels which an abduction causes. But Israel is a democratic and humanitarian country. To wipe someone out is a much more serious business. Just assume what the Italians or British or anyone else would say to a killing which occurred in their territory!'

The cost of a democratic country's intelligence service

causing death in a friendly democracy was illustrated by the crisis in 1985 in New Zealand–French relations following the blowing up of an environmentalist ship *Rainbow Warrior* in Auckland harbour in July 1985. The French authorities at Murorea in the South Pacific, where key tests on the French nuclear missile and the Hades tactical missile were to be carried out, were very concerned at the plans of environmentalists to disrupt the tests by sailing into the test area. The head of France's external intelligence agency (DGSE), Admiral Lacoste, believed that the simplest solution was to tow away the *Rainbow Warrior* if it entered French territorial waters around the testing site. But, given the importance of the tests, the head of the Centre d'Expérimentations Nucléaires on Murorea, Admiral Henri Fages, persuaded the French Defence Minister Charles Hernu that this would not be enough, and the latter ordered the secret service to 'prevent' the demonstration. The ship was blown up and a photographer was killed. Two of the French agents involved were arrested and this led to admission of official French involvement in the affair. The two were sentenced to ten years' imprisonment. In addition to causing a souring of relations between Washington and Paris, the affair brought about structural changes within French intelligence.

According to Harel, 'in my time as head of Mossad I made efforts in very difficult security questions to prevent the killing of a traitor.' There is also the question of a Jew killing another Jew. 'A man like Vanunu is a citizen under our jurisdiction and only our courts can, and must, judge treachery. We carried out some security operations just in order not to decide within the agency on a person's guilt but in order to turn them over to the courts. It is a lesson of what a democracy which finds itself in a grave situation like this should do.'

Even if Vanunu's killing had been expedient, avoiding the political and diplomatic fall-out which followed his abduction, a separate question is whether Mossad chief Nahum

Admoni and his colleagues would have been prepared to carry it out, aware that in earlier intelligence blunders – the killing of Arab terrorists after the end of the 1984 Arab hijacking of the 300 bus travelling from Tel Aviv to Ashkelon, and the 1986 Pollard fiasco involving the arrest of Jonathan Pollard, a US naval intelligence analyst who was subsequently given a life sentence for spying for Israel – Israeli politicians declined to carry the can.

'Israel had no choice. To let this guy run free in the world? Tomorrow he would have landed voluntarily or by force in Arab hands and they would squeeze the juice out of him,' Harel argued. For both the Arabs and the Soviet Union, it was a once in a lifetime opportunity to get the secrets of one of Israel's most sensitive installations. Moreover, the leak not only challenged Israeli security but, given Israel's pinnacle role as a western ally in the Middle East, it had important implications for the western alliance as a whole.

When the defence establishment first learnt that a nuclear technician was revealing Dimona's secrets to the world's media, they were faced with a number of questions. Principally, did Vanunu give information to foreign enemy agents such as Soviets, or to the Israel Communist Party which he had asked to join, or to Arab acquaintances including one who shared his apartment? Secondly, what information did he give the *Sunday Times*, including that not printed in the report, and to other media he approached, including *Newsweek*? The 6,000-word report in the *Sunday Times* was only about 10 per cent of the information Vanunu had imparted. A third question was, what would be the political cost from the impact, particularly in Washington, including Congress, from Vanunu speaking about his work?

Peres's decision to bring Vanunu home is also a product of his past. From 1952 to 1965 Peres was the Ministry of Defence's director-general, then deputy defence minister, as well as an architect of the nuclear policy of ambiguity.[42] The years endowed him with a security fixation, but the absence

176

of hard intelligence experience made him take a decision which would ricochet in foreign public and parliamentary criticism.

Another factor in Peres's decision appears to have been the need not to set a dangerous precedent. Peres said 'even though Vanunu's information about the nuclear weapons is untrue, Israel should still prosecute him because he does not have the right to discuss such matters. He violated state secrets.' 'A man cannot spit on his country about one of the most critical issues and get away with it,' a security source remarked. Not to do anything would mean that other dissident Israelis who had access to highly sensitive information could disclose it abroad without fear of accountability.

But was this largely a cosmetic claim to cover an action which contravened international law? After all, given diplomatic and public reaction abroad, would the abduction have been ordered had it not involved a highly-sensitive disclosure where the authorities were concerned what else and to whom Vanunu had divulged, beyond that which appeared in the *Sunday Times*? And given the patriotism and sense of duty which still pervades Israel over sensitive matters, was there a need to set an example? As *Maariv*, putting a brave face on the security leak, remarked: 'It is remarkable, despite hundreds or even thousands having access in Dimona, that Vanunu was the only one.'

Vanunu was not the first person to be brought from abroad for trial in Israel. The most famous case was that of Adolf Eichmann, abducted more than twenty-five years earlier. For Ben-Gurion – whose protégé Peres was – it was a case of bringing to trial an enemy of the Jewish people. There were striking differences between Eichmann and Vanunu. Vanunu had not murdered anybody, whereas Eichmann was not just an enemy of the Jews but an international outcast. Vanunu may have been an outcast for the majority of Israelis, but he was no international outcast. Moreover, he claimed moral goals for his action.

Then there was the case of Mordechai Keidar, recruited to the Mossad in the fifties, who killed his accomplice and stole his gun and a small amount of money. He was brought back, tried and convicted in secret. No one even knew he was in Israel until his release in 1974 from Ramle gaol. Avri Elad, a member of an Israeli plot to bomb British interests in Egypt in pre-Suez days, panicked and disclosed details. He was caught by Mossad agents. Again, it was only on his release from gaol in 1967 that his fate became known. The key difference between these cases and Vanunu was that the former were involved with foreign governments and the latter with a foreign newspaper, which by nature thrives on disclosure.

Although Defence Minister Itzhak Rabin and Shamir, then the foreign minister, were consulted in the decision to have Vanunu brought to trial as was Attorney General Harish,[43] the final decision rested with Shimon Peres, who as prime minister had responsibility for the intelligence services.[44] In a paradoxical sense Vanunu might be thankful that Peres was prime minister at the time. Had Shamir been in office (he took over two weeks after Vanunu arrived back in Israel), it may be asked whether the ex-Mossad station chief for Paris, experienced in the cloak and dagger of modern espionage, would have decided on a politically inexpedient course of action of abducting an important informer of an internationally respected newspaper. Instead Shamir was left to carry the can.

A disappearance some time after the controversy had died down could have been engineered, after interrogation abroad, and attributed to Arab agents or criminal elements. In the internecine war Palestinians have supposedly been victims of political rivalries in the Palestinian world. Vanunu's disappearance would have raised little concern at home.

There were other options. One was not to take any action. There was a certain value in letting a former nuclear technician advertise the country's nuclear capacity to foreign opinion. The photographs themselves were a scoop, but the message being carried by somebody who was breaking the law was that much more effective. Although Israeli officials were concerned whether Vanunu revealed to foreign agents or to the paper more information than would subsequently be published, Vanunu could have been expected to give the newspaper the most important information and the newspaper could have been expected to publish it. His revelations would have been put down as another uncorroborated report in a long series over the years. Instead, the abduction and trial served to confirm what Vanunu claimed.

Another option which deserved consideration was extradition. It was ironic that illegal means were used to bring to trial somebody who had broken the law. In 1962, for example, the West German federal government succeeded in obtaining the extradition from a neighbouring country of an employee of *Der Spiegel* following the disclosure of information about the autumn 1962 NATO manoeuvres. Israel's extradition agreements with both Australia and Britain – the two countries where Vanunu was known to be divulging the information – are limited to a specific list of offences, among them murder, manslaughter, piracy and hijacking, and do not include the unauthorised disclosure of official information. The only remotely related categories covered by extradition were fraud and bribery (Vanunu was to receive part of the proceeds from the syndicated sale of his story and from a book planned by the paper). 'Where the offence in question is not provided for in the UK–Israel extradition treaty, extradition is not possible,' said P. J. Monk of the British Foreign Office's Nationality and Treaty Department.

It was surprising that Israel's extradition laws had not been revised to the more modern 'no-list system' rather than a specific table of offences. According to Dianne Stafford of the International Branch of Australia's Attorney General's

Department, 'Australia's modern extradition practice has been to negotiate extradition treaties that apply to serious offences generally (carrying imprisonment of at least one or two years) without regard to the offence's denomination.' According to Monk, 'the crime would have to be an offence in both countries (i.e., the dual criminality system)'. Given that both Australia and Britain have an Official Secrets Act, Vanunu's crime would have been covered. Had Israel had a no-list extradition treaty with Britain it is possible that Vanunu's action would have been seen by the Thatcher government as a political offence. A clue to this was the British government's rejection of Meir Vanunu's request for political asylum on the grounds that he faced prosecution rather than persecution. Herself fighting against the publication of Peter Wright's account of Soviet infiltration of Britain's intelligence services, Thatcher was sympathetic to the problem facing Peres, but apparently the question of extradition was not raised when Peres spoke to her before Vanunu's abduction. Extradition might have been complicated by Israel's policy of ambiguity on her nuclear development. And had Vanunu known and revealed more secrets from Dimona, or had he gone to, say, a Scandinavian country where his action would have been seen as that of a pacifist, extradition would not have been possible.

Even more alarming is the fact that Israeli officials have failed to draw a lesson from the affair and include the unauthorised disclosure of information in its extradition treaties by adopting the 'no-list system'. 'Extradition is for criminal offences not political offences. Most governments would view the disclosure of information as a political offence,' said Robbie Sabel, the legal adviser to the Israeli Foreign Ministry. This is erroneous. All recently negotiated US extradition treaties, for example, have abandoned the list of offences system in favour of the 'no-list' and dual criminality systems. And, according to Rex Young of the US Department of Justice, 'a number of these contain provisions which could serve to make disclosure of classified information an extraditable offence.' Given the number of Israelis who previously had access to sensitive information who now live abroad, as well as cases of foreign correspondents who once abroad revealed information banned by the censor, a revision of Israel's extradition system is germane.

An alternative accusation, which would have avoided abduction or disappearance, would have been computer espionage.[45] An example was in the late 1980s, when a West German computer science student managed for two years to gain secret access, through global communications networks, to military information in more than thirty computers in the United States. Undetected, he obtained data relating to nuclear weapons, intelligence satellites, the Strategic Defence Initiative, the space shuttle, and the North American Air Defence Command. The West German, moreover, was able not only to read material stored in the computers, but could print it out as well as alter the original information.

The *Sunday Times* had transferred on to their computer the two-day briefing which Vanunu had given Dr Frank Barnaby as well as subsequent sessions between Vanunu and the Insight reporters. 'While the computer used in the Vanunu investigation was not on-line to anywhere, and a number of files were used specifically for this investigation which only certain people had access to, the computer itself was accessible to anybody in the building,' a member of the Insight team said. Israel could have ascertained what information Vanunu had given other than what had appeared in the published report by gaining unauthorised access to one of the cables at the *Sunday Times*'s Wapping site. It would have to be assumed that whatever Vanunu might have revealed to Arab sympathisers or even enemy agents was in the detailed testimony he gave the paper, and it could certainly be assumed that a news organisation's computer system would not be particularly secure against intelligence surveillance in contrast to, say, the computer system of a defence establishment.

After having eavesdropped on Vanunu's debriefing, Israeli agents could have disrupted the *Sunday Times* computers and the report being prepared for publication by the paper, by affecting them with viruses or other disruptive programs. Both eavesdropping into computer systems and disruption of their programs had not been properly covered by English criminal law, and in the past, Israel's defence establishment had applied computers to defence needs with some sophistication.[46] Electronic, photographic and radar intelligence had become tools of Israeli intelligence since the fifties.

Yet, the strategy chosen was bringing the man home.

The Israel defence establishment enjoys a dominating influence in external intelligence matters and the Israeli Foreign Ministry is left with a subordinate role in policy-making. Defence's kingpin role reflects the external threats faced by Israel; the absence of formal diplomatic ties with many developing and eastern countries; and the commitment to support Jewish immigration, including from distressed countries where exit is not sanctioned by the government.

According to David Kimche, former director-general of the Israeli Foreign Ministry and a former senior Mossad officer, 'a problem we have had on many subjects is that the defence establishment has not always understood the political connotations of some of their activities. It's very difficult because it's inbuilt: the people in the defence establishment don't always understand the importance of the political side. It's a very sad and sorry thing but this is the fact.' The same lack of political finesse was evident in Israeli involvement in the Irangate affair; by supplying arms for the release of hostages held by the Hizbollah and other groups, Israel ignored the principle it has promoted of not giving in to terrorist demands. Some in the Mossad look on operations like the Vanunu abduction as too overt and too politically dangerous, indulgences which no modern espionage service should allow itself. This feeling was particularly noticeable in the 1970s during the Mossad's war in Europe against Palestinian terrorists, and the hand of the critics was strengthened when Israel was suddenly attacked by Egypt and Syria in 1973. The Mossad's preoccupation with James Bond-style operations had diverted the agency from its primary task of evaluating military intelligence.[47]

During the last twenty years, the Israeli intelligence establishment has come under greater parliamentary and public scrutiny. The Pollard affair did not involve the Mossad directly (it was run by a scientific liaison unit in the Israeli Ministry of Defence) although the agency should have been aware of it. It severely damaged US–Israeli intelligence ties, as well as leaving an Israeli spy – an American Jew – serving a life sentence, causing considerable embarrassment to the American Jewish community.[48] It raised basic questions about the very nature of overseas covert operations. Israel's political echelon, which described the affair as a 'rogue operation', claimed they had no knowledge of it, despite the crucial information Pollard supplied. In the Israeli air attack on PLO headquarters in Tunisia in October 1985, for example, Pollard had supplied the information about Soviet, French and US ship movements in the Mediterranean at the time, enabling the seven Israeli planes to fly the 4,800km round trip undetected. Pollard also supplied information on Tunisia's and Libya's air defences, such as how far Libyan radar could reach.[49]

Questions were raised about the Mossad after the 1982 Lebanon war and the agency's exaggerated expectation of the reliability of the Phalange Christians as allies. They had also been raised in the aftermath of the Gibli-Lavon affair in the fifties, when an Israeli sabotage ring in Egypt was arrested. In addition to the 1973 surprise attack by Egypt

183

and Syria at the outset of the Yom Kippur War, the evaluative abilities of military intelligence came under scrutiny after it failed to forecast the beginning of the Intifada uprising in December 1987. But the Mossad has not undergone the thorough overhaul which its domestic sister, the Shin Bet, did in the mid-eighties.

The overwhelming majority of Israelis backed the decision to bring Vanunu home. Typical was *Maariv*'s reaction: 'We are not moved by the fact that someone took the trouble to bring Vanunu to Israel. We say "Well done" and we don't give a hoot whether he was brought legally or by subterfuge, by sea or by air, alive or dead. And if he has not been brought here, we will encourage every initiative in this direction.' The liberal daily *Haaretz* chimed, 'No foreign state can prevent Jerusalem from bringing a traitor and spy to Israel.' The paper expressed understanding for 'the need to minimise the dissemination of information on sensitive matters' such as nuclear research, and said that the only area of the whole affair which should arouse concern, and for which the public required an explanation, was the security leak. The only dissident press voice was *Al Hamishmar*, the organ of the left-wing Mapam: 'How far does Israel's jurisdiction extend? Is it permissible or not to bring persons to Israel through the use of coercion – which is perhaps appropriate for spy movies and irresponsible regimes, but not for lawful states?' it asked. 'Israeli public opinion must discuss all these issues without exposing – be it a millimetre – what is or will be considered a bona fide military or security secret.'

Shamir, who had since taken over as prime minister, replied to questions about the affair: 'Israel will say what it finds correct to say and will fulfil its obligation to its citizens.' The reply was reminiscent of his comment about the Pollard matter: 'What happened is usually known to those in the know, and whoever does not know should continue not knowing.' However patriotic the former Mossad officer was,

184

he had low regard for public and parliamentary accountability in the rough and tumble of Israeli politics. Although his attitude may have been more fitting for Israel twenty years earlier, the seventy-year-old politician was not out of tune with the rightward direction which Israel's increasingly oriental population has taken: the attitude is that national security matters should be left to the defence establishment which 'knows best'.

Reaction or no reaction at home, the fall-out abroad serves to pinpoint attention on the way the original decision to abduct Vanunu was made. It was taken in the inner Cabinet comprising Prime Minister Peres, Defence Minister Rabin and Foreign Minister Shamir without even key advisers. Nor was the full Cabinet consulted either before the abduction or afterwards.[50] On 16 November, seven weeks after Vanunu left Britain, the full Cabinet was briefed by Shamir. As questions were increasingly raised in Britain and elsewhere about Vanunu's disappearance from London, Israeli ministers informally expressed dissatisfaction with the handling of the affair. 'We appear as a non-law-abiding country but one which kidnaps its citizens,' a minister said. By taking decision-making out of the formal procedure, then Prime Minister Peres made a decision[51] to abduct an informer of an internationally-respected newspaper without weighing the full consequences. And by later initiating Israel's confirmation that Vanunu was back in Israel, Peres committed a primary transgression of covert espionage, public confirmation of an operation.

Heading an open democratic society, which operates under the rule of law, and making key intelligence decisions which may involve perjury or even killings, is not an easy one. According to Arye Naor, cabinet secretary of Menachem Begin's first government, the continuous state of emergency in Israel which results in leading decision-makers focusing on the short-term operative dimension, the political disintegration of coalition government, and the lack of Jewish tradition of government, all lead to a failure of policy planning. 'All efforts to establish "think tanks" or any other sophisticated process of analysis and decision have been swept away by sceptical prime ministers,' Abba Eban notes. In order to improve political supervision of the intelligence community, Shamir decided in 1987 to revive a secret Cabinet group, the 'X' Committee, which at one time reviewed sensitive operations. The group had fallen into disuse in the mid-1970s because Israeli leaders no longer saw a need for such broad supervision over covert intelligence. The Vanunu Affair reconfirmed the need for the prime minister to have his own adviser on intelligence matters, somewhat akin to the National Security Council in the United States, who would gather intelligence reports from the different strata of Israel's defence establishment and provide political advice.

More alarming was the lack of legislative control over the intelligence community. Most Israeli parliamentarians were prepared to leave the Vanunu Affair behind the closed doors of the Defence and Foreign Affairs Committee and its intelligence subcommittee rather than discuss it in open plenary. Yet four of the committee's members – Eliahu Ben-Elissar, Yossi Sarid, Sarah Doron and Pessach Grupper – were critical of delays in the inflow of information to them and demanded a faster and better service. Some blamed the lack of information partly on the absence for some of October and November of Abba Eban, chairman of the Defence and Foreign Affairs Committee. Only on 17 November was the committee and its intelligence subcommittee briefed by Prime Minister Shamir.

The lack of information was not peculiar to the Vanunu Affair. Parliamentary committees were also kept in the dark for months during the Shin Bet affair in April 1984. No one briefed either committee (truthfully) when the two captured Arab terrorists were killed. Nobody briefed either committee when the deputy head of the Shin Bet, Reuven Hazak, spoke to Prime Minister Peres and Attorney General

Itzhak Zamir about the role played by the agency head, Avraham Shalom, in the cover-up. In the Irangate affair, the government failed to update the committees on Israel's involvement in the arms deal, and Shamir resisted pressures for an official commission of inquiry into the Pollard matter. When Abba Eban announced that the Knesset's Intelligence Subcommittee would conduct its own investigation, Shamir went so far as to threaten to forbid government officials from testifying. Only after US criticism was a two-man panel set up, but it was neither empowered to compel witnesses to testify nor were its conclusions binding on the government.

The question of governmental accountability to the legislature on intelligence matters had come to a head some months before the Vanunu Affair with the establishment of the Rotenstreich-Shalev Committee to review the relationship between the executive, the legislative and the security services. Its unpublished report is said to have recommended certain obligations of control, supervision and reporting, but these had not been fully implemented by the time of Vanunu. The matter came up again in an internal memo written by Micha Harish to his colleagues on the Defence and Foreign Affairs Committee in January 1987 which pinpointed two problems in the committee's functioning. In addition to revamping fundamentally the channels for the flow of information to the committee from executive branches of government, Harish argued in favour of the appointment of permanent expert advisers to the committee. 'The politicians do not exercise the sort of vigilance that we expect of them,' argued Professor Amnon Rubinstein, a Knesset member who has led a campaign for a written bill of rights to be incorporated into the Basic Laws which make up Israel's constitution.

Lack of debate about the morality of abducting a person from abroad was no surprise. The Mossad is perhaps unique among modern intelligence services in that it is not merely an arm of government like MI6 or the CIA, or an alternative government like the KGB; it is part of the fabric of the nation. It is neither mocked nor hated but is respected for the part it has played in establishing the modern state of Israel and for safeguarding it. For Israeli citizens, as well as many people abroad, particularly Jews, it epitomises the essence of the valiant David who through stealth, bravery and daring is able to overcome the obstacles which face him. Yet, even if it is not addressed by most people, the affair raises profound moral questions.

It is one thing for those who engage in covert action to have no automatic right to be free from the very behaviour they use, but it is another for civil servants to be forcibly brought from one territory to another in contravention of international law and conduct. It offends the basic concept of national sovereignty. And Vanunu was no longer even a government-employed official; he was a civilian. He possessed secrets of the most important kind, and he had broken the Official Secrets Act which binds officials who have access to secret information to observe silence unto the day of death. If Vanunu could be kidnapped, cannot anybody who breaks the law and reveals information about, say, his basic training during national service? It was the enormity of Vanunu's crime which decided the Israeli government to act illegally in bringing him back to stand trial, rather than any intrinsic difference between these two cases. And if Vanunu may be abducted, can say a Soviet Jewish scientist who emigrates to Israel, or an East European emigré in the west, to determine how much information they may have revealed to their hosts about their former country? And may Iran, Libya or Iraq take steps against dissidents among their nationals in foreign countries?

One could conclude that Israel's intelligence community operates without any moral criteria. According to Benjamin Beit-Hallahmi of Haifa University, 'the cynicism of Israeli political discourse is reflected by the absence of any moral considerations in discussion of policy.' As an example, he cites a proposal to forbid arms sales to dictatorial regimes being turned down within the Labour Party caucus in 1982 even before getting to the Knesset. To ask basic moral questions would, he says, undermine Zionism. An Israeli adage runs: Everybody is out for himself in this world, and nobody really cares about us, so we have to be selfish – like the rest of the world.

Yet serious questions of morality in Israeli public affairs have through the years been raised even regarding certain aspects of intelligence behaviour. A commission of inquiry into allegations of the systematic maltreatment and torture by the Shin Bet of security prisoners and perjury of testimony, chaired by Moshe Landau, a respected former president of the Israel Supreme Court, grappled with two fundamental questions that affect a country faced with the threat of terrorism against their civilian population: permitting the use of extra-legal measures without eroding the moral and democratic principles upon which such states are founded; and defining the limits of such measures without inhibiting the effectiveness of the security services. The commission unreservedly ruled out the use of perjury in court by intelligence agents. It called for an end to the use of such methods, as well as calling for new trials to be held. The primary tool of the interrogator should be non-violent psychological pressure 'via a vigorous and lengthy interrogation using various strategies including acts of deception'. If, however, this fails, 'the exertion of a moderate measure of physical pressure is not to be avoided'. If the Shin Bet continues to operate outside the law 'control is one day liable to fall into the hands of an unscrupulous person'.

Another example is the considerable debate among informed opinion which followed the Shin Bet affair in which two Arab terrorists were killed after the civilian bus hijacking, during which a girl soldier in the bus was killed. Civil rights and left-wing groups campaigned for measures against those responsible for the deaths of the two terrorists, and official

189

inquiries were conducted. The head of the Shin Bet agency resigned after allegedly committing perjury involving the framing of a senior army officer for the killing. Even some Mossad officers have questioned the morality of assassinations which sometimes result in the killing of innocent people.[52]

The Vanunu abduction, concerning a leak about a very sensitive military installation, satisfies many people's criteria for covert action, but it must be asked whether less covert means could have been used – particularly given that his disclosures posed no immediate danger to the country's survival.

Vanunu's revelations about Israel's atom secrets were the result of one of the biggest security lapses in the history of the Jewish state. The lapse was doubly disturbing because Vanunu was no spy and had not hidden his pro-Palestinian views. 'If an overt security risk like Vanunu could get away with it, imagine what someone more subtle could have achieved,' a security source remarked. Knesset member Haim Kaufman asked, 'Who knows how many Vanunus there are who have passed state secrets to foreign sources?'

The nuclear research centre has an intricate system of security. These include an electrified fence, sand within the perimeter fence which is raked periodically to betray intruders' footprints, and missile batteries which have orders to shoot down any aircraft that strays into the airspace above – as one Israeli pilot found to his cost in 1967.[53] According to the *Sunday Times*, the fleet of buses that brings the staff to work passes one cursory security check some five kilometres before reaching the reactor, and a more rigorous one a kilometre before the entrance.

Security at Dimona was originally in the hands of a specially established Office of Special Tasks, run by a former Ministry of Defence security officer, Benjamin Blumberg.[54] His task was to ensure that Dimona's secrets did not leave the research centre, and was later broadened to include the

acquisition of materials for the centre from abroad and information about foreign nuclear projects and developments.

That Vanunu was able to leave the country with the information and the films when he was under suspicion as a security hazard by the Shin Bet, which has overall responsibility
for security at Dimona, indicates that the Vanunu Affair
may not have been a once-only security lapse. It involved a
whole series of hiccups, unjustified complacency and exaggerated trust. As Zeev Schiff of *Haaretz* and Israel's foremost military commentator put it, 'the right hand of the
security didn't know what the left hand was doing. All the
parts of the engine rotated on their axles, but no one was
properly connected to the other.'

As a result of the leak, a major investigation was under-
taken. Measures were reportedly taken by the Israeli Atomic
Energy Authority against senior officials at the Dimona reactor, including its head.[55] Scientists and technicians were
questioned about possible links to Vanunu.[56] A senior Shin
Bet officer was reportedly dismissed as a result.

In one sense, the absence of an independent investigation
into the fiasco is surprising. After all, there has been no
shortage of state commissions into recent controversies
involving Israel. These include the Agranot Commission into
military intelligence failures on the eve of the 1973 war, the
Kahan Commission on Israel's involvement in the Phalange
massacres at the Sabra and Chatilla refugee camps in Lebanon, and the Bejski Commission after the collapse of Israeli
bank shares in 1983. Even the intelligence services have not
escaped the eyes of independent tribunals. But, in the case
of Vanunu, the bipartisan approach to the nuclear issue and
to maintaining a position of ambiguity meant that public
discussion of the security failure and the revelations themselves was muted.

The question remains whether the intelligence services
should be left to investigate themselves. To allow them to
do so not only enables a cover-up of or by those responsible,

but is a dereliction of legislative control over the security services. A request by Geula Cohen of the right-wing Tehiya party for a Knesset debate on security procedures at Dimona, and specifically how Vanunu could have been employed there, was withdrawn under pressure from the government. When Professor Amnon Shaki of the National Religious Party raised the question in March 1987, it was passed to the Defence and Foreign Affairs Committee. Yet earlier, in November 1986, committee member Yossi Sarid complained that 'to the best of my knowledge no discussion of the security lapse has yet occurred' within the closed doors of the committee. In early December Prime Minister Shamir told the committee that the Vanunu Affair was a serious security flop, and that the matter was being investigated and conclusions drawn.

To understand the Shin Bet's position and how it is perceived within Israeli society, a brief history may be useful. The origins of the (General) Security Services, Sherut Bitachon, abbreviated to Shin Bet, were established in 1949 with responsibility for internal intelligence. Its first head was Isser Harel. The Shin Bet had some 1,000 personnel, of whom about 550 were staff officers according to a CIA 1977 estimate.

Prior to the state's founding the intelligence section of the various Jewish underground groups led a fairly free existence in their two-pronged war against the British authorities and against Arab elements, but afterwards the Shin Bet had to work within the legal limits which a democratic state imposes upon its intelligence service. One of its first tasks in the aftermath of the War of Independence was to crack down on such right-wing groups as the Irgun (Etzel) and the Stern Gang (Lehi) which opposed David Ben-Gurion's conciliatory stance towards the Arabs. In the following years, Shin Bet's attention turned towards various left-wing groups which Harel feared were the targets of Soviet infiltration.

The Israeli Communist Party, members of which had ties with the Soviet embassy in Tel Aviv, was placed under surveillance. More controversial was the decision for similar action with Mapam, then the chief opposition party. Ben-Gurion was charged by some with using information gleaned for political rather than security purposes. Mapam is no longer under surveillance but, according to a 1979 CIA report, surveillance of various far-left groups – as well as far-right groups – has continued to this day.

Shin Bet established a considerable track record in counter-espionage. Notable was the arrest of Dr Israel Ber in March 1961. Ber, a military scientist, had become Ben-Gurion's trusted military adviser, but he had been long suspected by Harel as a Soviet agent. He was arrested after Shin Bet officers spotted him meeting a Soviet diplomat. A year earlier, Professor Kurt Sitte, who headed the physics unit at the Haifa Technion was arrested for spying for the Czechs.

None the less, the glamour of Israel's intelligence services has generally attached to the Mossad, with its dramatic kidnap of Eichmann from Argentina and its underground war against Palestinian leaders.[57] Because the Shin Bet is responsible for internal security, since 1967 the daily work of its operatives has concentrated upon security in the administered territories – a thankless task. In the last few years, image and reality notwithstanding, the Shin Bet's decline can be attributed to a number of self-inflicted wounds. The period 1984–7 was dogged by the 1984 bus hijacking and the cover-up on orders from its chief, Avraham Shalom, regarding Shin Bet responsibility for the deaths of the two Arab terrorists. When the Zorea Commission investigated the killings, the Shin Bet managed to get one of their officials on to the commission, who succeeded in focusing the commission's attention on an army officer, Brigadier-General Itzhak Mordechai, as the guilty party. The Attorney General reached the same conclusion, but an inquiry by the Israeli

Army Advocate General cleared Mordechai. The affair would have died at this point had not other Shin Bet officers, including its deputy head, revolted against Shalom. However, Prime Minister Shimon Peres backed him but, eventually, after receiving a presidential pardon, together with ten other officials, Shalom resigned. The scandal rocked the Shin Bet to its foundations.

Barely had those pages closed than the Shin Bet found itself embroiled in another scandal involving the framing of a Circassian IDF officer, which, in turn, led to the allegations that similar methods of falsifying evidence – as well as using force to extract confessions – had been part and parcel of Shin Bet behaviour in the territories since 1967.

It is therefore not surprising that when the head of the Mossad complained to Peres about the Shin Bet fiasco over Vanunu and pressed Peres to launch an investigation of the service, Peres, in his last days as prime minister, declined. He argued that 'the Shin Bet had suffered enough'. The scandals had not only confirmed fundamental weaknesses in the organisation but had tarnished its many successes in aborting terrorist plots and solving other security cases.

The Vanunu Affair was of course a different type of problem. It didn't involve the Shin Bet hierarchy, but was a breakdown in security procedures and coordination between the Shin Bet and the Dimona authorities. Even so, Geula Cohen launched an attack on it not for its bureaucratic failings but for employing 'left-wingers'; had they not been there, she claimed, greater care would have been taken to terminate Vanunu's employment earlier. 'Why do people who believe in meeting the PLO need to work in the Shin Bet, whose task is to stop meetings with the PLO?' she asked. Yitzhak Shamir, who had just taken over the prime ministership from Peres under the rotation agreement which exists between Labour and Likud, said that the employment of a man with known left-wing sympathies in Israel's nuclear facility was a serious mistake.

Measures taken to improve security at Dimona presumably included not employing people of extreme political views, keeping a check on any changes in ideology of existing employees, and better routine security inside the research centre. Other measures could also be taken. For example, in the aftermath of a series of espionage cases in the US, including the Walker family spy ring for the USSR, the US army established a toll-free telephone number enabling people to report on workers with access to sensitive places or information who arouse their suspicions. In its first year it received over 2,000 calls. There is an obvious requirement to check such reports with the utmost care, but this does not stop somebody from leaving the country and revealing the information abroad – apart from their awareness that they may share Vanunu's fate. In the absence of extradition arrangements covering the unauthorised disclosure of information, no society can be 100 per cent foolproof.

Cohen's attack was levelled more against the Shin Bet than Vanunu, and therefore appeared as a further episode in the long-running political battle for legitimacy between Israel's Right and Left. Nevertheless, her remarks – and their rejection by left-wing politicians – had deeper implications: whether officials in an intelligence service or other sensitive defence posts are able to carry out their tasks, like other civil servants, irrespective of their political views. Support for this came from a surprising quarter, Raful Eitan, then a party colleague of Cohen's. Eitan is also a former chief of staff of the Israeli army. He called Cohen's view a double-edged sword, arguing that 'today's rulers might purge holders of the opposite view, and tomorrow's rulers might purge the security men left in their jobs.' Heads of sensitive organisations have adequate means for checking trustworthiness. 'I know a great many loyal people who today could be described as members of the leftist camp, and who are just as outstanding fighters and loyal Israelis as everyone else, if not more.'

It is ironic that the Labour Party's Ben-Gurion, who served as defence minister in addition to being the first prime minister of Israel, set the precedent that Leftists should not be employed in sensitive posts. Another member of the Tehiya Party, Professor Yuval Neeman (one of the architects of Israel's nuclear policy), then identified with the Mapam and was initially barred by Ben-Gurion from being appointed deputy head of Israel's military intelligence. Subsequently, Ben-Gurion was persuaded that Neeman was no longer politically active in Mapam. By the same token, those with right-wing views would not be employed in certain internal security posts. Indeed, while Ben-Gurion allowed former members of the pre-state underground groups of the Irgun, led by Menachem Begin, and the Stern Gang, one of whose leaders was Itzhak Shamir, to serve in the external intelligence arm, the Mossad, he did not want them in the Shin Bet. Although there have been brief periods since the inception of the state in which left-wing parties have been regarded with suspicion, nowadays, with the exception of the Communist Party, even members of far-left parties are in highly sensitive posts. One example is a Member of the Knesset, Ran Cohen, from the Citizens Rights Movement, who holds a high military rank in the reserves. Merit is the key, but one remaining exception is recent Jewish emigrants from the Soviet Union, in the knowledge that the KGB infiltrated some of its agents into the ranks of Soviet Jewish arrivals.

The liberal-orientated *Haaretz* editorialised that in a free society even those who support a Palestinian state should not be discriminated against in the general labour market; however, 'in sensitive places people whose political views are likely to be translated into actions should not be employed.' *Haaretz* was discussing Vanunu rather than the Shin Bet. The question comes down to whether a worker can carry out his task responsibly without allowing any personal views to influence it; Vanunu was not able to do so. Without a commission of inquiry, it is unclear whether those Shin Bet officers and Dimona officials responsible for security at the reactor failed because a political view may have consciously or subconsciously influenced them not to weed out Vanunu. But the combination of the nuclear element and the involvement of the security services ruled out an independent inquiry. Had its effects been more immediate, such as a nuclear accident, it is most unlikely that a public commission of inquiry could have been avoided.

7. THE NEWSPAPER AND THE INFORMER

The *Sunday Times*'s relationship with Vanunu graphically illustrates the responsibilities and tensions of the news reporter-informer relationship. It raises questions regarding the obligations of the news organisation to protect the informer when his or her life may be endangered through revelation of the information, its obligations when things go badly wrong, and the obligations of the informer to co-operate with the organisation.

Vanunu was not the first informer whose fate was to become a matter of concern for the *Sunday Times*. Anthony Mascarenhas, an Indian journalist living in east Pakistan, witnessed the rebellion and fighting which resulted in the independent state of Bangladesh, including the atrocities committed by west Pakistan in an attempt to quell the rebellion. He approached the *Sunday Times* to tell his story and, like Vanunu, requested that his name not be attached. But Harold Evans, the editor, said his name had to be attached because it was an eyewitness account. It was clear that he would be unable to go back to west Pakistan. Evans paid him some £15,000 for the story, which ran for two weeks, but recognised Mascarenhas's account as a continuing commitment, sending him back to bring his family out and absorbing him on to the paper's staff. Mascarenhas was spellbound both by the paper's integrity and by its journalistic instincts to recognise the story's significance.

The newspaper devised a plan to ensure Vanunu's safety

which on the face of it looked fairly secure. First, the *Sunday Times* planned to organise an international seminar on Israeli nuclear weaponry as a follow-up to the paper's exposé. The seminar, to be attended by internationally respected strategists, would address the dangers not only for the Middle East but for the world as a whole as a result of the nuclearisation of the region. One reporter envisaged the newspaper's report on the seminar including a diagram showing the prevailing wind factor from any nuclear explosion. The *Sunday Times* also planned for Vanunu to give evidence before a US Congressional Commission on nuclear proliferation.

But come the end of 1986, Vanunu would need, in Andrew Neil's words, to 'open a new page to his life in a new place'. 'We knew we couldn't guarantee his safety for the rest of his life. The Israelis have a long memory,' Insight editor Robin Morgan remarked. He told Vanunu, 'You will be kidnapped, and taken back and punished. You will want to go home because it's your home. "That's my problem, not yours," he replied. His point was a philosophical one. He wanted the information to be known,' Morgan said.

A number of countries were discussed by Vanunu and the newspaper as places where he might make his new life. In addition to Britain, these included Canada and the United States (both his girlfriend, Judy Zimmet, and his brother, Meir, lived in Boston). Australia was also mentioned, but Vanunu had not been enamoured of his four-month stay there. 'What interests them is to drink beer,' he said disparagingly. Another possibility was New Zealand: Stephen Milligan, the paper's foreign editor, knew David Lange, the prime minister and an ardent anti-nuclear campaigner, and believed he could arrange for Vanunu to get citizenship. 'In practice,' said Bruce Page, a former Insight editor, 'you have to find a very specific environment. The newspaper has to be very intimately involved with the government in question.

That means he would need to settle in Britain. You need to lay out a lot of positions with the ruling party and the opposition. You could improvise on it afterwards. But you have to have it ready before,' he said. Neil says, 'We told Vanunu that we would try to help him get citizenship when all this was over.'[1] But the paper made no known approaches beforehand presumably because it thought Vanunu's case for application would be stronger once he had become an international political personality. If Vanunu had foreign citizenship and had given up Israeli citizenship, an idea that he himself was toying with, it could have discouraged the Israelis (assuming they were aware of the change) from planning to abduct him in the knowledge of the diplomatic repercussions which would follow.

Mordechai Vanunu aspired to teach philosophy, as he had begun to do at Ben-Gurion University prior to his departure from Israel. While the *Sunday Times* did not pay Vanunu for the original disclosure, arguing that they do not pay informers, they recognised Vanunu's need to build a new future for himself and offered an arrangement: he would receive part of the second rights from the sale of the exposé to foreign news organisations, earnings from appearances and interviews with the media, and royalties, the percentage to be agreed upon, from the book the Insight team were planning to write, for which the publishing house Collins had offered a substantial contract.

During Vanunu's debriefing by Dr Barnaby and the Insight team in September, considerable thought went into the need to protect him. During the crucial days of the debriefing, Vanunu, Barnaby and the Insight staffers stayed at Heath Lodge, a country guesthouse outside London. They thought Vanunu was well protected, but this did not prevent the run-in with Yoram Bazak in London. So well had the newspaper disguised Vanunu's identity that a year afterwards the proprietor of Heath Lodge still had no idea who his mysterious guest had been.[2] After Vanunu was abducted,

Neil said 'if Vanunu had stayed within our care and protection he wouldn't be back in Israel.'[3]

This is questionable. Even if Vanunu had adhered to the *Sunday Times*'s wishes and stayed at Heath Lodge, the possibility remains that somebody determined to might have located Vanunu in the country by following journalists' travel movements there. Further, in at least one instance, a researcher-cum-minder unwittingly allowed Vanunu to walk into what might have been a trap. This was on Wednesday, 17 September, a week and a half before Vanunu disappeared. The 'minder' was Wendy Robbins, who had just graduated in modern languages from Leeds University, and was spending the summer as an intern researcher on the Insight team before she commenced a journalism course at City University. (Today Robbins is an assistant producer of BBC 1's 'Panorama'.) Robbins joined Vanunu for a dinner engagement with Yoram Bazak, whom Vanunu had bumped into, seemingly coincidentally in London's Regent Street.[4] Ironically, in Australia Vanunu had given Peter Hounam Bazak's name as a reference. When, at dinner, Vanunu asked him rhetorically what his reaction would be if he were to divulge information to the media about his former workplace, Bazak, visibly shaken, replied that he would find a means to get him back to Israel and into prison.[5] This should have alerted Robbins. Instead, Bazak and his girlfriend Dorit took them back to their room at the Royal Scot Hotel. 'It was one of the first stories I had worked on in my life. I knew nothing about conspiracies. To me the thought that the Israelis had sent somebody to bump into him on Regent Street was inconceivable. I argued with Peter Hounam and Robin Morgan "It's a coincidence. I'm sure it's a coincidence." '[6] According to Robbins, Bazak's girlfriend telephoned Israel. 'Bazak asked Motti not to go downstairs to drink something, as if he was afraid that he would flee,' she said.[7] The Insight team's published account of this encounter, while mentioning the dinner date, does not mention that

201

the Insight researcher and Vanunu went to Bazak's hotel room, nor the phone call to Israel and Bazak's request that Vanunu should not leave the room. The incident destroys an assumption by Morgan and Neil that somebody would not try to abduct Vanunu in the presence of *Sunday Times* staff. When, according to Robbins, Bazak asked Vanunu not to leave the hotel room[8], it ought to have sounded a danger signal. 'It didn't really occur to me that somebody could grab him,' Robbins remarked.[9] She was given no instructions on what to do in the event of somebody attacking him. It appeared to her that the function of the 'minder' was less to provide security for Vanunu and more to ensure that he was not bored.[10] 'She was only a junior trainee. We should have been more careful about the way we looked after him. While some were busily checking the story, others who were looking after him did not do as good a job as they probably should have,' an Insight reporter said.

In the days before the *Sunday Mirror* came out with its story, when Vanunu had already been debriefed – or 'milked' as one staffer put it – and the Insight team was busy checking the story, security for Vanunu appeared to be less stringent than it had been.[11] It was then that Vanunu met Cindy at Leicester Square. 'People couldn't be bothered to entertain him. We had what we wanted, and he was more or less left to do whatever he liked,' said Robbins. Peter Hounam was an exception; his journalistic responsibility expressed itself in his standing by his news source from the initial meeting in Australia to this day. Another researcher said that 'there was a certain naivety among us about the possibility that he could still be kidnapped after he had given us all the information.'

On Tuesday, 23 September, Vanunu was moved from his old hotel to the Mountbatten Hotel. As the paper admitted, Vanunu's car could have been followed by somebody trying to locate where he was staying.[12] Even though the Insight team may have failed to suspect a film crew standing outside

202

the paper's Wapping offices photographing a picket line as being Mossad agents[13], it was sheer carelessness and laziness for Vanunu to be moved in a car rather than, say, a closed van.

The paper had considered using professional security guards – but the idea was rejected. Notwithstanding the *Sunday Times*'s self-confidence in its ability to protect Vanunu, a newspaper's resources are clearly more limited than the state's. During the period immediately around the publication of Vanunu's exposé, Neil devised a plan for Vanunu to take a tour of Britain. 'I wanted that he should take a bus tour around Britain so that he would be on the move all the time. But he wouldn't hear of it', Neil said.[14] He would have been surrounded continuously by a group of thirty tourists, including two of the paper's reporters and a photographer, making it, Neil thought, impossible for anybody to kidnap him. He would have been booked under a fictitious name. It would not necessitate crossing borders, hiring cars (which require passport identification in the case of foreign visitors), registering with hotels, using his driver's licence or credit cards.

Neil could have used the four weeks the paper was in touch with Vanunu to prepare the ground with the British government. Bruce Page believes that Neil should have contacted officials saying, 'we have coming up a very difficult story that could have very profound implications in British relations with Israel. When it comes out it will be explosive, and I am telling you now so that you can get your act together.' Having sown the seed with officials, they should have approached Mrs Thatcher, with whom Murdoch had good ties. But the newspaper was anxious to preserve confidentiality lest information be passed from MI6 to the Israeli authorities.

More than any other aspect of the Vanunu Affair, it is the incident of Guerrero, who introduced the newspaper to

Vanunu, taking the story to the *Sunday Mirror*, which published a report casting doubts on the story, that raises the question of whether the *Sunday Times* was in any way responsible for Vanunu's abduction. On the weekend of the *Sunday Mirror* publication, which followed the Insight team taking the story to the Israeli embassy for its reaction, Vanunu, according to the paper, had grown more and more restless and complained about the delay in the story's publication. Feeling vulnerable, lonely and desperate, Vanunu fell for Cindy's suggestion to fly to Rome. He told the paper, Morgan said, that he was going to look after himself, lose himself in a crowd. 'He couldn't take the risk of somebody following *Sunday Times* reporters,' said Morgan. 'He'd just seen his picture in a national newspaper, in a foreign country that he'd visited only once before. He'd known us for four weeks – and he's going to trust his life to us.'

When Vanunu first met Guerrero several months earlier, in Australia, Guerrero showed him a picture of himself interviewing Issam Sartawi, a Palestinian moderate who had been murdered by extremists. It quickly convinced Vanunu that Guerrero and he were thinking along similar lines. It was not long before the two talked about holding a press conference where they would call for Itzhak Shamir and Yasser Arafat to sit down together.

That the *Sunday Times* decided to follow up the story on looking at Vanunu's photographs which Guerrero showed them in London implied an obligation by the news organisation to work with the Colombian, even though the paper was already suspicious of him. 'Guerrero was a very frustrating person to deal with,' Hounam said. While a more delicate treatment of Guerrero in Sydney might have been appropriate, such as avoiding any actions which might be construed as going behind his back, the paper could not have been expected to bring him to London with Vanunu. And yet, at this stage – with his hot property en route to London with Hounam – that he feared he might still be eased out of the deal, notwithstanding the letter promising him the first US$25,000 of earnings from any agreement between the *Sunday Times* and Vanunu.

It's a very insalubrious situation where a news organisation is very keen to reach a source but the middleman is the last person in the world they would like to deal with. If a news organisation thinks that it will not be able to deal with the middleman they ought to abandon the story. Once they went ahead with the story, it implied a commitment not only to Vanunu but also to Guerrero. It is always risky for any news organisation to concentrate on an informer rather than a middleman, and it must face the cost of the latter going off to another news organisation, and the consequences of that. Precisely because of Guerrero's unorthodox character, it showed a lack of expertise not to deal with him with caution.

But Guerrero is even more responsible than the *Sunday Times* for the consequences of his decision to approach the *Sunday Mirror*. As far as is known he had no instructions from his client, Vanunu, to do so. He admits Vanunu behaved with integrity and intervened with the *Sunday Times* on Guerrero's behalf, insisting that he still be kept in the picture. If Vanunu had gone behind his back and the *Sunday Times* had come to a deal with Vanunu which cut Guerrero out, Guerrero could have turned to the courts. But this, of course, was not the case.

To its credit, on hearing that the *Sunday Mirror* was planning to publish its account, the *Sunday Times* sent two journalists to Vanunu at his hotel, and emphasised the need to take great care of him. Nevertheless, after the report came out, Vanunu was clearly upset. Talking that Sunday evening by telephone to McKnight in Sydney Vanunu said he was 'upset by it all, and he thought that the *Sunday Mirror* story might have damaged his credibility so that the *Sunday Times* would not publish it at all. He spoke with great fear for his safety,' McKnight said.

In a letter to Judy Zimmet in March 1987, Vanunu appeared to hold both the *Sunday Times* and Guerrero responsible for his ending up back in Israel. 'My original programme was from Australia to go to New Zealand, and from there to Hawaii, and from there to Los Angeles and to New York. Oscar Guerrero and the *Sunday Times* sent me here, to the Israelis.' Ivan Fallon, deputy editor of the *Sunday Times* said, 'We should not have lost him, and next time round, if there is a next time, we would take far better care of him. We were very naive. We did not believe that the Israelis would go to the trouble they actually did to kidnap him. Had we done we would have behaved differently. We did go to quite a lot of trouble, but obviously not enough. For that we do feel responsible.' But Neil, smarting from Vanunu's abduction, over the years has tried to put a brave face on his disappearance, and spoken of the considerable measures taken. Asked by the BBC whether he had something on his conscience regarding Vanunu's disappearance, Neil replied, 'It's not a matter of my conscience. He came to us, he knew exactly what he was doing. We spent five weeks checking the story and one of the problems at the end was that because it took so long, he got restless, and wouldn't stay in our care. If he'd stayed within our care and protection he wouldn't be back in Israel now.'[15] The 'care and protection' did not sustain itself in practice. Wendy Robbins said, 'There was no central plan or coordination in looking after Vanunu. Apart from Hounam who was genuinely more caring, the others had no interest in who he was or what he wanted to do. During the day it was milk, milk, milk. At night: find anyone to take care of him. During the first days Max [Prangnell] took him to his flat or visited him at his secret location. Hounam took him out. So did Peter Wilsher for dinner. But increasingly the better I got on with Mordechai, the more he wanted to spend time with me. In the evening it was left to whoever was sitting in the office. On at least one occasion Vanunu was left sitting in the office, all the reporters having left.'

Neil was quite within his rights to delay publication until he was certain the story was genuine. Insight had not told Vanunu that they would not publish; the opposite was true, that they attempted to reassure him of the paper's interest but that further checking had to be carried out. Nor was five weeks, when the paper first heard about Vanunu and his information, particularly long for checking such a complicated story. The paper had warned Vanunu about Cindy, whom Vanunu had first encountered days prior to the *Sunday Mirror* hoax story, cautioning that she might be an Israeli ploy. 'We suspected something was going on,' Neil said. Nevertheless, had Guerrero been handled by the *Sunday Times* with greater dexterity and professionalism, Vanunu's photograph might not have appeared in the *Sunday Mirror*. Furthermore, Neil's claim that 'if Vanunu had stayed within our care and protection he wouldn't be back in Israel now' appears to be ill-founded. The physical protection which the *Sunday Times* gave Vanunu has been shown to be wanting. Moreover, there is every reason to believe that if the Guerrero episode had not occurred, Israel would have found other means to woo Vanunu from Britain.

Another question hangs over whether the *Sunday Times* may have indirectly and unwittingly contributed to Vanunu's capture. It concerns the visit by one of the paper's reporters to Israel in early September to check some of Vanunu's personal details with his neighbours and friends in Beersheba. 'You can never be sure that you aren't raising suspicions. We have to be very careful. We do it all the time', Morgan said.[16] But the paper admitted that after its reporter talked to one girl, an army reservist who spoke to her military superior, Israeli authorities had been put on guard. There was also an unnecessary risk taken in sending back to London on open telex and telephone lines from Australia the information drawn from the initial interviews with Vanunu. Unable to check the information's accuracy in Australia there was a clear need to send it back quickly to Insight colleagues in London. But there was no need to risk possible interception of the information by an intelligence service when mail could have been sent by express courier service. The open floor plan of the *Sunday Times* building was not conducive to keeping Vanunu hidden. The Insight desk is not far from the features desk and the news desk. 'Everybody knew there was this Israeli in the office. The news desk knew what we were doing,' Robbins claimed. 'People would speculate: "Is he genuine or not . . ."' she added. 'I don't think enough care was taken to keep him away from the rest of the media operation,' Hounam said, 'not that I think that caused direct troubles. It would have just been easier.' Questions of judgement also arise because when Mordechai Vanunu first contacted the *Sunday Times* he said that he did not want his name connected with the exposé. Peter Hounam insisted that if the information was going to be published it had to be with Vanunu's name on it because its value was that for the first time somebody who possessed inside knowledge of the Dimona reactor was revealing its innermost secrets. It took Hounam some time to persuade Vanunu that his best security against being the target of a Mossad operation was to attach his name to the paper's exposé. There would have been a story even had Vanunu's wish for anonymity been respected because the fifty-seven photographs which he had taken inside the Dimona complex were themselves of international significance. Of course the story had added value with Vanunu's name. But this should have been weighed against the real danger to Vanunu.

No internal inquiry was apparently carried out within the newspaper regarding Insight's handling of Vanunu, his protection during and after his debriefing, or how reporting and checking evidence forewarned Israel despite the fact it would offer certain lessons for future investigations regarding the handling of characters like Guerrero, security for informers prior to publication, and creating the best conditions for their survival after their exposure. When reporter John Swain disappeared in 1976 in Ethiopia, there was criticism among some staff, including Insight reporters, alleging the editorial executives had endangered Swain's life in sending him to rebel-held Eritrea. As a result Harold Evans instructed the paper's legal adviser, James Evans, to carry out an internal inquiry. Fortunately Swain turned up safely. After David Holden, the paper's chief foreign correspondent, was found murdered in Cairo, in 1977, an inquiry was launched. But the bulky file was closed, at the request of Holden's widow, after evidence was discovered linking Holden to an intelligence organisation. When *Stern* magazine was duped into buying the Hitler Diaries an internal inquiry was set up, but criticism of its objectivity produced calls for an investigating commission independent of the magazine's editorial and publishing staffs. These were rejected by the magazine's publishers, Jahr.

Investigative journalism involves checking information. Notwithstanding questions about certain claims made in the paper's Vanunu exposé, Insight executed this with considerable professionalism. But investigative journalism also involves protection of news sources, among other things. In this respect, Insight displayed poor judgement, and some inexperience. At the psychological level, the paper may have been slow in responding to Vanunu's needs when the *Sunday Mirror* published its report. On the other hand, there is evidence of some sensitivity being displayed. After debriefing him about his work at Dimona, some members of the team debriefed him at some length about his life while others were checking the scientific information partly, according to Morgan, 'because we were trying to keep the guy out of circulation.'

But, as an Insight reporter admitted, 'Vanunu was always in control of the story. We never signed an agreement [one was due to be signed prior to publication, two days after Vanunu disappeared]. He could say to us "I don't like the way you are treating me. I will leave. I'll keep the story and go somewhere else!"' They acceded to his request to move from the country to London. One day, instead of attending a planned meeting with Insight, Vanunu 'insisted' on meeting Cindy briefly. Then came his 'decision' to go away for a few days ostensibly to the country, but in reality with Cindy to Rome. He failed to take his own security seriously. According to Robbins, 'the pseudonym names which the paper gave him were a joke for him. We would get into a taxi and he would start up with the driver, "I am John Smith . . ." He often said to me, "Ah, Wendy, something terrible will happen before I go to my island. They will get me." But he didn't seem to do anything about it. He couldn't be bothered to get worried about it. Totally fatalistic.' Vanunu should have been made to understand from the beginning, when he first made contact with the paper, that the paper would only investigate and publish the story if he accepted the terms of protection offered by the paper. A member of the Insight team said: "The difficulty I didn't anticipate is that you have to insist on the full cooperation of the person whom you are protecting because if you don't, if he walks about, then he is prey to anyone who wants to get him. Had we have signed a conventional Fleet Street contract with him, we could have probably had some hold over him and said, "Look, you are going to have so much money: stay out of London, stay in the guest house we are putting you in"'.

It was not surprising that Neil's reaction on learning of Vanunu's disappearance was one of 'extreme anger', according to an Insight reporter. Neil felt he had provided Morgan with all the financial support he required in checking the story. But the real question was whether Neil – and ultimately Murdoch – had provided sufficiently experienced reporters to do the job. Notwithstanding that some of the younger Insight reporters had done some investigative stories, apparently only Hounam and editor Morgan could be said to have truly solid investigative experience. The overall make-up of the team contrasts negatively with the experience which Insight teams in the sixties and seventies possessed. For example, when Godfrey Hodgson headed Insight in the late sixties 'Phillip Knightley was an extremely experienced reporter who worked on newspapers and had edited a magazine in Sydney. John Barry had won a press award, John Fielding came from the paper's Business News, and Mark Ottaway had considerable reportorial experience,' Hodgson said. The errors made by the Insight team in the Vanunu investigation reflected the lesser experience of journalists on the paper's staff as a whole.

'There was a time in the early and mid-seventies when you could say that the brightest bunch of journalists in the British papers were on the *Sunday Times*,' media commentator Philip Kleinman said. 'You had some twenty bright reporters. The ideas came from them. Evans, like Denis Hamilton beforehand, gave them their head. Light attracted light: because there were bright guys there others wanted to join. Today, the *Sunday Times* have good, mediocre, and bad stories, like everybody else.' Nicholas Faith, a former reporter on the paper, is more critical: 'To retain its readers' attention, the *Sunday Times* has to provide them with a steady stream of new slants, new stories, exciting insightful glimpses into the news behind the news, and that requires a depth of talent which simply cannot be bought overnight.' A story like Dimona requires journalists of wide experience. Unless a proprietor provides the resources to attract the required journalistic talent, an editor has to ask himself whether he should go after such a demanding story, however newsworthy it may be.

When Vanunu disappeared with Cindy from London on 30 September, the paper did not immediately publish the information because they were not certain he was in Israeli hands. If he was not, this would have alerted the Israelis, who would have realised that Vanunu was no longer in the company of the paper's journalists and easier to pick up. In its three-page exposé on 5 October the only reference to his disappearance was hidden away in the side-bar article detailing how the paper had checked the story. It reported that Vanunu had become agitated after the *Sunday Mirror* had published a photo of him and, fearing for his safety, went to ground.

How did the paper's management and Insight team react after Vanunu had been abducted? There was a week's delayed reaction. On Tuesday, 7 October, two days after publication, members of the Insight team debated whether to inform the police that Vanunu was missing. Some reporters said they should not bother since he had gone off on his own. But Peter Hounam said the police should be informed, and when Hounam said that if the team did not agree, he would inform the police of his own accord, they agreed. A formal complaint was lodged with the police, who carried out checks at the Mountbatten Hotel but found nothing suspicious. Coffins which had been flown from Heathrow Airport to Israel were investigated, and they discovered that a coffin had been despatched on the day Vanunu disappeared. They tracked down the family and found it was quite innocuous. Inquiries were made with the Home Office, which controls immigration, but the police file was closed after a couple of weeks. The inquiries to the Home Office did not, according to one Insight reporter, 'go beyond the official level'. Robbins, who had left the paper to return to her studies, was asked by Insight whether Vanunu had been in touch with her. But she notes that she was not asked about anything suspicious which might have given Vanunu away and offer a clue to where he was. The foreign secretary, Sir Geoffrey Howe, was asked to make an official request to the Israel government for information. But a spokesman replied that 'we have no grounds for intervening with the Israelis'. When it was revealed that Vanunu had been abducted to Israel from Rome, the management was not reported as having approached either the Italian govern-

212

ment, or the British Foreign Office to take up the matter with Italy. Instead, the paper's Insight team provided, in good faith, information it had discovered regarding Vanunu's abduction to the judicial inquiry under Domenico Sica, set up to investigate Vanunu's claim that he had been abducted from Italy. Peter Hounam went to see Sica five times, providing the documentary evidence which the paper had gathered about Cindy and about Vanunu's abduction and which it used in preparing the articles on these subjects. Hounam made a statement to Sica regarding Vanunu's motives for speaking about his work. The paper also took Meir Vanunu to Rome to give his own statement to Sica.

There were precedents for *Sunday Times* journalists and informants disappearing or even being murdered. As mentioned earlier, in summer 1976 John Swain had been sent by the paper to report on the progress of the peasant army mobilised by the Ethiopian government against guerrillas in the northern province of Eritrea. Swain disappeared after leaving the town of Axum to the north of Addis Ababa, en route to the Tigrean province. He was the eighth Briton to disappear – kidnapped by Tigrean rebels. Only the previous year, during the communist takeover in Cambodia, Swain had flown as the only passenger on the last plane into the country's capital, Phnom Penh, before it fell. For two weeks he was confined with others in the French embassy, watching as the victorious Khmer Rouge took over the city. A long and arduous trek out of the country followed. Five pages of the *Sunday Times* were devoted to Swain's graphic account, 'Diary of a Doomed City'. It won him that year's British Press 'Journalist of the Year' Award.

The Ethiopian experience shows how a newspaper goes about finding and obtaining the release of a reporter who had disappeared. 'I talked to the foreign secretary a couple of times. That is really a formality. You do that to get the necessary backing and high-level thrust behind you. Then you deal with the senior official in charge of that area of the world,' Frank Giles said. While there were relations between London and Addis Ababa, it was not easy to begin solving Swain's disappearance given that it was only the early days of the regime and the province to which Swain had travelled was in rebel hands. The British ambassador in Addis Ababa, Derek Day, turned to the Ethiopian government for assistance. A British consul then began the trip to Makale, the capital of Tigre province which borders Eritrea, but was not allowed to continue because of the security situation. Nor did the authorities allow a *Sunday Times* journalist who went to Addis Ababa to search further north. Notwithstanding a dispute between the Sudanese and British governments, the newspaper obtained from President Nimeiry, who in the past had intervened on behalf of westerners missing in Ethiopia, a pledge of personal help to extricate Swain. He was finally released because an interview on the BBC World Service with Harold Evans, the editor, eased the rebels' suspicions that Swain was a foreign intelligence officer posing as a journalist. Anxious for favourable publicity, the rebels saw a certain value in releasing him.

When the body of the paper's chief foreign correspondent, David Holden, was discovered on the outskirts of Cairo in December 1977, two senior *Sunday Times* journalists flew to Egypt, and two others to Amman, where Holden had been prior to travelling to Egypt. By contrast, after Vanunu disappeared, and was assumed to have been abducted to Israel the paper sent only a junior member of the Insight team, Rowena Webster, to Israel. She did hire a leading civil rights lawyer, Dr Amnon Zichroni, who by coincidence was the lawyer Vanunu selected from a short list given to him by the prison authorities.

Vanunu was not a staff journalist with the paper. The degree of obligation was small. He came to the newspaper on his own volition, and was not in the same category as a staff man who disappears. 'Informers frequently disappear. He was not part of the *Sunday Times* staff in which case

214

there is a moral obligation to find out where he is. Rather there is an obligation to the family to find out,' a former *Sunday Times* staffer said. 'Like the guy who informs to the police is the "fink", so is the guy who brings us the story. It reflects an ambivalence or worldly cynicism that just because someone brings us a good story, that didn't necessarily mean they were angels. We realised they often had bad motives in bringing us the story. We didn't feel ourselves 100 per cent emotionally committed to the person'. 'Had he have been a Frenchman, or a German who had got kidnapped, we might have had a different view but because he was a Moroccan Sephardi there was not so much interest in his welfare. There were those in the office who were a bit contemptuous of Vanunu,' an Insight reporter said.

But Vanunu was no ordinary informer. He was one of the most important informers the paper had dealt with, during Neil's editorship. If there was limited rapport between the paper's staff and the oriental Israeli, the pride of the *Sunday Times* had still been wounded: a foreign government had abducted a very important informer. The limited reaction of executives on the paper is therefore most surprising. 'Most of those on the executive level had not come across a case like this before. Many of them did not believe that the Israelis could abduct one of their contacts from London,' an Insight reporter remarked.

There appears to have been a failure to use the wide British political contacts which a national newspaper normally has. 'Harry Evans would have been straight on to the proprietor. Thomson would have asked questions in Parliament,' Phillip Knightley said. Frank Giles, Neil's predecessor, said, 'I would start, as Neil did, to turn on the journalistic heat to try and follow the trial and reveal how he disappeared. If this failed I would go to the Foreign Secretary himself. I would talk to the senior official who looked after the security services in the Middle East. Other than that I'm not sure what I could do. Newspapers don't have missiles. I could imagine that if I was in possession of a secret which would gravely embarrass the government I would say to the Prime Minister "Unless you get me my informer back I would reveal your secret"'. A big surprise was the absence of any newspaper editorial after the Israeli Government formally issued its announcement that Vanunu was in detention in Israel.

According to Fallon, Rupert Murdoch – despite his good ties with both Thatcher and Israeli leaders – was not asked to take up the matter. 'The day we begin asking our proprietor to bring pressure is the day we allow him to put editorial pressure on us. That is something we would not even consider,' he said. The ideal proprietor-editor relationship is less one of excessively demarcated lines of responsibility and more one based on total non-interference by the proprietor in the running of a newspaper but ready availability if use of his contacts became genuinely necessary. By contrast, in the case of the *Observer* journalist, Farzad Bazoft, who was sentenced to death by the Iraqi regime, the chairman of the newspaper, 'Tiny' Rowland, turned to President Kenneth Kaunda of Zambia, whom he had known for many years. As a result, Kaunda, who had good ties with Saddam Hussein, sent a top-secret appeal to the Iraqi leader four days before Bazoft was hanged. (That was unsuccessful because Hussein had been inaccurately informed that Rowland's company Lonhro had supplied arms to Iran.) But a later appeal by Kaunda for the release of British nurse, Daphne Parish, who was with Bazoft at the time, was successful.

Had the *Sunday Times* not been directly involved in the publication of Vanunu's allegations, the absence of an editorial would be of no significance. Interest in security-related stories is a fact of media life. The *Daily Telegraph*, for example, enthusiastically printed details of Peter Wright's claims about Soviet infiltration of Britain's intelligence services even though editorially the paper disapproved of

216

Wright's action. The Israeli media, including the left-wing Mapam Party's *Al Hamishmar*, while editorially critical of Vanunu, carried long reports summarising the *Sunday Times* exposé; in some cases, including *Maariv*, the three-page story was reprinted in full.

Even Neil's statement when Vanunu was sentenced was devoid of direct criticism of the Israeli authorities for abducting its informer. In his statement Neil said that the paper understood that democratic government must protect secrets in the national interest and that most Israeli citizens regard Vanunu as a traitor. 'He committed an offence under Israeli law,' said Fallon. 'We believe in the rule of law. We have not objected to that part of the process – although we have not felt very easy that he was kidnapped and prosecuted. We have objected to the length of the sentence – absolutely out of keeping with the offence – and to the conditions under which he is held', Fallon added. Had Vanunu found sympathy among a significant section of the Israeli population, Neil's attitude to his abduction might have been different. In June 1990, after the Israeli Supreme Court rejected Vanunu's appeal against his eighteen year prison sentence, Neil, in an open letter to the Israeli president published in the paper, did lash out at the court's decision. He wrote that if clemency was not given to the abducted informer Israel would be behaving on a par with pre-revolutionary totalitarian regimes in Eastern Europe. But unless a newspaper editor is prepared to see the consequences of a disclosure to their conclusion, whatever the reactions of others, it is obvious that he should not have gone ahead with the investigation to begin with.

Meir Vanunu said: 'I have a very strong complaint about the way the *Sunday Times* behaved. They have failed to make any strong declaration regarding Mordechai's action. Did they think it was a moral one? They have ignored the whole issue since it began.' Fallon said that 'we weren't very

217

morally indignant that Israel had the bomb. Nor were we very morally indignant that Israel had chosen not to tell its own population or the rest of the world about the bomb. To us it was a matter of enormous international public interest that Israel did have the bomb and we thought the world should know and that the people of Israel should know – but that's up to the people of Israel'. The *Sunday Times* does not oppose possession of nuclear arms. The Vanunu exposé was not a campaign against Israel's possession of the bomb. The paper was against it not being shown. Only a connoisseur of the fine art of 'news consuming' could appreciate that the sole raison d'être of a news organisation is exposure, irrespective of a political connotation which could be misconstrued by others. But the British and Italian governments could hardly be expected to take up Vanunu's disappearance in a serious manner if the *Sunday Times* itself appeared half-hearted.

Coverage of the various stages of the Vanunu affair by the paper, and statements by Neil, suggests a lack of commitment. Less than two months after Vanunu disappeared, in an interview with *Haaretz*, Neil expressed no anger or criticism towards the Israeli authorities. Jollity even crept in. Asked by *Haaretz*'s London correspondent Shaul Zedka whether with Vanunu's disappearance the paper had cancelled plans to bring out a book, he replied, 'Now the book is much better'. Asked how Vanunu would be able to benefit from the book's profits, Neil replied, 'I really have to give it thought because it is possible that the Israel government would impound the money.' When the correspondent remarked that the money might then go to finance Mossad activities, Neil's reply was that he was 'prepared to pass the money to the Mossad if they will tell me how they took Vanunu from here'. 'To Israel, Vanunu was a traitor and we took no view on it,' said Fallon. 'We didn't feel very easy that Israel, under its own law, had prosecuted Vanunu, or even the fact that they kidnapped him. To us that was a very

218

interesting story too but we weren't very morally indignant about it'.

The only resources which Insight could draw on was embarrassing information. Insight, in the words of one of its team, 'leaked' information to MPs to raise in the House of Commons. Among the aspects of Vanunu's disappearance which Insight researched was how the Israelis trailed Vanunu in London, how they managed to draw him to Rome, the identity of Cindy, and his abduction from Italy. In revealing Cindy's true identity, Insight, Hounam said, 'showed what really happened. We didn't want to embarrass Israel, and if we do embarrass it, sometimes it's because there is something to be embarrassed about. They lied and said that a crime was not committed in British territory. We are proving that such a crime was committed.' 'We spent tens of thousands of pounds tracking down Cindy not just because it was a good story but because if we could resolve it it would be one of the best ways of advancing his cause', an Insight reporter said. Morgan said, 'the reportage might embarrass Israel to the point where they would have to let him off the charges and let him go.' He compared it to the media's influence in revealing the French secret service's role in the Greenpeace Rainbow Warrior affair. To believe that Israel would release somebody charged for disclosing one of the nation's most important secrets because of some embarrassing information in a foreign newspaper displays a poor appreciation of the media's influence in international politics. Morgan also said that Insight hoped to provide the evidence for the British government to act. 'The reaction at the highest level in the British government was "You bring us evidence to show a couple of Mossad agents hitting him with a sack of sand in the street and we'll act"', an editorial executive said. Ironically, while the paper reported on the roles of the Israeli and Australian intelligence services it failed to investigate any role played by MI5 or MI6, such as trailing Vanunu's movements in London, beyond reporting that two Special Branch men observed Vanunu's arrival at London airport accompanied by Hounam. Insight concluded that MI5 turned a blind eye to his disappearance but that they would not have tolerated any action on British soil. Yet Insight failed to examine whether MI5 was actually approached, and thus forewarned about Israeli intentions, or whether MI5 had actually told the Israelis that they would turn a blind eye. According to an Insight reporter 'It is true that you look at the broad canvas, i.e., were the security services involved? But we were more interested in the specific leads we had like Cindy and Rome. If we had a lead of a CIA involvement, we would also pursue it.' Some believed that too much time was being spent on the story, that the story was over, and that it was time to move on to other things. It was, therefore, not surprising that a long article which Hounam wrote at the end of 1987, after he gave evidence in the closed doors trial, describing the atmosphere and what he said, was reduced to a quarter of its original length. The reporting was not always accurate; the paper's report on the eve of Vanunu's trial in September 1987 carried the headline 'Sympathy grows as Vanunu trial opens'. It was not only untrue but the paper provided no evidence to support the claim. In reporting the information Meir Vanunu gave them about how his brother was abducted and taken to Rome, Insight claimed that Cindy wooed him with the promise of sex – but it was to happen only in her apartment, where she felt comfortable. How logical is it for a man on the run to fly to another country for sex just as he is about to have such a story published? Meir Vanunu denies ever having told the paper about the sex angle. 'They embellished truth with the part about the sex. I never told them that', he said.[17] According to him, the American offered to help Mordechai to contact the Italian press.[18] 'The newspaper was trying to sensationalise,' remarked Meir. 'He was a very philosophical man and they went and put a headline that the man went after sex,' he added. The brother's protestations notwithstanding, Vanunu flirted with the female reporters and researchers during the time that Insight was checking his story.[19]

Yet the newspaper has played a significant part in Vanunu's legal defence, recognising that it had an obligation to assist in Vanunu's legal expense, thus resolving the internal debate over the level of its commitment to Vanunu. Key proponents for legal assistance included Alastair Brett, the legal adviser, and Peter Hounam. According to Brett 'the affair has international ramifications, and has a major effect on the freedom of speech. If people cannot come to Britain and talk to a newspaper about what is happening in other countries because they are afraid they will be kidnapped, then it is a very sad day for the freedom of speech in Britain as well as internationally. Israel has behaved absolutely poorly: they have broken international law.' As soon as he disappeared, and before the Israeli Government even confirmed he was back in Israel, Rowena Webster had approached lawyer Amnon Zichroni, to turn to the Israeli Supreme Court with an application for habeas corpus; this, together with a number of other factors, led the Israeli Government to confirm finally that Vanunu was in detention in Israel. According to a member of the Vanunu family, interviewed in January 1988, the paper had contributed US$28,000 towards the legal expenses of the defence which are expected to total over $50,000. But one *Sunday Times* source insisted that, with the exception of a small payment made by the family to Zichroni after they dismissed him as defence lawyer, the paper has covered all the estimated US$50,000. In addition to Brett maintaining contact with Vanunu's defence lawyer, the paper has consulted international law experts in Britain regarding the best approach to take in the trial. Anthony Lester QC was consulted regarding the laws of conspiracy and kidnapping in order to ascertain whether British law was broken. 'We looked at the international ramifications of somebody finding themselves

221

charged in Israel when the charging state has committed an offence in bringing the person to trial in its jurisdiction,' a legal executive on the paper said.

Despite this, the *Sunday Times*'s participation in Vanunu's defence has not been total. It has been cautious in the way it has defined its legal involvement from the earliest days. Asked by an Israeli journalist in November 1986 whether the paper was paying for Vanunu's defence, Neil replied 'No, we aren't involved in it. Vanunu is paying his lawyer'. Another aspect of the paper's limited involvement was that, despite early expectations, no senior executive from the paper, or from its parent group News International, volunteered to testify on Vanunu's behalf: only Hounam did so. The lack of complete involvement was tempered, according to Brett, 'by the fact that Vanunu very largely caused his own problems by ignoring the advice given to him by the *Sunday Times*. But we can't say we don't have any responsibility at all because he is facing the treason charges as a result of having given the material to us.' Given, however, that the paper and Guerrero may bear some responsibility for Vanunu's abduction, it needs to be asked whether these two parties have a responsibility greater than they have demonstrated.

The assistance which the *Sunday Times* gave at the legal level and its series of disclosures on how Vanunu was abducted to Israel might be seen, by people wanting to make public important information which might result in their prosecution or worse, as proof that in such an event they could expect the paper's support. Yet a closer look has shown this to be only partially correct. It is true that a news organisation's resources are limited, but precisely because of this the paper ought to have turned to other potential sources of support, notably in the government, more than it apparently did.

Yet one must also question Vanunu's motives for going with Cindy to Rome. Given Meir Vanunu's claim that his brother wanted to take up Cindy's offer to introduce him to the Italian press – Vanunu presumably believing that following the *Sunday Mirror* story on the Nuclear Conman the *Sunday Times* might no longer go ahead with his account – it was tantamount to taking the story to another newspaper, which reduces the level of responsibility of the newspaper for supporting Vanunu's legal defence after his abduction. But the *Sunday Times* never reported that Mordechai Vanunu went to Rome for this purpose; they suggest he went to spend a few days with his friend only to return prior to publication and to sign the contract with the newspaper.

8. (3 METRES × 2 METRES) × 18 YEARS

The shroud of ambiguity which the Israeli authorities placed over the diplomatic and intelligence aspects of the Vanunu affair also characterised Vanunu's trial. But while denial and disinformation are part of the diplomat's craft, the independence of the Israeli judiciary and the rule of law changed the rules of the game. The judges, though they would be encumbered by limitations in discussing the nuclear subject, reached a considered verdict. However, the omission in the Israeli penal system of a law specifically prohibiting unauthorised leaks to the news media left the judiciary with the task of charging with treason and espionage somebody who had leaked classified information to the media for the proclaimed public good. The case raised a number of important questions about the relationship between the state and the individual, but the judges were to confine themselves to interpreting the existing law. This conveyed an incorrect impression that the court simply passed the 'buck' it was handed by the government on to the prison authorities, which, in turn, confined Vanunu in his 3m×2m cell for an enforced eighteen-year-long silence.

Israel's nuclear secrets and a Mossad abduction had made Vanunu's legal defence an undoubtedly prestigious case. The media interest and the thought of the *Sunday Times*'s backing encouraged a number of lawyers to offer their services to the Vanunu family. But Mordechai Vanunu had already picked the name of Amnon Zichroni from a list of lawyers approved to see classified material, which was given to him by the prison authorities after he was returned to Israel in October 1986. A veteran lawyer of left-wing causes, Amnon Zichroni was a founder of the former leftist political party, 'Haolam Hazeh' (This People), for whom he had been elected to the Knesset. As a young recruit to the Israeli army, he refused to serve and went on a hunger strike. He had fought law cases for those appealing religious legislation, and conscientious objectors to the 1982 Lebanon war. He is thought to have been the first lawyer to have proved the innocence of somebody charged in Israel with espionage, and during the time Vanunu had been a student at Beer-sheba's Ben-Gurion University, he had turned to Zichroni on behalf of Arab students on the campus.

Zichroni's style of maintaining ties with the Israeli establishment, including the intelligence community, aroused the concern of the Vanunu brothers. Zichroni was a personal friend of Yossi Ginnossar, a senior Shin Bet officer who, according to Meir Vanunu,[1] led the team which interrogated his brother. Days before Vanunu's case was due to come up before the courts in March 1987, Mordechai, on Meir's initiative, dismissed Zichroni. Meir was concerned that Zichroni was not raising the matter of the abduction, and also wanted the issue of the non-legitimacy of nuclear weaponry tested in the court room. In the months since his brother's abduction, Meir had increasingly linked the case to the international anti-nuclear movement. During the mystery over Vanunu's fate immediately after his abduction, Zichroni refused to break the stringent censorship and admit that his client was back in Israel and under arrest.

Asked on the BBC radio programme *The World at One* (10 November 1986) by presenter Brian Widlake, 'Where is Mr Vanunu being held?' Zichroni replied: 'I cannot comment.'

Presenter: 'Have you discussed with Mr Vanunu how he got to Israel from Britain?'

225

Zichroni: 'I cannot comment.'
Presenter: 'But have you discussed that with him?'
Zichroni: 'I cannot comment on it. . . .'
Presenter: 'Does Israel have the British equivalent of the Official Secrets Act?'
Zichroni: 'We have a special act which deals with such cases.'
Presenter: 'Would I be right in thinking that Mr Vanunu is subject to that act?'
Zichroni: 'I cannot comment on it.'
Presenter: 'Mr Zichroni, you're being excessively cautious, can you tell me why?'
Zichroni: 'I cannot even comment on your last question!'
Presenter: 'On why you're being cautious?'
Zichroni: 'Yes.'
Presenter: 'Is this because you are under some pressure from the Israeli authorities?'
Zichroni: 'I am not under pressure, but I cannot comment on it.'

It was little comfort to the Vanunu family that Zichroni had been instrumental in getting the authorities to lift the veil of secrecy and confirm that Vanunu was alive and in custody by threatening to go to the High Court to obtain this permission.

Zichroni's replacement, Avigdor Feldman, had a solid reputation as a human rights lawyer. He had defended Arabs appealing deportation orders, Druze residents of the Golan Heights, and had got the administration order imposed on Palestinian activist Faisal el-Husseini reduced by half. Former legal adviser to the Israel Association of Civil Rights, Feldman had over the years been concerned about the poor legal services available to Arabs and the lack of overall success in Arab appeals to the Israel Supreme Court. He is one of the Israel monitors of the New York-based Human Rights Watch group. The holder of an MA in international law, he had been a visiting scholar at Harvard University, and as a young lawyer a member of Zichroni's legal practice for fourteen years. For the poet intellectual turned lawyer, the Vanunu case had a number of significant and stimulating issues which could have long-term implications: the rights of the individual against the state and the limits of how far an individual may act; how a democratic society grapples with the nuclear issue and whether Israel could set her own rules.

Before Feldman took over, he talked at some length with Vanunu to determine what he meant by wanting Feldman to 'politicise the case'. While such issues as the morality of nuclear weaponry and legislative control over the nuclear research programme could be presented in the courtroom within the framework of the legal arguments, Feldman was not going to delegitimise the court system. The line of legal defence which he proposed was that Vanunu had acted from ideological motives, and had not damaged state security in revealing the nuclear secrets. He would claim that the opposite was true: Vanunu had wanted to 'assist' the public and inform them of the nuclear programme so that they could reach a viewpoint on the subject. Nor had he sold any secrets to an enemy; he had leaked them to a newspaper.

Underlying the alternative strategies of Feldman and Zichroni was a difference in outlook about the place of politics in the courtroom. According to Zichroni, 'Law is an undoubtedly professional matter, the courtroom a forum for a completely legal message. Law is a language not understood by everybody.' He admits that there are situations where a political overtone can help the defendant, in countries where the court system does not function properly. According to Feldman, 'the law itself is a product of political institutions. The function of the law is to find a legal peg on which to give political expression to the customer. Vanunu expects that his legal defence will search in the penal system for something which justifies and defends his motive.'[2] Given

227

Vanunu's desire to bring the nuclear issue to public attention, the change in lawyers had a certain irony in that Zichroni is by temperament a more publicity conscious lawyer than the retiring Feldman.

Inevitably, the cloak of secrecy which enveloped Vanunu's arrival back in Israel spread to his trial. The judicial system allows for a 'closed-doors' trial for security reasons, and a number of security-related trials, including espionage, have been so conducted. The only information to reach the public is a brief notification at its end that a person has been found guilty and the name of the offence. Vanunu's trial, which opened at the Jerusalem District Court in August 1987, following a delay to enable the new lawyer to prepare, had two security-related aspects: the nuclear arms issue and Vanunu's abduction.

Before the trial began Feldman appealed to the court for it to be open. Given Vanunu's wish to raise the question of the morality of nuclear weaponry, and his argument that the public had a right to nuclear information, the openness of the trial was particularly important. The popular image Vanunu had acquired as a traitor and a spy had to be dispelled and his true motives understood.

But the court rejected Feldman's appeal, insisting that proceedings be held behind closed doors. Hopes were dashed that only that part of the trial which dealt specifically with Dimona and the abduction would be closed. Indeed, Feldman had argued that even the information about Vanunu's work at Dimona was no longer secret now that it had been published in detail in the *Sunday Times*. The same was true of the abduction story, which had also been followed up by the newspaper. But the prosecution countered that there was additional information which witnesses – from, for instance, Dimona and the security services – might raise in testimony, and Vanunu might have additional information which he had not yet divulged.

At the forefront of the authorities' fears was the 'palm' incident when Vanunu, arriving at the courthouse in November 1986 for his remand to be extended, held out to waiting reporters the palm of his hand on which was scribbled, 'Hijacken in Rome'. Not only were the public and the media denied access to the proceedings, but extraordinary measures were adopted to prevent any possibility of Vanunu's having contact with the outside world. He was brought to court each day in a police transit van with its windows blacked out, and entered the courthouse through a rear entrance where a sacking canopy had been erected to shield him. He was made to wear a helmet to stop him from shouting to waiting journalists, and police sirens drowned anything he tried to say. The courtroom was partitioned off from the rest of the courthouse, and windows were boarded, which produced complaints from the judges about the intolerably stuffy atmosphere in the courtroom. A mere handshake offered by Vanunu, who wanted to thank witnesses who had come especially from abroad, was a matter of negotiation with the Shin Bet, requiring the intervention of the judges.[3]

A separate problem the security services sought to address was how to keep defence witnesses – most of whom had come from abroad – from journalists waiting outside the courtroom, or from disclosing, after leaving the country, what had happened in the courtroom. One witness, the *Sunday Times*'s Peter Hounam, was warned by Israeli officials that if he revealed details of his testimony he could be extradited from Britain and brought to trial in Israel.[4]

Implicit in the judges' designation of the information as secret, and in the decision that the trial would be behind closed doors, was an indication of what their verdict would be. Not only would that section of the trial dealing with Vanunu's work at Dimona and his abduction be closed, as would the testimony of the prosecution witnesses, but so would the testimony of defence witnesses, including experts

229

from abroad whose evidence was mainly philosophical or based on information already known.

The prosecution did not oppose the principle of the testimony of defence witnesses being open to the public but, if it were, they and the security services would demand that Vanunu be removed from the courtroom. Vanunu agreed to this so that nuclear debate in the court could be public, but the judges decided that it was more important for Vanunu to be present at his trial than that it should be open to the public. Also rejected was the possibility of defence testimony being fed to journalists in an adjoining room because there might be an outburst from Vanunu. There were two other possibilities: one was for Vanunu to sit in a special soundproof booth (as had been used in trials in Germany of members of the Baader-Meinhof group) with directional glass to enable him to see the courtroom but not for anybody in the courtroom to see Vanunu, lest there be a repetition of the palm incident. The other possibility was for the proceedings each day to be published, after vetting by military censors, which was agreed.

Defence and prosecution lawyers met at the end of each day to agree on what could be released, but in practice the system was ineffective. For example, after the prosecution allowed the testimony of one foreign expert, Professor George Quester, in its entirety, much of it was blue-pencilled by the military censors.[5] And when Feldman wanted to release some of Mordechai Vanunu's description of his background – his childhood, studies, army service and political views – the judges objected, saying that its publication might infer that the judges were sympathetic to his testimony. The only sentence permitted from testimony lasting two days was 'I did this from ideological motives.'[6]

By taking a maximalist rather than minimalist view of security concerns, the judges in effect encroached upon the democratic principle of open trials. The credibility of the trial and its verdict were not enhanced by the judges' action. But according to one witness, Dr Frank Barnaby, 'the judges made no effort to cut short the testimony. They allowed, as far as I could see, the defence as much time as was needed to make the case and they listened with interest. Genuine interest, I think.' Accounts of the trial (including this chapter) were largely dependent on incomplete titbits of information which trickled out of the courtroom.

There were, in essence, two court cases. Parallel to the charges of disclosing official secrets, Vanunu was attempting to put the state of Israel on trial for abduction. He insisted that he was not going to prison for, say, fifteen years without the illegal manner of his being brought to trial being raised. Shortly after he was brought back to Israel, the security services and Vanunu had engaged in some plea bargaining. Vanunu would be charged only with aggravated espionage and not with treason if he agreed not to raise the subject of his abduction.[7] But once Vanunu had divulged that information on the palm of his hand, the offer was withdrawn. It could have knocked three to five years off the eighteen-year sentence he was to receive.

At the outset of the trial the Minister of Defence had used his powers to issue an order barring the court from discussing either Vanunu's work at Dimona or his abduction, on the grounds that this was likely to impair the security of the state. Under the Penal Law (Section 128) a court can order that the accused or his counsel not be present at a particular legal proceeding or not inspect some particular evidence. Said an official: 'It was a funny situation. Vanunu knew – or thought he knew – what was true or not. There was an assumption that the prosecution lawyer knew what was true or not. The only persons that could not know were the three judges.' Avigdor Feldman appealed to the Israel Supreme Court to lift the ministerial order, saying that it would be impossible for the defence to be conducted under these

231

conditions. He intended to claim that the court had no jurisdiction over Vanunu because he had been brought to Israel illegally. Feldman also planned to challenge the admissibility of the confessions the Shin Bet had obtained from Vanunu during his interrogation, by getting his client to testify about his feelings and reactions during his journey from Italy and his initial imprisonment.

Judge Gavriel Bach, known for his humane legal rulings, took the rare step in Israeli legal history of limiting the Defence Minister's order, and decided to let Vanunu describe how he was brought to Israel, how he was held, for how long, and what his feelings were. It was the first time, according to Bach, that a defendant was being prohibited from giving testimony at his own trial, and Bach ruled that the court had to be convinced that the state's security would indeed be impaired to justify limiting Vanunu's evidence. Quoting another liberal maverick of the Israeli judiciary, Judge Aharon Barak, Bach said that a judge had to weigh the relative importance of each piece of evidence, between complete unimportance and vital relevance. When this had been done, a comparison had to be made with the importance, from the point of view of state security, of not disclosing the evidence. If its importance for the accused outweighed considerations of security, its disclosure could be authorised in the interests of a fair trial. Bach ruled that Vanunu could relate the way he had been arrested abroad, how he had been brought to Israel and imprisoned and his feelings and fears during the entire period. That the trial was behind closed doors reduced the danger of evidence being disclosed.[8] The decision, and its publication, sent a minor shockwave through senior ranks of the intelligence community. However, Bach said, Vanunu could not name the country where he had been arrested (even though he had already named it in the palm incident) or the place where he had been held, the identity of his abductors or even the type of transport in which he had been returned to Israel.

232

These, Bach argued, were irrelevant to the trial and would only make it cumbersome.

The first task for Feldman was to argue that since Vanunu had been brought to Israel illegally, the court had no jurisdiction. If the judges accepted Feldman's argument Vanunu would have to be freed. There was a precedent in US law (which is admissible in Israeli courts): the prosecution of a drug-smuggler, Francisco Toscanino, who had been sentenced to a long prison term for smuggling a great quantity of heroin. A US federal court of appeal overturned a lower court's decision on the grounds that he had been abducted from South America by US narcotics agents and brought drugged to the United States. Until the federal court decision, US justice had drawn a veil over what happened before a trial, saying that it was irrelevant how a person was brought to court.[9]

There were precedents, too, in Israeli law for people having been brought to Israel by the use of force. Most notable was Adolf Eichmann, in charge of logistics in the systematic Nazi extermination of the Jews, who was abducted from Argentina in 1960 by Mossad agents. The court had rejected Eichmann's defence that it had no jurisdiction, arguing that the court was not interested in how a person was brought to trial. What was relevant was whether it had legal power – which it had over anybody in Israeli territory. One difference between the Eichmann and Vanunu abductions was that while Argentina had waived its right in the case of Eichmann, Italy was not known to have done so regarding Vanunu.[10] However, only states, in contrast to individuals, had standing in international law and could claim its infringement, and there was no extradition agreement between Israel and Italy. Unless someone had been extradited under an existing treaty, the court would not investigate the circumstances in which a person was detained and brought to Israel.[11] Yet there have been developments in international humanitarian law. According to the International Covenant

233

on Civil and Political Rights (Article 9) 'no person should be subject to arbitrary arrest or detention', which includes the abduction of a person by agents of one state to another state. Thus, argued Feldman, Israel, which has incorporated the Universal Declaration of Human Rights into its legal system, was obligated to return Vanunu to Italy.[12]

The court rejected Feldman's argument,[13] – its precise reasons were not made known – in line with the principle that a court could try anybody under its jurisdiction and was not concerned how that person had reached its jurisdiction. The Vanunu family hoped that Mordechai's abduction would be raised in the Italian courts or at the European Court at Strasbourg, but Feldman was sceptical given the verdict of the Italian prosecutor, Judge Sica, that Vanunu was 'an Israeli agent'. Feldman preferred the possibility of suing the Israeli government because its official agents had used force to bring Vanunu to Israel.

Had Vanunu's trial been open, the comparison made by his lawyer would hardly have scored points in the public eye, where his image was already tarnished as a traitor. But whereas Eichmann was a murderer, accused of crimes against humanity, Vanunu's crime was political. The comparison could even be turned on its head: the finger pointed at Eichmann could also be directed against a state which Vanunu claimed possessed nuclear weapons.[14]

Feldman also tried to scuttle the trial by claiming that the confessions taken by the Shin Bet, on which the prosecution case was based, were given by his client under great psychological pressure. Vanunu had reportedly been brought back to Israel in the dark cabin of a boat, and then imprisoned in a closed, airless cell. The Shin Bet had given Vanunu the impression that he would be imprisoned for years without anybody knowing.[15] The confession which Vanunu claimed he was forced to sign included the statement that he had received money from the *Sunday Times* for the story, and this profit motive gave the prosecution reason for charging that Vanunu intended to commit treason.[16] Vanunu waited for his opportunity to describe in graphic detail his treatment at the hands of the Shin Bet, but he kept within the boundaries of the revised order of the Minister of Defence and did not refer to the transport used to get him to Israel or the country from which he had been abducted.[17] Throughout the trial two Shin Bet agents sat at his side to put their hands over his mouth in case he disclosed something classified. Months earlier, Vanunu had tried to evade his guards at a court hearing to say something to the judges, but the guards had pulled him away.[18] If Feldman could get the court to accept that the confessions had been obtained under great psychological pressure, the prosecution's charges would be invalid. But Israeli courts allow evidence obtained by illegal means, provided those means do not affect its reliability. In the United States, by contrast, to deter law enforcement agencies from employing illegal tactics, 'the fruits of the poisoned tree theory' prohibits a court from using such evidence even if there is no reason to doubt its reliability.

The head of the police serious crime squad and Yossi Ginnossar told the court that Vanunu's mental condition was good,[19] and the judges decided to accept the confessions, saying they had been obtained with a reasonable amount of pressure.[20]

The prosecution case against Mordechai Vanunu appeared clear cut. According to the charge sheet Vanunu, on commencing a training course at the nuclear research centre at Dimona, had signed a declaration which committed him to observe secrecy about his work, and was told of the importance of this. But, particularly from the beginning of 1985, he had collected, prepared, copied and held in his possession classified information. He visited top-secret areas of the nuclear research centre and photographed 'top-secret objects' and installations, and hid the information at home.

This information allegedly included the physical and organisational structure of the centre, classified 'developments' there, classified operating procedures and production processes, and 'codenames of terminology of various secret developments'.

In Australia, continued the indictment, Vanunu gave a man named Guerrero, 'who presented himself as a journalist', secret information as well as photographs he had taken at Dimona. 'When he passed the information to Guerrero, and subsequently to the *Sunday Times*, the accused intended to impair the security of the state. The accused delivered the information in the knowledge that it would be published by the newspaper, and that it would in this way be likely to reach the enemy. By his acts, the accused intended to assist the enemy in its war against Israel.'

The most obvious section of the criminal law regarding state security and official secrets under which to charge Vanunu was 'aggravated espionage'. According to Section 113

> (b) A person who delivers any secret information without being authorised to do so and with intent to impair the security of the State is liable to imprisonment for life
>
> (c) A person who obtains, collects, prepares, records or holds possession of any secret information without being authorised to do so is liable to imprisonment for a term of seven years; if he thereby intends to impair the security of the State, he is liable to imprisonment for fifteen years.

The charge that Vanunu had impaired the security of the state suggested that the information he gave the *Sunday Times* was accurate. But, anxious that the charge-sheet should not undermine the posture of nuclear ambiguity, officials were quick to point out that under the law it was irrelevant whether the information was accurate or not. 'Secret' information could include signs reading 'Keep Out' surrounding the nuclear research centre.[21]

236

The Vanunu file was in the hands of Dorit Beinish, the deputy state prosecutor, and Uzi Hasson, head of the Justice Ministry's fiscal department, who could call on considerable experience in criminal appeals to the Israel Supreme Court. The two were considered the best team to handle this sensitive case; they had previously served on a controversial so-called 'Jewish Underground' trial when some Jewish residents of the West Bank had been given sentences of up to life imprisonment for the murder of Arab residents, and Beinish had become the butt of personal attacks and criticism from the political Right. As the Beinish–Hasson team put the final touches to the Vanunu indictment of espionage, a charge of treason was added. Its addition reflected differences between the Shin Bet and the Justice Ministry, and within the ministry.[22] According to Section 99

(a) A person who, with intent to assist an enemy in war against Israel, commits an act calculated so to assist him, is liable to the death sentence or to imprisonment for life.
(b) For the purposes of this section, 'assistance' includes delivering information with intent that it fall into the hands of the enemy or in the knowledge that it may fall into the enemy hands; and it is immaterial whether or not war is being waged at the time the information was given

Notwithstanding that prosecutions have a tendency to include the maximum number of charges, the treason charge raised some official eyebrows because Vanunu had given the information not to an enemy but to a news organisation. Some thought that it would be difficult to convict Vanunu on this count.[23] There were also disagreements inside the Justice Ministry about what sentence to demand. The Attorney General, Yosef Harish, wanted to press for the death penalty, given the seriousness of the charges,[24] but other officials argued for life imprisonment, saying that a death sentence could be imposed only if the offence was committed during a period of armed hostilities, i.e. war. The only death sentence ever carried out in Israel's history was that on Adolf Eichmann, but Harish relied on a legal interpretation that Israel, in the absence of peace with neighbouring states, was in a constant state of armed hostilities. However, the final decision was to demand life imprisonment.

Not contesting the prosecution's key charge that Vanunu had provided the information to the *Sunday Times*, Avigdor Feldman rested his defence on two questions: Did the information damage Israel's security? And did Vanunu intend to damage the country's security? Feldman claimed that the information did not damage Israel's security because reports that Israel possessed the bomb had been published earlier, and something which everyone knew could not be considered secret. There is a point at which common knowledge is a contradiction in terms with the notion of secrecy.

A difficulty which Feldman had to overcome was the government's order banning discussion in the courtroom of such questions as whether the exposé had caused damage or whether it was true, on the grounds that it implied Israel might have the bomb.[25] Feldman sought to overcome this by inviting foreign experts to testify that the information was already known. Professor George Quester of Cornell University, who has written widely on the arms race, said that there was nothing new in Vanunu's testimony. 'Every country in the world,' Quester told the court, 'including the Arab states, the USA and the Soviet Union assume that Israel has the nuclear bomb. The superpowers and the Arab states determine their policies accordingly.' In the fourteen months between the time of the *Sunday Times* article and his appearance in court, in January 1988, Quester noted that there had been no international pressure on Israel on the nuclear question. Nor had Arab states made any special declarations or taken specific positions on the issue. This proved, Quester argued, that Vanunu's 'exposé' did not reveal anything new.[26] Dr Frank Barnaby, called by Feldman, also said there was nothing knew in the revelations.[27]

238

The defence had prepared a chart which listed earlier published reports on Israel's nuclear capability.[28] The reprocessing facility referred to by Vanunu had already been noted by Fuad Jabber, author of *Israel and Nuclear Weapons*; by Steve Weisman and Herbert Krosney, authors of *The Islamic Bomb*; and by Peter Pringle and James Spigelman in *The Nuclear Barons*. An arms expert had a year earlier estimated on NBC news that Israel had at least one hundred nuclear warheads, and possibly over 140. The reactor's enlarged megawattage had been reported in 1982 in a book by French journalist Pierre Péan.[29] But the chart had not found any earlier claim than Vanunu's that Israel had thermonuclear bombs.

In contrast to Barnaby and Quester, another witness subpoenaed by Feldman, Shimon Peres – prime minister at the time of the Vanunu exposé, and an architect of Israel's nuclear research programme and its posture of nuclear ambiguity – testified that Vanunu had damaged state security. Peres appeared to contradict a comment he had made in November 1986, a month after the story appeared, when, addressing a closed meeting of Knesset members of Israel's Labour Party, he said that the *Sunday Times* article had not weakened Israel.[30] Another reason why his testimony was a disappointment was because he stuck rigidly to the government order and refused to answer Feldman's questions on Peres's sources for claiming damage to state security or how that security had been impaired.[31] Labelling the government order 'an interference in the judicial process', Feldman appealed again to the Supreme Court to lift it. Judge Gavriel Bach, who again heard the appeal, lifted one of the five forbidden themes which, according to Bach, was 'very essential and important to Vanunu to be addressed'.[32] Yet Peres still failed in his three-page written response to deal with some of the twenty questions Feldman had raised.[33]

It was paradoxical for Quester to argue that Vanunu's

claims had been common knowledge because this implied that the *Sunday Times* 'scoop' had no value. The newspaper itself had noted Professor Theodore Taylor's view, on being shown Vanunu's testimony, that the Israeli nuclear programme was more advanced than any previous reports Taylor had seen. Barnaby told the court that part of the value of the paper's exposé lay in the fact that the information came from somebody on the 'inside'.[34] In claiming this, Barnaby was in effect destroying Feldman's case that there was nothing new in the revelations to warrant Vanunu's being charged under Section 113 with passing 'secret' information. The weakness in Feldman's argument was that there was no real knowledge about Israel's nuclear capability – there were assumptions and evaluations.

Feldman's second line of defence concerned Vanunu's aims in making his disclosures. His client had no 'intent to assist the enemy' (Section 99) or 'to impair the security of the state' (Section 113). His goal was to inform the Israeli public and the world community about the nuclear programme. Feldman quoted Section 94, found at the beginning of the penal law chapter on state security and official secrets:

> An act shall not be regarded as an offence under this chapter if it has been, or appears to have been, done in good faith with intent to bring about, by lawful means, a change in the structure of the state or the activities of any of its authorities or in the structure of a foreign state or the activities of any of its authorities or in the structure or activities of an agency or organisation of states

Through Vanunu's breach of the law the public would be informed of something previously hidden from them, and would then express opinions through the democratic process.

'There must be some sort of equilibrium: how can a citizen vote if he doesn't know? Is the Likud government for or against nuclear weapons?' Feldman asked.[35]

240

Peter Hounam told the court that he 'was the first person from the paper whom Vanunu met. We did not pay him money, but only covered his expenses. I told the court that in our meetings Vanunu emphasised that he acted from ideological motives. Money did not motivate him.'[36] Hounam had not seen Vanunu since he disappeared in London. 'I said, "Look after yourself and keep fighting" and he said, "Thank you very much, Peter". It was a very emotional moment for both of us. Tears came into his eyes,' Hounam said.[37]

Feldman had subpoenaed Abba Eban, chairman of the Knesset's Defence and Foreign Affairs Committee, which formally has legislative control of nuclear policy, in order 'to expose the non-democratic process through which decisions were made, even key committees didn't know.'[38] Eban's testimony 'helped Feldman to construct his line of defence,' – an extreme one of claiming civil disobedience.[39] At the Nuremberg trials it had been recognised that an individual was not only obliged to refuse to carry out an 'illegal' order but had to do everything in his or her power to see that the order was legal.[40] Since Dimona was not open to international inspection and Israel had not signed the Nuclear Non-Proliferation Treaty, Feldman posited that Vanunu was under a moral obligation to reveal the information despite having been sworn to secrecy.

Feldman had wanted to call Professor Richard Falk, an international lawyer at Princeton University, who had defended conscientious objectors conscripted to serve in Vietnam. But the judges said Feldman could include Falk's views in his summing-up at the end of the trial.[41] The various experts and witnesses Feldman was bringing to testify that Vanunu's ideas were held by internationally-respected academics were turning the court into a university lecture hall.

The claim that Vanunu was under a moral obligation to act as he did was not universally accepted. Whereas a nuclear capability used as a first strike weapon was illegal, the legal

241

status of a capability used as a deterrent was undecided. A separate question concerned Feldman's interpretation of Article 94 that Vanunu's disclosure had been 'in good faith with intent to bring about, by lawful means, a change'. Feldman's interpretation of the law opened a Pandora's box whereby any ideologically motivated person could break the law. It was difficult to conceive that the Knesset, in drafting the law on the security of the state, had this in mind.

However, the major question to occupy the court in considering Vanunu's aims concerned the legal meaning of 'intention'. Israeli law, like some other legal systems, differentiates between motivation and intent. Motivation concerns the basic goal of an alleged criminal; intent concerns the means used to reach that goal. Throughout the years Israeli courts have not been interested in the motivation of an individual – although it can be relevant for sentencing – but in the intent or action of an individual as it affects society, or, as in the Vanunu case, the security of the state. Vanunu was not unlike a doctor who, wishing to undertake heart research, takes the heart from a living person for laboratory examination. The person, of course, dies. The doctor did not want to cause the death, but would be charged with murder because it was highly probable that the person would die. The legal definition of intent is one who foresees the results and in so doing accepts them. Thus, in 1960 the Czech-born professor, Kurt Sitte, was convicted by an Israeli court of passing secret information to foreign agents even though he did not wish to harm the security of the state but did so out of concern for the welfare of his relatives. In its ruling the Israeli Supreme Court said that 'in offences against state security a person is responsible for such consequences of his action as are highly probable.' According to the law on treason 'assistance to enemy in war includes intent that it shall fall into the hands of the enemy or in the knowledge that it may fall into the enemy's hands' (Section 99b). The drafters of the law appeared to be concerned that where the security of the state was at stake, society would not be adequately protected. A more narrowly defined law could, for example, leave outside the law the individual motivated by ideology, as distinct from one whose motivation was, indeed, to harm the state.

Given the wider definition of intent in Israeli criminal law to embrace the probable effects of an action – irrespective of whether it was the actual goal – Feldman's task was not an easy one. This was particularly true regarding the charge of espionage, according to which 'a person who delivers any secret information without being authorised to do so and with intent to impair the security of the state is liable to life imprisonment.' Even the unauthorised gathering of information made Vanunu liable for a seven-year imprisonment (Sections 113 (b) and (c)).

The prosecution had a weaker case with the treason charge. It was pushing the matter to accuse Vanunu of having 'intent to assist an enemy in war against Israel', even though 'assistance includes delivering information in the knowledge that it may fall into enemy hands'. Vanunu acted in good faith and never intended to 'assist the enemy'. Feldman argued that the law should have been drafted as 'a person who assists an enemy in war . . .' The fact that it read, 'a person with intent to assist an enemy in war' suggests that a special type of intent was required. Feldman also proposed that assistance to an enemy including mere knowledge that the information might fall into its hands (stated in Section 99 (b)) first required the special intent which preceded 'assistance' in Section 99 (a).

The prosecuting lawyer, Uzi Hasson, countered that it was impossible to enter a person's heart to determine his intention: intent came from the action itself.[42] Judge Shalom Brenner challenged him. 'If you say that Vanunu intended to pass secret information to an enemy, then why did he not go to the enemy? Why did he require an intermediary, that is the *Sunday Times*?' Hasson replied somewhat lamely, 'It

243

is not possible to know the unequivocal reason for this.'[43] The judges were not convinced that Vanunu's action could be equated with treason; they passed the onus of proof from the defence, which would have had to prove Vanunu's good intent, to the prosecution which now had to prove the opposite.

In contrast to Feldman's intellectual explanation of Vanunu's motives, Uzi Hasson presented the court with a socio-psychological analysis of the man.

'In personality terms Vanunu was an introverted person, egocentric, a loner, of composite and complex mental-build, who concluded that he hadn't found his place in Israeli society and the country. His life search in general, and in particular in Israeli society, led him more and more to the Left, coming near in outlook to the Arabs.' According to Hasson, 'the more Vanunu's inclinations grew in these directions, the more hostile he became to the nuclear research centre. This feeling grew in the 1982 Lebanon war and after it, and hardened when he was scheduled for dismissal. The cancellation of the dismissal notice did not change his feelings; indeed, insulted, he decided to give in his notice. He resigned because, according to him, his superiors wanted to be rid of him. The interruption of work, and the insults beforehand (which originated in the conversations and warnings from security personnel following the discovery of his left-wing tendencies) strengthened his decision – reached at the beginning of 1985 – to cut himself off from Israel and begin a new life abroad, and aroused a desire to take revenge against all those who had caused him that pain.' This may also have been the reason, Hasson said, for changing his religion.

'Vanunu is an intelligent person,' Hasson continued, 'who in spite of his social background made majestic efforts to advance, and to achieve a more respectable position than his parents and family had. Regrettably, he could not; nor

244

did he raise a family. His routine work, without hope, and perhaps even opportunity, of advance in it brought him to the conclusion that he had not achieved anything in his life. And from this', Hasson argued, 'came his desire for self-publicity, to do something significant which would take him out of anonymity and prove his uniqueness. The possibility of monetary, or other, benefit (required for starting a new life) was among the reasons' for his act, even though, Hasson admitted, 'there was no direct proof that, Vanunu managed to receive any significant payment from the *Sunday Times*.'[44]

The judges were divided over the question of what motivated Vanunu. In a majority decision, the presiding judge, Eliahu Noam, and Judge Brenner, accepted Hasson's description, which in effect nullified Vanunu's claim that he was ideologically motivated. Judge Zvi Tal, however, said that the overriding factor was ideological – 'a world outlook which concretised during Vanunu's activism at the Ben-Gurion University. Vanunu was on the far Left of the political spectrum.' In trying to determine Vanunu's true motives, the judges looked for earlier evidence of his anti-nuclear predisposition. A letter he had sent to his brother, Meir, before flying from Australia to Britain, was of some importance for Judge Tal. Vanunu told Meir that 'he had decided to do it primarily from political motivation. Even though I left Israel and don't want to be involved I am returning to the involvement. I feel it is my obligation to publicise the information.' But Judges Noam and Brenner thought the letter was an attempt to justify his action 'because for any intelligent person the action amounted to treachery towards his motherland'. The ideological explanations were there to disguise any suggestion of his being a spy or traitor. To understand Vanunu's motives, the two judges said, one had to take into account his desire to join the Israel Communist Party, and his subsequent desire to cut his ties with the country and not return. They also said that Vanunu's diaries showed a constant wish for self-publicity and a financial incentive, but did not support a strong ideological motivation.

Yet Israeli press reports about the diaries suggested that Vanunu's progressive thinking was most present. The absence of diary entries about the bomb or his work at Dimona could be to his credit, in that he had been careful not to reveal the classified information even in his own diary. He did not discuss his work even with his family or ex-girlfriend. What might have persuaded the judges otherwise would have been indications of legal activities after he left Dimona such as press articles of anti-nuclear content or his involvement in interest groups. The judges seemed unaware that, while staying at King's Cross in Sydney, Vanunu was actively involved in a workshop on peace, which also focused on the nuclear arms issue. The Noam–Brenner line, if generalised, would imply that an individual's self-proclaimed political views and actions are tied to deep socio-psychological forces rather than to intellectual and rational consideration. Also implied in Hasson's picture of Vanunu was that he was 'extreme' on the nuclear issue as he was on other political matters such as the Arabs and the future status of the West Bank. It would indeed not be surprising for an individual who reached a broadly radical outlook on life to be anti-nuclear.

The three judges wrote their judgement together, but until the week of the verdict (at the end of March 1988) they pondered at length whether Vanunu should be sentenced for espionage only or for treason as well.[45] They finally reached a unanimous decision that he was guilty of both espionage and treason. The court rejected every one of the arguments brought by Feldman. Of the defence that the information had been given to a newspaper and not to a foreign agent, the judges said that publication in a newspaper was in effect testimony that Vanunu 'intended to bring all information he had gathered and publish it for the knowledge of every enemy of Israel even without making direct contact with them.'[46] Of the argument that 'assistance to an enemy' had to prove damage in practice, the court said that 'damage' could be measured in the very prohibition of the act, even if the enemy did not use the information. And on the question that 'assistance to the enemy in war' was limited to periods of armed hostilities, the court said that '. . . in war' included periods between wars because most Arab countries had been in a continuous state of war with the Jewish state. The court also rejected the argument that information about Israel's nuclear capability had been published earlier (but their reasoning was censored).

Feldman had also argued that the charge of aggravated espionage did not apply to Vanunu since he did not have 'intent to impair the security of the state'. Whereas the section on treason explicitly stated that 'intent' included merely 'the knowledge that the information may fall into enemy hands', no such definition of 'intent' was given in Section 113 on espionage. The judges ruled that Section 99 defined the essence of 'intention' for Section 113 as well. Their interpretation is questionable, because the penal law on state security and official secrets is itself divided into six articles, among them 'General Provisions', 'Espionage' and 'Treason'. If the wider interpretation of intent had been intended by the drafters of the penal law to be applied in other sections dealing with state security, this should have been included under the General Provisions at the beginning rather than under a specific section, namely, that dealing with treason. The judges, in effect, had applied a ruling on one specific article from another separate specific article, Treason.

Notwithstanding that two of the judges rejected the ideological motives Vanunu claimed, the court concluded its ruling by noting that 'the worst crimes in the history of humanity have been done from ideological motives. No ideological goal sanctifies the use of illegal means. Moreover, the danger from ideological criminals is perhaps greater than from other types of criminals.' Quoting law professor Itzhak Zamir, the court said that ideological criminals not only transgress the law but place the state infrastructure itself in danger. Since they are often seen in positive terms, they become a focus of identification for their respective causes, and will take measures and violence 'perhaps to the extent of rebellion and uprising against authority, that is, against democratic society'.

When the judges announced their verdict, Vanunu addressed the court and said that he did not regret publishing the information, but with hindsight he would not have done it. As he read the sixty-page verdict he could not hide his disappointment, and intermittently put his head in his hands. Vanunu had expected to be found guilty of espionage only. 'I am not a traitor, I didn't intend to damage the security of the state. I am very disappointed that the court did not accept the message which I tried to give it: that I did what I did for ideological reasons,' Vanunu said to Feldman.[47]

He was sentenced to eighteen years' imprisonment, less than the twenty demanded by the prosecution. His being held in solitary confinement, cooperation in the Shin Bet interrogation, and expression of some regret in his final statements to the court all contributed to the judges' decision to reduce the sentence. Had the issue of the bomb exercised the Israeli public, it is most questionable whether Vanunu would have been given the harsh sentence he received.

Asher Vanunu's reaction to the verdict and sentence was: 'Mordechai didn't murder, he didn't rape. He had good intentions. Nobody understood him.' But his father, Shlomo, said: 'My honour has gone. It is a disgrace to the family. But this is my son. Do you know a father that doesn't love his son? What can I do? We were more successful with our daughters: they married men of (Jewish) learning. And this son destroyed our life and honour.' In London, Meir Vanunu, who like Asher had hoped the court would not find Mordechai guilty of treason, attacked the court 'for not succeeding in rising above narrow state interests, and pronouncing on the nuclear issue in general.' There would be an appeal to the Supreme Court, and he would lobby international public opinion against the sentence.

The Vanunu trial had parallels with a case before the US courts, involving a civilian naval intelligence analyst, Samuel Loring Morison, who also worked as a part-time American editor of the London-based *Jane's Fighting Ships*.

In 1984 Morison gave US satellite photos of a new Soviet aircraft-carrier he had spotted on a colleague's desk to *Jane's Defence Weekly*. The Reagan administration used the 1917 Espionage Act to charge Morison with espionage. He was the first person ever to be so charged by a US court for leaking classified information to the news media. Morison contended in his defence that in passing the Espionage Act Congress had not intended that espionage apply to leaks to the news media. He invoked the First Amendment, pointing out the danger of a citizen being tried for thus leaking information. But US circuit judge Donald Russell rejected this. 'The mere fact that one has stolen a document in order [to] deliver it to the press, whether for money or for other personal gain, will not immunize him from responsibility for his criminal act. To use the First Amendment for such a purpose would be to convert the First Amendment into a warrant for thievery.' In October 1985 he was sentenced to two years' imprisonment.

There were similarities and differences in how the Israeli and US courts dealt with the respective cases. If in the Vanunu trial much of the discussion concerned whether to extend his crime from espionage to treason; the Morison trial never considered this: it was a question of whether or not it was a case of espionage. Two of the three judges, while agreeing with Russell's verdict, were concerned with the media's and the public's right to know. Judge James Wilkinson said that 'the First Amendment interest in informed popular debate does not simply vanish at the invocation of the words "national security".' In the Morison defence as well, questions of motivation, and of actual damage to the security of the country, were raised. The US government contended that Morison, by making public the photographs, had alerted Soviet intelligence to the capabilities of US satellite intelligence-gathering techniques. The defence argued that the Soviets were aware of the capacity of US satellites, and even had a stolen manual of the KH-11 satellite which had been used to take the photos. They also argued that Morison, a patriot, was warning of the Soviet threat. But Judge Russell said that he had been fired not 'by zeal for public debate' but by 'self-interest' to ingratiate himself with *Jane*'s.[48]

The key arguments Avigdor Feldman raised in Vanunu's defence in the Jerusalem District Court were heard again at the appeal before the Israel Supreme Court in May 1989. A tendency for the Supreme Court to discuss broader legal questions – in the Vanunu case these included such basic definitions as motivation, intent, assistance to the enemy, damage to state security – gave Feldman hope that it would recognise some of the weaknesses in the penal system on which he pinned his client's defence, and which he had unsuccessfully raised at the earlier trial.

It was noteworthy that the appeal, before three Supreme Court judges, was chaired by Meir Shamgar, president of Israel's Supreme Court. A former advocate-general of the Israeli army, Shamgar had a particular interest in defence matters, and has shown a general inclination to accept prosecution claims in classified intelligence evidence.[49] Yet, while advocate-general he had introduced the application of international law to the military administration of the West Bank and Gaza, and later, as the government's law adviser, made it possible for residents of the West Bank and Gaza to appeal to the Israel Supreme Court.

Feldman restated his argument that the law of treason – 'a person with intent to assist an enemy in war' – implied a special type of intention. That treason was mere knowledge that the information might fall into enemy hands presupposed this special intent. Vanunu never had intent to assist the enemy. But Judge Shamgar rejected the need to prove 'certainty' concerning the result of his actions; a 'high probability' was sufficient. A person was assumed to intend the natural and probable consequences of his actions.

Feldman argued that Vanunu's motives had been incorrectly interpreted by the majority of the District Court, Judges Noam and Brenner. Hasson's portrait had been one-sided, and he asked the Supreme Court to accept the minority opinion of Judge Tal that Vanunu had been motivated primarily by ideological factors. But the Supreme Court said that under Israeli law motive was immaterial regarding criminal responsibility. The law existed to protect the organs of government and was interested only in the intent of a person as expressed by their actions. Shamgar quoted British judge Lord Devlin that 'rebels and high-minded spies could be heard to argue that defeat in battle would serve the best interests of the nation because it would be better off under a different régime.' There could be no question of good faith where a person published secret information in the knowledge that there was 'a high probability' that the publication would damage state security, Shamgar said. Feldman then argued that the Vanunu exposé, rather than causing damage to state security, had heightened perception of the country's nuclear capability. Shamgar replied that Vanunu did not have authority to decide what was in Israel's defence interests; that authority rested with the government.

According to Professor Mordechai Kremnitzer, law dean

of The Hebrew University, Jerusalem, Vanunu's action could have helped an enemy, but treason was an inappropriate offence to charge him with. It went too far: 'One needs to distinguish between information given to the media and the normal type of espionage for two reasons. First, when something has appeared in the media it is possible to take steps to repair the damage, which one is unable to do when the information was conveyed in secret. The injured country has an advantage when it knows what the enemy knows. Second, the treason charge comes close to stopping freedom of expression and the public's right to know. There is a difference between going to a foreign intelligence agency and to the media. There should therefore be a separate offence in the penal system for revealing classified secrets to the public.'

Feldman repeated his argument that, under Section 94, Vanunu had acted in good faith to bring about a change by lawful means, through pressure from informed public opinion. Shamgar said that 'the attitude that ends of motivation satisfy the means is the antithesis of democratic rule.' There was no contradiction between democracy and secrecy: all free states recognised the right of competent authorities to enforce secrecy for the protection of the state. It appeared that Vanunu had confused democracy with anarchy. Feldman countered that '"secret" was what the authorities saw fit to guard as secret'. In a narrow sense, nuclear issues were under legislative control because Section 113 (d) recognises a category of information 'that the security of the state requires its being kept secret – information which the government, with the approval of the Knesset's Foreign Affairs and Defence Committee has declared to be secret.' Nuclear information was one of these.

Notwithstanding his concern for defence interests, Shamgar has a reputation for defending the freedom of expression. In trials involving libel, for example, he has given more importance to freedom of expression than to an individual's reputation. In rejecting Feldman's appeal, he was in effect saying that nuclear matters should remain secret. Shamgar sees the Supreme Court as a seismograph of public attitudes, and notes that laws require public legitimacy. Wide public support for Israel's possession of nuclear capability, and agreement that the subject be secret, creates the strong emotional public involvement with Shamgar knows is a key to national security. But, in a wider sense, criticism by members of the committee itself over the years about their being inadequately briefed by government officials suggests that Shamgar's perception of the legislative control on nuclear matters by this committee is inaccurate. His judgement also ignored the rights of minority groups in a democracy to be informed and to discuss this issue of crucial importance. Shamgar lost an important opportunity to focus attention on these lacunae in Israel's democracy.

Shamgar also questioned whether Vanunu really wanted to reach the Israeli public. After all, why publish the information in a British newspaper, whose Israeli audience was minuscule? 'Rather, it was a blow at Israel from abroad in front of all its inhabitants,' Shamgar claimed.[50] The judge failed to deal with the censorship which existed in Israel on all nuclear matters prior to Vanunu's exposé. Although fringe interest groups had campaigned against nuclear weapons, there had been no debate on the subject among the wider public. Where Feldman's argument that Vanunu had acted in good faith to bring about lawful change may be questioned, was that Vanunu (as Shamgar argued) could have breached secrecy in a less drastic way. Notwithstanding the lack of formal procedures, he could have contacted the State Comptroller's Office or the chairman of the Knesset's Foreign Affairs and Defence Committee. In going to a leading foreign newspaper Vanunu had breached secrecy on a wanton scale.

The defence derived some satisfaction from the trial itself. A debate on the nuclear issue was held in the end – even if the press benches were unoccupied and the rest of the world could not follow it. The judges were there, as was history, if only for the record, and international experts had come to testify. Even if the debate-of-sorts was not essentially about whether Israel should have the bomb, and whether its possession is morally justifiable, the questions cropped up within the framework of Vanunu's motivations and whether he had impaired state security. It was the first time an Israeli court had addressed itself to the status of nuclear weaponry in international law and the rights of the individual to disclose official secrets to the media. The minority opinion that he had been ideologically motivated gave Vanunu some hope that the Supreme Court would address the deeper-seated issues which underlay the State of Israel v Mordechai Vanunu. The innate truth that there is no nuclear debate in Israel, and that this lack is actively encouraged by the government, had added to these hopes. But the rejection of the appeal, and of a request for a re-appeal at the end of 1991, put paid to Vanunu's challenge to the government and Knesset. With the closing of legal channels, the realisation that he would be released from prison only in 2004, or at the earliest in 1998, induced a period of depression and helplessness.

Vanunu has been in solitary confinement since October 1986. His cell in an isolated wing of Ashkelon prison measures three metres by two metres; it has a bed, shelf and table and a small window above head height. The cell has a drain which doubles as a lavatory and a shower. Initially, his light was kept on for twenty-four hours a day, and there was a close-up camera because the authorities feared he might damage himself. He spends much of the day reading; his choice of literature is eclectic: Thomas Mann, T. S. Eliot, Kafka, Spinoza, Shakespeare. He is allowed out to an isolated exercise yard for two hours, and he does yoga on his cell floor.

The solitary confinement is characterised by an almost total absence of contact with the outside world. The only people he can talk to are his family, whom he is allowed to see for half an hour every two weeks, or an hour once a month. All meetings are in the presence of the prison governor or senior prison warder and a security agent. He can see his lawyer any time he wishes; in practice once a month or once in two months. He is not allowed to see any friends; early in his imprisonment the authorities refused to let him see a former girlfriend because, they said, he had passed secret information and might still do so. Seeing his relatives and his lawyer is hardly compensation for forming or maintaining relationships. The authorities agreed to his using cassettes, which could be vetted, but Vanunu is not given access to a telephone, a privilege accorded most Israeli prisoners. A small consolation is a radio, generally forbidden in Israeli prisons because prisoners might fight over the tuning in to stations. He listens often to the BBC World Service, and he also has a television set. He reads the English-language *Jerusalem Post*, and his brother has arranged subscriptions to a number of magazines. According to his lawyer, 'Vanunu reacts to world events. He is most interested in the nuclear arms question both within the Middle Eastern context like Iraq, and the superpower context and US–Russian arms reductions.'

Initially, he kept up a wide correspondence notwithstanding the rigorous censorship of his outgoing mail. He has written to the Israeli media and politicians on nuclear matters, and to individuals like Peter Hounam and Frank Barnaby. But by 1990, the fourth year of his imprisonment, he wrote seldom, even to his close brother, Meir, in London. In a letter to Meir in early 1991, he wrote, 'I have written you many letters – but they don't let me send them to you. I have a lot to tell. But they're still using their powers to close my mouth – but they're unable to close my brain. When I am free, I will speak . . . I have nothing to lose.' Another contact was a priest who used to celebrate communion once a month, mostly on Sunday. The Reverend John McKnight, who converted Vanunu to Christianity, writes about once a month.

Vanunu is not the only security prisoner in Israel held in solitary confinement.[51] In the long term, such prisoners suffer a variety of psychological and physical disorders including emotional disturbances, impairment of concentration and ability to think, loss of reality, neuroses, sleep disturbances, headaches, dizziness, low blood pressure, and circulation and digestive problems. While for the first years of his imprisonment Vanunu was concerned with his trial and the court appeal, there is now little for him to hope for. At the beginning, he had delusions that he was being followed by the security services. By 1991 he had spells of dizziness, a lack of balance, and difficulties in concentrating.

Asher Vanunu, another brother, attempted to get some left-wing Knesset members to improve his prison conditions, but with little success. So did the Israel Association of Civil Rights. According to Avigdor Feldman, the solitary confinement is routinely renewed every six months by the prison governor upon instructions from the Shin Bet without apparent recourse to the courts. Feldman appealed to a Jerusalem court in 1991 to have solitary confinement ended, but the prosecution charged that the incident of Vanunu's palm message was evidence of his determination to continue disclosing information. There had also been instances during prison meetings with his family, during one of which, according to a secret agent named Boaz, Vanunu told his brothers 'about the place from where he was brought to Israel, the vehicle in which he was brought and the methods employed to bring him there'. According to Boaz, he asked his brothers to arrange for the information to be published abroad.[52] In his correspondence with foreign organisations he pressed them to continue to publish additional information.

Feldman claimed rather than solitary confinement Vanunu

should be brought to trial in the event of his disclosing more information. Underlying the policy of solitary confinement was a clash between what Vanunu saw as his right and responsibility to disclose information and what the authorities saw as their right to protect secrets. Some perceived solitary confinement as an attempt by the security authorities to seal Vanunu's lips by driving him crazy.

Judge Zvi Cohen said that Vanunu had completed five years in conditions of isolation. These were without doubt difficult, but the key was in Vanunu's hands. Yet, Cohen added, the authorities also had an obligation to take the sting out of the 'information which Vanunu still wants to publish', and recommend that another prisoner, chosen by the prison governor, join Vanunu in his cell. The judge's decision was a first step towards the eventual end to solitary confinement. Although Feldman suggested that Vanunu at least try it for an experimental period, Vanunu – suspecting the cell-mate would inform on him – turned down the offer, claiming that the authorities did not have the right to decide who the cell-mate should be.

Amnesty International, which sent observers to his trial and appeal, has called his conditions of imprisonment 'cruel, inhuman and degrading', and a category of ill-treatment one level below torture. They claim that steps could be taken by the prison authorities to ensure Vanunu did not disclose more information as well as 'protecting' him from 'other prisoners', another reason given for his isolation, without solitary confinement. These included a prison warder nearby when Vanunu is with other prisoners.

His solitary confinement engendered sympathy among anti-nuclear groups around the world. Organisations like the Bertrand Russell Peace Foundation and the Association for Peace in Italy lobbied local politicians as well as the Israeli authorities, and engaged in informational activities. For these groups, Mordechai Vanunu was a way to draw public attention to the danger of nuclearisation in the Middle East.

There was most interest in western Europe, in particular Britain and Italy, and also among groups in Australia. Lack of enthusiasm in the United States caused Vanunu sympathisers to claim a 'conspiracy of silence' between the US administration, Congress, and the media, but the real reason was the lack of US official reaction to the Israeli nuclear programme which, in turn, contributed to lack of public interest in the subject. Church groups supporting anti-nuclearism as part of their activities for peace and justice, notably those within the Quaker movement, the Anglican Church, and the United Reform Church or United Church, have taken up the Vanunu cause. Some dozen support groups in both Britain and Australia write letters to Vanunu, according to McKnight, 'to help him feel that he is not forgotten'. Other church leaders have been hesitant to enter potential conflict with Israel and the Jewish community.

By the end of the eighties, sympathy for Vanunu began to permeate to liberal and socialist politicians. Following the rejection by the Supreme Court of his appeal, the European Parliament called on President Herzog to pardon Vanunu. Failing this, aid and scientific cooperation between the European Community and Israel could be 'delayed'. But the realignment of the Middle East in the 1991 Gulf War, with Israel identified with the US-led coalition, resulted in these agreements being implemented. The Vanunu issue has occasionally been raised in individual parliaments: the Green Party in Germany has taken it up, and left-wing politicians in Italy have pressured their government to pursue Vanunu's abduction from Italy. Internationally-acclaimed scientists who identify with the anti-nuclear lobby have added their names to appeals to the Israeli authorities.

Vanunu has been nominated for the Nobel Peace Prize, and in 1987 he was awarded 'the Right Livelihood Award', worth US$25,000, a sort of alternative prize dealing with issues such as ecology and anti-nuclearism. There has been considerable discussion in Amnesty International about

258

making Vanunu a Prisoner of Conscience. He fits Amnesty's classification because he is non-violent, and his action was motivated by conscience, but since he disclosed military secrets (which a country has a right to under international law) the organisation withheld the status. He joins a group which includes Daniel Ellsberg, not accorded the status for disclosing the Pentagon Papers, and Nelson Mandela, who backed armed struggle.

The campaign on Mordechai Vanunu's behalf is spearheaded by his brother Meir, an articulate Hebrew University law graduate. He has contacted a great number of politicians in various countries, and is a featured speaker at conferences on nuclear issues. He has tried to walk a thin line of aligning himself with the anti-nuclear movement while ensuring that prominence is given to his brother's plight. The ultimate measure of success would of course be his brother's release, but Israel has steadfastly refused to bow to what amounts to fringe group pressure on this sensitive matter. The campaign is a public relations annoyance, little more, but it has ensured that the Israeli authorities know there are groups monitoring his condition.

More widely, the Israeli nuclear theme has been addressed – but mainly within the anti-nuclear movement. Vanunu never conquered the wider public attention or the international political agenda. As superpower rivalry ended, concern with the nuclear proliferation was replaced by issues such as economic recession, unemployment and the environment. And even though the 1991 Iraq war reminded people of the danger of non-conventional weaponry in the region, there was no fall-out for Vanunu's personal fate.

9. A Consensus of Silence

A truly democratic government which follows a policy of ambiguity in nuclear development or in any other sphere of official policy has still to reconcile itself with the principle of governmental accountability. The Israeli case is a litmus test of the tensions involved. According to David Kimche, former director-general of the Israel Foreign Ministry: 'Every democracy has a policy of ambiguity about certain subjects. No democracy reveals everything because no democracy wants to be self-defeating. The problems facing Israel cannot be compared to western Europe. A democracy has first and foremost to preserve its democratic existence as an entity and that's what we are doing. It is a mistake to say that everything in a democracy has to be open.' But does it have to be an either/or situation? Should public discussion of even the broader issues around the nuclear option be officially discouraged?

There remains in Israel a widespread public deference to authority on the broad range of questions relating to national security. The *'sacredness of security', or kedushat habitachon*, permeates a society which throughout its forty-odd years' existence has had to face threats to its very existence. Referring to the Davidic psalm, 'The Guardian of Israel will neither slumber nor sleep', a public opinion poll in 1986 asked Israelis whom they saw as the 'Guardian of Israel.' Fifty-seven per cent replied the Israeli army, 17 per cent God, 13 per cent the state of Israel, 10 per cent the people of Israel, 2 per cent the United States, and 2 per cent said everyone must guard themselves.

'In the Israeli mentality there is a recognition that there are secret things on nuclear matters going on. The government knows best and doesn't fool around. Also, there are more immediate problems which come before the nuclear issue,' said Menachem Shalev, diplomatic correspondent of *Davar*. 'I am just amazed how much the nuclear issue fails to arouse Israeli public interest,' remarked Peter Hounam. The large segment of Israel's population of immigrants from eastern Europe and from Arab countries, neither of whom had experience of democratic participation, has only compounded this attitude. There is also a conscious recognition by many Israelis that freedom of access to information, particularly regarding defence matters, is not an absolute value, such as in some other western countries, but is a relative one which has to take its place with other values around the absolute of national survival. 'The public accepts the ambiguity: if we are not sure we have the bomb we don't have to think about it,' Professor Dan Horowitz of the Hebrew University argued. According to Mordechai Gur, a former Labour Party minister, and himself a former chief of staff, 'The public knows quite well that as a result of the continuous threat by the Arab countries we have to survive and take measures in order to survive. No Israeli wants to know all the details. If you ask most Israelis they don't have the feeling that they are being kept in secrecy.'

The media have been under tight military censorship regarding all Israeli nuclear-related material lest this weaken the image of ambiguity. But while a detailed discussion of Dimona remains in the realm of the most forbidden, unless foreign sources are quoted, there has been an opening up of the subject. In the sixties even indirect mention of Israel's possessing a nuclear capability was blue-pencilled by the censor, because it made Israel's nuclear option too visible. When early in 1967, prior to the Six Day War, Zeev Schiff,

Haaretz's military correspondent, wrote a series of articles which included Arab perceptions of Israel's nuclear potential, it was banned by the censor, Colonel Walter Bar-On, on the grounds that it was based on what the Arabs were saying and not on what the Israelis were saying. *Haaretz* has been subject through the years to requests from Israeli officials not to publish matters relating to the nuclear issue; on one occasion when the censor's guidelines did not allow for a particular item to be banned, a senior Israeli official approached the paper's editorial board arguing that its publication would encourage an 'undesirable' public discussion in Israel. The paper turned down the request.

Military censorship is integral to Israel's deterrent posture. Thus, in April 1986, journalists were barred by the censor from reporting remarks made by an army briefing officer on the possibility that Syria might be in a position to use chemical weapons against Israel. At the end of 1986 military spokesmen began to speak more openly about Syrian possession of chemical weaponry. Today, with the considerable undermining of the ambiguous image, there has begun to be an easing of the censor's limitations of discussion of the broader issues involved. It parallels greater public and media sceptism of the military in general which followed the 1973 and 1982 wars. Prior to the 1973 war, correspondents acceded to the censor's requests not to publish intelligence warnings about Egyptian and Syrian military manoeuvres lest it arouse public concern. Had these warnings been published, the national emergency call-up might have begun earlier, resulting in many fewer casualties.

Acquiescence in censorship by the Israeli media need not be contrary to the theory of a free press. A democracy may impose its own limitations on freedom of expression, such as artistic freedom, as well as on matters concerning national security so long as these are determined by the people rather than the government. A 1987 public opinion poll commissioned by Tel Aviv University's Jaffee Centre for Stra-

262

tegic Studies found that of the Israelis questioned, 78 per cent favoured secrecy regarding Israel's nuclear capability. When, in the aftermath of Vanunu, Hannah Zemer, editor of *Davar*, raised the nuclear issue in the paper, she, as well as other Israeli editors who had done so, was inundated with letters from readers, including reservist army officers, claiming the newspapers had divulged Israel's secrets to the enemy, even though the material had been cleared by the military censor.

Where the foreign media are concerned, the level of commitment to respecting information which a foreign public may desire to remain secret is minimal if non-existent. 'What if a foreign government is using secrets to cover incompetence or prejudice or political bias to militate in its own political interest?' asked Godfrey Hodgson, a former Insight team staffer. 'Our business is to disseminate news if we think it is important, not to calculate to the nth degree a possible consequence of publication. Unless there is a specific danger to life, the function of the press is to publish.' According to former *Sunday Times* editor Frank Giles, 'the argument that the revelation of Israel's nuclear secrets could have led to an escalating nuclear arms race in the region is the argument of the statesman and not the editor. The possibility of escalation is very hypothetical. If the *Sunday Times* had discovered, say, that the Pakistanis or Indians had a nuclear capability, it would have been a first-rate news story, and one of major world interest. But if there was clear-cut evidence that publication would lead to an innocent man's death, such as a British secret agent, or possibly someone of another Western country, I would certainly withhold the story.'

In Israel, the imposition of censorship is what determines the foreign media's compliance with the country's view of national security interests. Thomas Friedman, the Pulitzer Prize Jerusalem correspondent of the *New York Times* from 1984–8 did not investigate the Israeli nuclear story. 'Why

263

waste my limited resources of time and energy for a story I can't publish unless I am thrown out of the country,' he asked. 'And why', he added, 'get thrown out of a country for a story that is already known?' According to Charles Richards, then Jerusalem correspondent of the *Independent*, London, 'with the exception of the Israeli nuclear story, and one or two other matters, censorship doesn't affect my work as a foreign correspondent.' When, in the early sixties, David Rubinger, *Time*'s photographer in Israel, snapped the Dimona reactor from beyond the perimeter fence, he had 'a night-long argument on the phone with the censor. I won in the end because I convinced him that the American U-2 spyplane could shoot more than I could ever photograph from the ground. To this day it's the only picture of Dimona that has ever made it through censorship.' Gideon Berli, who worked for Deutsches Presse Agentur, the West German news agency, and was a former chairman of Israel's Foreign Press Association, said, 'We can do a little more than the Israeli media on the nuclear story but in practice we are limited because we have no sources.' Berli, who was an Israeli national, added: 'I respect the importance of this subject for the safety of the country much more than selling it as a good news story. If other journalists are not doing it, why should I play Vanunu?'

In a statement made in March 1988 after Vanunu's sentencing, *Sunday Times* editor Andrew Neil acknowledged that democratic countries had to protect their secrets in their national interest. He noted that for most Israelis Vanunu was a traitor, but pointed out that in other democracies citizens know whether their country has nuclear weapons and that only with such information can they make enlightened decisions. Further, it is in the general interest for countries which are nuclear to be identified. Neil's statement creates as many questions as answers. His underlying premise was that Israelis did not know that Israel possessed a nuclear capability. In a public opinion poll in January 1986, nine months before the *Sunday Times* publication, the Jaffee Centre for Strategic Studies found that 92 per cent of Israelis questioned believed that Israel already had nuclear weapons: 54 per cent of those asked were sure that Israel had nuclear weapons and 38 per cent thought that Israel did but were not sure. Only 7 per cent did not think Israel had, but were not sure, and only 1 per cent said they were sure that Israel had not. It was a considerable increase over a survey commissioned in 1976 by *Haaretz* which found that 62.3 per cent thought Israel possessed a nuclear weapon. Only 4.3 per cent, however, thought that Israel did not possess one. A third of those asked, 33.4 per cent, said they did not know.

A second question concerns Neil's – as well as Vanunu's – premise that Israelis wish to debate the subject: 78 per cent of Israelis support the policy of secrecy. Moreover, 'the general interest to know who is a nuclear power and who is not' carries much less weight given the Israeli consensus in favour of ambiguity.

Taken to its logical conclusion, this would mean that a news organisation should not reveal foreign news which a particular society wishes to remain secret. 'Is it any obligation of Israel to tell you, or anyone else, every secret matter that we have in this country?' asked Israeli minister Ehud Olmert rhetorically about the *Sunday Times* disclosure. For Dr Frank Barnaby, the dilemma is, 'On the one hand I believe that people should not break the law. On the other hand, Vanunu's argument about the consequences for world security, which I sympathise with, overrides issues of national security. If a person feels strongly about it his duty overrides any official secrets act.' In his statement Neil said that nuclear matters were of world concern. Hounam added: 'It could drag other states into a nuclear war.'

But what did Neil hope to achieve since the Israeli population believes the country possesses a nuclear capability? The questions of the public's rights and of the responsibilities of the foreign media to it remain unresolved. At best, Neil sketched a muddled defence of the free media. At worst, he attempted to rationalise publication of a good scoop. 'The security considerations', an editorial executive said, 'were never part of our decision-making in the Vanunu investigation. It is not part of our job to consider Israeli security. If we had to balance the argument it would have been that nuclear secrecy is a bad thing and if we are in a position to throw some light on it we have a duty to.' Asked whether the *Sunday Times* would reveal the inner workings of a secret British nuclear facility, he remarked 'We wouldn't try!'

The clash between Israeli national security and the foreign media in the guise of the *Sunday Times* resurfaced three years later with the Sheikh Obeid affair, when the paper's roving Middle East correspondent broke Israeli censorship regulations and revealed that Sheikh Obeid, a Shi'ite cleric, abducted from southern Lebanon, claimed that two of three Israeli soldiers which had fallen into Hizbollah hands, and whose release the Israelis were demanding as the price for the release of the cleric, were dead. The Israeli army claims that until proven otherwise missing soldiers are presumed alive. The Israeli army had an interest in recommending that the claim that two of the soldiers are dead be censored because Israel's negotiating position is weakened if her expectations are lower. Israeli officials were concerned about US pressure to free Obeid in exchange for the American hostages held in Lebanon. From a news organisation's perspective, non-publication in the interest of gaining the release of hostages cannot be justified by saying that it might perhaps – but only perhaps – contribute to the hostages' release.

On Friday, 26 September 1986 the Israel Editors' Committee was called into urgent session by Prime Minister Peres. 'It was quite unexpected – at the very unconventional time of 2 p.m. on the eve of the Sabbath. We were afraid that Peres was going to tell us that war was going to break out that same evening,' remarked Hannah Zemer. As recounted earlier, Peres told the assembled editors that the *Sunday Times* was about to publish the revelations of the runaway technician and asked them to abstain from seeking Israeli reactions to the story for the first forty-eight hours. It would have been impossible to stop any discussion in the long term. After the first forty-eight hours editors would be free to print whatever they wanted after clearance from censorship. The concern was not so much Israeli public reaction or even US reaction but Egyptian and other Arab world reaction.

Even though Israeli officials had known for nearly a month that Vanunu was in touch with the *Sunday Times*, Peres convened the committee only after the newspaper had turned to the Israeli embassy in London for its reaction and it seemed clear the paper was about to publish. Initially, Israeli editors told Peres that they could not abstain from reporting reactions and comment, but after Peres explained that anything coming out of Israel would make things more sensitive, no objections were raised. 'It was an appeal to our patriotism, and we complied with it,' one editor said. 'I am a responsible Israeli,' said Ari Rath, editor of the *Jerusalem Post*. It was not a difficult choice for editors for another reason. They did not know what the *Sunday Times* was going to publish. Even if they had some idea, no editor had the type of detailed information about the nuclear research centre which the *Sunday Times* had. The Israel Journalists Association, which had previously criticised the Editors' Committee as an institution which enabled officialdom to gag the press, later met to condemn both Peres and editors. Although in the end none of the assembled editors objected to Peres's request, a formal vote was not taken. And Gershon Schocken, the publisher and editor-in-chief of *Haaretz*, went away believing that Peres's request had not been accepted. After the *Sunday Times* published some nine days later, an editorial *Haaretz* planned to publish alongside a reprint of the three page *Sunday Times* disclosure was impounded by the censor. In protest the paper left its editorial column blank. About 70 per cent of a planned editorial in *Al Hamishmar* was also censored.

The misunderstanding between Peres and *Haaretz* originated in the absence of any objections. At a subsequent meeting of the Editors' Committee, editors decided that in future a formal vote should be taken when a government minister requested non-publication of a specific piece of information. However, this would still leave the minister in the vulnerable position of having to volunteer information before obtaining the editors' agreement not to publish it. It was finally agreed that at the beginning of each meeting the chairman would clarify the rules of the game, and that the information would be non-publishable only if everybody agreed to it by vote there and then.

Ironically, the editors have never discussed among themselves the question of the lack of reporting on nuclear issues. Individual quality newspapers, including *Haaretz*, *Davar* and *Al Hamishmar*, have carried articles since 1986 on the broader question of nuclear policy, although these have mostly been by outside contributors rather than, say, the specialist correspondents. The mass circulation afternoon newspapers, *Yediot Aharonot* and *Maariv*, have not discussed the issue. 'I will let someone write about it once a year because the subject has been exhausted,' said Iddo Dissentschik, editor of *Maariv*. By contrast, *Hadashot*, a multi-coloured tabloid established in 1984 and the only national newspaper not to belong to the Editors' Committee, attempted to raise reader interest by focusing on Mordechai Vanunu's own story. Since 1990, and the build-up to and aftermath of the Gulf War, including Saddam Hussein's threat to 'scorch half of Israel' with chemical weapons, the Israeli media have reported at length on the non-conventional arms aspects of the Arab–Israeli military balance – within the confines of a rigorous censor's blue pencil on information about the Israeli nuclear capability.

London bureaux of the international news media summarised the *Sunday Times* exposé. Their correspondents in Israel – who do not enjoy a status similar to the Editors' Committee – were censored in their reporting of Israeli reaction, including material which had appeared in open sources. Two-thirds of the despatch sent by Ian Murray, the correspondent of *The Times*, was censored. His protests were in vain. 'It is I, not you, who is the judge of what can damage Israel's security,' the censor told him. Later, in limiting access to information about Vanunu's abduction, his being charged, and the trial behind closed doors, Israeli officials were not only attempting to limit disclosure of the circumstances in which Vanunu was brought to Israel but also the renewed lease of life which the abduction story gave to the original *Sunday Times* disclosure.

Vanunu's goal 'of opening up the subject to debate' had been partly achieved. In the fifties and sixties scientists and politicians who attempted to raise the matter received officially-inspired threats. Eliezer Livneh, a Knesset member of the ruling Mapam party, who attempted to raise debate on the nuclear question, was called in by Israeli officials and warned that charges would be brought against him. In 1976 the first programme in *Second Look*, or *Mabat Sheni*, Israel Television's flagship current affairs programme, which was entitled 'Israel's nuclear option', was banned by the Israel Broadcasting Authority's director-general 'because the subject is delicate, and would arouse public discussion much beyond what had been discussed up to that time'. 'The function of television is to report information and not cause public discussion,' the director-general, who is a government appointee, added. A book, *None Will Survive Us, the Story of the Israeli A-Bomb*, by lawyer Eli Teicher and journalist Ami Dor-On was banned in its entirety by the censor in 1980, and its authors warned that they would face fifteen years' imprisonment if they ever revealed its contents. When Dan Raviv, CBS Radio correspondent in Israel, reported the banning of the book, and the book's claim about Israeli –South African nuclear cooperation, he became the second foreign correspondent in Israel's history to have his press credentials cancelled.

Writing about nuclear and non-conventional warfare at all was rare, and journalists were discouraged from doing so. 'There is no doubt that this was an error, and I include myself among those responsible for it,' said *Haaretz*'s Zeev Schiff. 'The result has been that the majority of writings about nuclear weapons in Israel and the Middle East has come from foreign sources, not a few of which were full of basic errors, and, what is worse, also written with the intention of harming Israel.' These words were written in a special issue of *Politika*, the intellectual review of the Citizens' Rights Movement, which was devoted to the nuclear subject. Ironically, during the Vanunu Affair Schiff did not address the nuclear issue in the wider circulation pages of his newspaper.

Yet it would be incorrect to say that there had been no debate within informed circles or that there has been no organised opinion on the subject. A number of groups surfaced over the previous twenty-five years which campaigned on an anti-nuclear platform. These include a group led by Hillel Schenker of *New Outlook*, Mapam's intellectual review; and the Committee for Nuclear Disarmament in the Arab–Israeli region in the sixties, whose leaders included Professor Yeshayahu Leibowitz, the scientist and philosopher. More recently a group formed around Professor Avner Cohen of Tel Aviv University and co-author of *Nuclear Weapons and the Future of Humanity*.

As early as 1964, a serious study of Israeli nuclear strategy, *Nuclear War and Nuclear Peace*, by a former head of military intelligence, Professor Yehoshafat Harkabi, appeared in Hebrew and went immediately into a second printing. In

1966 it was published in English. Yigal Allon, the former Labour minister, articulated his thinking in *A Curtain of Sand*. Academics like Professors Shai Feldman and Yair Evron, and journalists like Avraham Schweitzer of *Haaretz*, the late Haggai Eshed of *Davar*, and Ephraim Kishon have discussed the issue. But discussion has often been in circumlocution. Thus, at the foot of an article in the Israeli academic journal, *State, Government and International Relations*, by Alan Dowty, then of the Hebrew University, articulating the unambiguous case for nuclear ambiguity, was appended the disclaimer: 'This article is based entirely on published sources. The author had no access to classified information, he is not linked to the Israeli government nor did he receive official or background guidance in preparing this article.'

At the parliamentary level the question of nuclear capability has been brought up by left-wing members over the years. In November 1987 Mattityahu Peled of the Progressive Peace List tabled a no-confidence motion because of the government's failure to respond to an Egyptian proposal for a nuclear-free zone in the Middle East. 'Israel's nuclear policy endangers Israel by encouraging an Arab arms race,' he argued. Replying, a deputy government minister said that Israel supports a nuclear-free zone as part and parcel of a wider peace agreement between Arab states and Israel. But with broad bipartisan support among Likud and Labour, the main political parties, for the nuclear option and the policy of ambiguity, no wide parliamentary discussion which might stimulate discussion among the public at large has resulted. The question has surfaced in the Knesset when related matters have come up: when two nuclear reactors were purchased from France in 1984, Meir Wilner of the Democratic Peace List charged that they were to be used for defensive–military purposes rather than civilian purposes as the government claimed. Health safety from radioactive waste came up in June 1988 in a debate on the environment. But no full discussion took place after the *Sunday Times* disclosure. Opening a debate on the general political situation, two days after the exposé, however, Yair Tzaban of Mapam, which also supports a nuclear-free zone, said that 'even though the subject has captured the headlines – in a sensational manner from every perspective – it is forbidden to use this as an excuse to sweep the issue under the carpet.'

'Who is Vanunu to pass a judgement about decisions which were made in a democratic process in a democratic country?' asked Minister Olmert. He would have been right in almost any other sphere of public policy in a country characterised by vigorous debate and political infighting. But Vanunu's claim that crucial decisions in Israel's nuclear programme were taken outside the parliamentary process, and even without the full consent of the Cabinet, is well-founded. At the time of the building of the nuclear research centre at Dimona, the Knesset's Defence and Foreign Affairs Committee had received only a general summary of the project – and that only after it had been published in the newspapers. The decision to build the reactor was kept even from members of the Knesset's Defence Budget Committee, which is usually informed of fiscal matters even if they are top secret. Prime Minister David Ben-Gurion did not inform the Knesset about the nuclear reactor until 1960, when under pressure from the US administration; he reassured Knesset members that it was for peaceful purposes only. There was a great outcry in the Knesset, with indignant charges of concealment levelled at the government. Haim Landau of the right-wing Herut Party and a member of the Defence and Foreign Affairs Committee complained that 'the most important fact regarding the atomic reactor was not made known to us, and that was deliberate subterfuge.' But Ben-Gurion was steadfast: 'security' justified the silence. *Time* claimed that the plutonium processing plant was constructed at Ben-Gurion's and Moshe Dayan's initiative without the Cabinet's knowledge or consent. Today, nuclear arms policy is discussed by the 'forum of four', comprising the prime minister, defence minister, foreign minister and finance minister.[1]

Nuclear policy is the responsibility of the Defence and Foreign Affairs Committee, which meets behind closed doors. In a reply to a request to discuss the committee and nuclear arms policymaking, then committee chairman Abba Eban, told the author: 'I have jurisdictional responsibility on the nuclear development problems and on the Vanunu affair, but precisely for this reason I would be unable to discuss them with you.'

But surely criticism of a lack of government briefing of the committee on a range of sensitive issues, including intelligence, must raise doubts about whether the committee does fulfil and has fulfilled its constitutional role in nuclear arms policymaking. In concluding that Israel possesses between one hundred and two hundred nuclear warheads, Dr Frank Barnaby has asked whether its nuclear programme has 'got out of hand with the nuclear scientific community quite understandably from their perspective wishing to produce yet better and more sophisticated nuclear weapons.' Vanunu's, and Barnaby's concern at the lack of legislative control was shared by no less a personage than Levi Eshkol, who as prime minister forced the resignation in the sixties of the chairman of Israel's Atomic Energy Commission, transferred the commission from the Ministry of Defence's auspices to those of the Prime Minister's Office, and filled the board with civilian experts. Both the government and the Defence and Foreign Affairs Committee need to take steps to reassure those Israelis who disagree with the policy of ambiguity that proper legislative control is maintained in nuclear policymaking.

The loss of political control is a direct result of the ambiguity policy. The intense secrecy in building a reactor and a plutonium processing plant was a condition for France's

273

willingness to build them. According to Dr Francis Perrin, head of the French Atomic Energy Authority at the time, the secrecy was necessary because of French–US relations. Under an earlier agreement between Paris and Washington, the US allowed French scientists who had worked on nuclear weapons in Canada during the Second World War to return to France and use their knowledge there, provided that secrecy would be maintained. France, Perrin said, believed that Jerusalem would keep French involvement secret.[2] Despite the value which Israeli policymakers appear to see in the continuation of this tradition of secrecy, they must find a golden mean between maintaining the desired ambiguous image and the need and value of wide public discussion.

Public debate in other countries may be divided among those such as India, Argentina and Brazil where, like the United States, Britain and France, there is wide public debate, and those such as Pakistan where support for the bomb is equated with patriotism, where a critic could be labelled anti-Islamic, and where no public debate on the nuclear programme has ever been permitted. Those in Israel advocating public discussion of the basic nuclear issues include some favouring ambiguity. Yair Evron, for example, has argued that 'in a democratic society, a learned and open debate about the implications of strategies that concern the very existence of that society is essential. The problems connected with nuclear issues are so complex that it is doubtful whether prudent and effective policies and strategies could be planned and executed without open and elaborate discussions. Given the reality of non-conventional arms and the possibility of escalation, Israeli officials have an interest in there existing a consensus of support for the nuclear option.'

In addition to the pragmatic arguments, a minority has the right to express its views on subjects of basic importance to a society's existence such as the nuclear issue, whatever the majority view, and to demand some degree of accountability from the government. The lack of public discussion

about the nuclear question is reflected in seemingly contradictory findings on public attitudes. A 1976 *Haaretz* poll
found that 77 per cent of Israelis questioned favoured possession of the bomb. Of these 69 per cent supported its
possession unconditionally as opposed to 8 per cent because
of 'no other choices'. However, in the 1986 Jaffee poll, in
which 78 per cent of those questioned supported the policy
of ambiguity, 46 per cent did not agree to 'switch to nuclear
weapons in order to deter the Arabs', and 28 per cent 'certainly did not agree', while 22 per cent agreed and 5 per cent
'certainly agreed'. But while in 1986 64 per cent opposed the
use of nuclear weapons under any circumstances, less than
two years later this went down to 47 per cent. Of that 47 per
cent, 96 per cent said it would be acceptable to use nuclear
weapons as a response to a nuclear attack by another nation,
58 per cent in order to avoid defeat in a conventional war,
and 52 per cent 'to save many lives'.

The now wide popular Israeli belief that the country does
possess a nuclear capability, noted earlier, means there was
little purpose to or justification of Vanunu's act of disclosure.
Whether the public's belief is correct or incorrect is largely
irrelevant, since Vanunu's story agrees with this belief. Had
his claim differed significantly from this consensus belief it
might have had greater justification. And had somebody
who had worked at Dimona spoken publicly about his work
prior to the mid-seventies, when public knowledge about
Israel's nuclear development was even hazier, it could have
also been justified. While Vanunu was correct that nuclear
decision-making has been without proper legislative control,
his act of disclosure served no clear purpose. History cannot
be revised. For good or bad, technocrats and a couple of
senior ministers made policy.[3] Vanunu seemed unaware of
how widespread public belief was in Israel that the country
possessed nuclear capability.

In the aftermath of the Gulf War there was an increase
in Israeli public support for nuclear development. A Jaffee

Centre poll conducted after the war found that 91 per cent of Israelis questioned favoured development of a nuclear weapon; in 1987 78 per cent had said so. Even more noteworthy was an astounding increase in the Israeli public's willingness to deploy nuclear weapons: 88 per cent of those asked said after the war that they would tolerate use of nuclear weapons. Only 53 per cent had said so in 1987, and a mere 36 per cent in 1986. If Vanunu did not know about the level of public support for nuclear policy, an alternative explanation for his action was that he was overwhelmed by concern at what he saw happening at Dimona, and was grappling with the profound moral questions involved. Vanunu's aims ought to have been two-fold. First, to have made his goal the education of the Israeli public as to the evils (as he saw them) of non-conventional armaments by, for example, working among Israeli youth in peace education, which exists in many countries including Scandinavia. In spite of its support for a nuclear capability, it is noteworthy that 78 per cent of respondents in the 1991 poll were willing to abandon all non-conventional weapons provided the enemy did so. Second, he could have encouraged a public already aware that the country had a nuclear capability to lobby for adequate legislative supervision, even if, given the policy of ambiguity, only behind the closed doors of a Knesset committee. One may argue from a practical as well as moral viewpoint that there was limited value to Vanunu's deed, and he will now spend a good portion of his life in prison, devoid of any influence.

Though Vanunu did not reveal evidence of imminent health or environmental dangers from Dimona, he helped to draw attention to governmental secrecy regarding nuclear development and its environmental effects. Vanunu told the *Sunday Times* that 'low level' but still dangerous radioactive waste, produced mainly in the reprocessing plant, had for many years been mixed with tar, sealed in barrels, and buried in disposal sites about a kilometre from Dimona. In time, a radio active leak from the barrels could contaminate the Negev Desert's water table. Vanunu also claimed that the reprocessing plant released airborne pollution and radioactive gases. He said that especially toxic gases are sometimes released into the atmosphere from the Dimona facilities.[4] According to Barnaby, however, Israeli scientists regularly test radioactive contamination and, based on Vanunu's description, Barnaby concluded that Dimona's health and safety standards were reasonable. Yet Israeli officials have become concerned that nuclear waste from Dimona may have entered the water resources, as are environmental lobbyists and the mayor of the town of Dimona.

Information given by Vanunu about the disposal of nuclear waste (and included in Barnaby's book, *The Invisible Bomb*) was the subject of discussion by Israel's Nuclear Security Agency which oversees the Israeli Atomic Agency.[5] There are three known cases in Dimona's thirty-year history of the health of workers being damaged, including cancer, as a result of contact with dangerous substances at the centre. Legal hearings in some of these cases were held behind closed doors. In 1990 the works committee at Dimona took the step of turning to a Hebrew University health expert for advice on workers' exposure to dangerous substances.

The Chernobyl disaster in April 1986 – which occurred when Vanunu was in Australia – was an influencing factor in his decision to go public with his account. An official inquiry into the level of radioactive fall-out in Israel from Chernobyl found that 'Israel was totally unprepared and unorganised to deal with a nuclear accident in a distant country. Measures taken to deal with the fall-out were ill-organised and unplanned.' The report had been banned by the censor lest it arouse public discussion about the consequences of nuclear energy development. According to

277

Mattityahu Peled, then a Knesset member, 'the Israeli public has a right to know, as do publics in all other democracies, where radioactive waste is stored, how distant this is from populated areas, or in what level at sea it is buried, and what are the levels of danger of radiation reaching places of settlement.' Examination of Israeli agricultural produce by government inspectors after Chernobyl was done only selectively despite high levels of radiation being discovered, the produce even being turned back by the West German authorities. The Israeli customer was not notified, nor was it made public that during one week after Chernobyl children (who are five times at risk compared with adults from radioactivity) were exposed to one-tenth the radioactivity they absorb during an entire year.

Built thirty years ago, the Dimona reactor is relatively old, and a fire broke out there in 1991, say US officials. According to Paul Leventhal of the US Nuclear Regulatory Commission, it suffers from safety problems, and Israel has been looking for a new reactor. The US administration made Israel's purchase of an American reactor conditional on Israel signing the Nuclear Non-proliferation Treaty, which would require opening Dimona to international inspection. When Israel turned subsequently to France, and later to Russia, for a reactor, Washington applied diplomatic pressure on those governments not to sell to Israel. The government is now contemplating building its own reactor with locally-produced and foreign parts. According to Science and Energy Minister Professor Yuval Neeman, 'Israel has all the date and technology required to build a nuclear reactor which will be secure from both environmental and security aspects.'

'I broke the taboo. Now others will come. Nobody can stop it,' Vanunu wrote to *Maariv* in September 1987. Few came. Vanunu had much less impact in Israel than he had hoped. No major public debate on the nuclear issue occurred, and without much official effort the breach in the taboo healed itself. Vanunu 'died' less than two years after the *Sunday Times* exposé. Meir Vanunu said, 'nobody can expect that after twenty-five years of taboo suddenly because of something even as dramatic as this, things will be turned upside down and totally open in public. There is a definite start in public interest. What is published today is a lot more material that before would not have been published.'

The debate has been confined to informed and organised opinion, and academic symposia were held to consider Israel's nuclear options. The 1987 volume of the *Middle East Balance*, published by the Jaffee Centre for Strategic Studies, included a section on non-conventional weaponry in the Middle East. But the discussion has failed to spill over to the public at large. Confessing to some disappointment nine months after the *Sunday Times* publication, Mordechai Vanunu bemoaned that 'nobody wants to challenge the establishment, which is succeeding in removing the issue from the public agenda.' During and after the Gulf War there was probably greater informed discussion in Israel about non-conventional strategy than at any other time, and while the Vanunu exposé contributed to making this discussion more intelligent, it would be wrong to exaggerate his impact in stimulating the discussion. It was the war, the missile attacks on Israel, and the Bush proposal for regional arms control, which provoked the debate.

Vanunu did not want merely to inform Israelis about Dimona; he wanted to arouse internal concern. There is evidence that in other countries public discussion of nuclear and other types of weaponry has contributed to arms reductions. In the United States, for example, the debate over the neutron bomb was stimulated by revelations in its development stage, eventually leading to the decision not to deploy the weapon. Public concern in the US about atmospheric pollution has led to limitations on nuclear tests, and the M-X missile program was reduced following public criticism, including opposition from those in the vicinity where the missile was to be based. Public opinion has also had an effect on the outlawing of certain types of warfare and the use of biological and poison gas agents.

Israel's Left (to be distinguished from the left-of-centre Labour Party) oppose the idea of Israel's possessing any nuclear capability and favour a nuclear-free zone in the region. In an article in *Al Hamishmar*, which caused some controversy, Gideon Spiro, a peace activist, compared Vanunu to a parent who punished a child for wanting to stick a metal wire into an electric socket. 'If a parent who prevented their child from being electrocuted were brought to trial on charges of child abuse, they would think that the system had gone mad. Vanunu feared that if the government succeeded in sticking a metal wire (a nuclear one) into a socket it would electrocute us all in a nuclear death.'

Al Hamishmar's Yael Lotan was more circumspect, and compared Vanunu to the Israeli public's reaction to the 1982 Lebanon war. Dubbed 'Operation Peace for Galilee' by the Israel government it had as its goal ending the reign of terror caused by the PLO in southern Lebanon on Israel's northern settlements in the Galilee. 'Most people supported the Lebanon war. Today this has been reversed. The majority now know that it wasn't a war but simply bloodshed caused by a few leaders who wanted to "impose order" in a neighbouring country by force.' Even the left-of-centre *Davar*, the trade union movement's daily, said, 'Vanunu's claim that the citizenry are hidden from knowing about the nuclear programme cannot be refuted entirely because military censorship nullifies most of the reports without any connection to their level of accuracy. But the way to advance his struggle should have been via the Knesset and the government.'

Three months after the *Sunday Times* publication the Committee for a Public Trial for Mordechai Vanunu was formed. It had three objectives. First, that Vanunu should receive a public trial instead of the closed-doors trial the authorities had decided on. Second, that the campaign's focus should be less on Vanunu's personality and more on the nuclear issue. Third, to encourage public debate on the nuclear question as a means of getting the country to sign the Nuclear Non-proliferation Treaty. This committee succeeded the Israel Committee for the Prevention of Nuclear War which had been established in the aftermath of the Chernobyl disaster. It made negligible headway in reaching out to the Israeli public.

Israel's Left was divided over whether Vanunu's action was a positive or a negative step. Some like Yoram Nimrod, a Haifa University historian who since 1963 has campaigned in favour of an open debate on nuclear policy, says that 'Vanunu's disclosure was damaging. People will identify the cause of a non-nuclear Israel and nuclear disarmament with the treason of Vanunu.' Approached by Asher Vanunu to support his brother's goals, Israeli public figures declined to be identified with Mordechai Vanunu. Yossi Sarid, Knesset member for the Citizens Rights Movement, attacked Vanunu for the manner he had chosen to advance his goal: divulging the secret information to a foreign newspaper. Retired General Aharon Yariv, head of the prestigious Jaffee Centre, whose *Military Balance* said that the exposé raised Israel's nuclear posture, declined Asher Vanunu's request to make a statement to this effect, or to give testimony at the trial. And Levi Morav, a left-wing journalist, argued that 'a public debate did not require colourful pictures of the reactor which Vanunu brought to the *Sunday Times*.' Although Mapam has over the years campaigned for a nuclear-free zone in the Middle East, only the Progressive Peace List, which had two members in the 120-seat Knesset, publicly backed Vanunu.

Vanunu burnt his bridges, and the natural revulsion in Israel for him as a national traitor was not surprising in a country which is still without peace with most of its neighbours, and which faces an escalating Arab arms race. It is difficult to conceive how Vanunu could have made a dramatic impact on public opinion in Israel without some really sensational disclosure of information. If his dramatic revelations failed to achieve political change, could Vanunu, in Ehud Olmert's words, have 'made an attempt within Israel's democratic system which allows for an absolute freedom of speech, more than in any other country in the world, to fight for his opinions?' The business of lobbying by a pressure group is an arduous and exasperating matter in the freest societies, often with small results to show at the end of the day. Democratic theory may allow for an interest group to lobby the public and policymakers for change, but if the issue cannot be discussed because the subject is too sensitive the democratic system shows its shortcomings. Had Vanunu attempted in the sixties to debate the issue, it is fairly sure that officialdom would have intervened. Although former members of the Israel Atomic Energy Commission subsequently campaigned against the defence orientation which they said nuclear development was taking, there are the other cases of official discouragement of public and media discussion of the nuclear subject. Even before 5 October 1986 a pool of information and data had trickled into the public domain from foreign sources, enabling some limited discussion, but only after this date could informed discussion seriously take place, and debate has still not extended to the level of the wider public.

Shimon Peres, in appealing to the patriotism of the Editors' Committee not to discuss the *Sunday Times* exposé, was saying that the higher goal of 'national security' had to take precedence over the democratic process. Whether or not the law had been broken was irrelevant. Peres was in effect saying, 'No, Mr Vanunu, wide grassroots public discussion of nuclear arms issues cannot take place in Israel.'

Vanunu may have carved himself a place in the international liberal conscience. But Israelis, facing serious external threats, and not having debated the issue, dismissed him as a national traitor. His disaffection with his country, culminating with his conversion to Christianity, fuelled the image. Yet, with growing concern over the spread of non-conventional weaponry among Arab states, discussion of the nuclear issue received a breath of life. In the event of a disaster at one of Israel's nuclear reactors, the nuclear arms issue will certainly enter the public consciousness. Such a horror could well result in mass public pressure for arms control or nuclear disarmament. But, barring such a catastrophe, and given both the continuing fears of annihilation and long-term electoral trends towards the Right, opinion polls suggest that the debate on the nuclear issue would be far from what Vanunu hoped to achieve.

AFTERWORD

The interface between Vanunu's moral conscience and that of Israel could not have been resolved in a more unsatisfactory manner than the tragedy of his eighteen years in solitary confinement. True, it is unlikely that in any other democracy in conflict, the clash between disclosure of highly classified information on a subject for which there is a consensus at home, including a consensus that it should remain secret, would have been resolved in a different way. In a non-democratic country it would be 'resolved' more quickly and brutally. But the lack of the resolution of this interface is a weak point in the democratic model of government. At no stage in the judicial proceedings against Vanunu did any judge acknowledge that up to 1986, and even after that, no system existed to enable the Israeli public to receive official information and have an informed discussion on the nuclear issue. A democracy where citizens are informed of sensitive national security issues only through that information being published abroad is weak.

The founding fathers of Israeli democracy 'based' the availability of 'sensitive' national security information upon those trickles which, by hook or by crook, authorised or not authorised, reach the public domain. A democracy should be a self-contained system with a formal mechanism for monitoring sensitive national security information which should be classified, and declassifying the remainder. The short-term diplomatic consequences of a policy of ambiguity need to be balanced with the long-term requirement for adequate data for the public to reach intelligent and informed decisions. Had such a system existed, Mordechai Vanunu's name would be unknown.

Democratic societies also require means by which those concerned about government inefficiency or other matters of public interest can report them and not have to resort to unauthorised leaks to the media. In the eighties Israel adopted the 'Whistleblower' rule, under which an official witnessing corruption may bring it without fear of dismissal to public knowledge or report it to the State Comptroller's Office, body which inspects the efficiency and working of government. However, this rule does not extend beyond corruption, and certainly not to allegations such as Vanunu's concerning inadequate legislative control of nuclear policy.

To close the file, Vanunu, in the context of requesting a presidential pardon, should regret his action of revealing classified technical information and undertake to discuss only the broader issues. He should do so even in the likelihood that the Israeli court does not revise its generalisation that Vanunu 'confused democracy with anarchy'. Vanunu – already a 'box office' attraction – may be able to achieve more for his cause outside the prison cell.

As evidenced by the personal treatment Mordechai Vanunu has received and is receiving, the Israeli public, the government and the judiciary remain in the pre-Vanunu era. The nuclear theme remains sacred and unquestioned. Only a nuclear catastrophe may turn somebody labelled a traitor into somebody who lived ahead of his time. For the public to make that leap and question nuclear weapons and their morality may come only with the experience of their totality. Had Vanunu made his disclosure in a climate of intense public debate about nuclear weapons, it is most unlikely that the courts would have given him the sentence he received. His exposé, in providing a pool of data about the nuclear programme, enabling a more informed discussion of nuclear options, earned a place in the history of Israeli democracy, the peculiarities of the Israeli censorship system, and the foibles of public opinion.

Yet morality and conscience are relative rather than absolute values. In 1986 Israel lived in a Middle East where after forty years of conflict only one Arab country had formally come to terms with the Jewish state, and where there was a hostile trend towards Islamic fundamentalism. National survival is a moral value, and a strong Israel, including its nuclear deterrent posture, was seen by most Israelis as meeting that value. For most of them the Vanunu Affair revisited the dilemma of how an open society protects its secrets. In one sense the affair confirmed that the open society may survive and prosper as much as a closed society while enjoying the benefits of openness. The vast majority of officials who have access to sensitive information do not reveal it, thanks to efficient security procedures. Open societies like Israel have a grey area in which former officials are able to participate in the democratic process even when they use the information, experience and insight gained officially to form their judgements. For example, two of the board members of the Israel Atomic Energy Commission who resigned in the sixties subsequently led a group opposing Israel's nuclearisation. And while Vanunu was warned by the authorities not to join the Communist Party while working at Dimona, nothing stopped him doing so when he left.

In another sense, the Vanunu episode underlined the vulnerability of the open society. People exit and enter; the national media may be unable to publish security secrets, but there is little stopping the foreign correspondent. Once a disclosure is made, the open society can do little to prevent the fall-out. In the Vanunu case, official Israel had the good fortune that it was not in the interests of foreign governments, friend and foe, to blow up the matter.

NOTES

1. *Going Nuclear*

1. Louis Beres (ed), *Security or Armageddon: Israel's Nuclear Strategy* (Lexington, Lexington Books 1986).
2. *Time*, 12.4.1976.
3. Ibid.
4. Ibid.
5. Andrew & Leslie Cockburn, *Dangerous Liaison* (New York, HarperCollins 1991).
6. Haaretz, 5.10.1986.
7. Fuad Jabber, *Israel & Nuclear Weapons* (London, Chatto & Windus 1971), p. 114.
8. Leonard Spector, *The Undeclared Bomb* (Cambridge, Ballinger 1988) p. 386–7.
9. Spector, op. cit. p. 168.
10. Spector, op. cit. pp. 386–7.
11. Steve Weisman & Herbert Krosney, *The Islamic Bomb* (New York, Times Books 1981), p. 114.
12. Pierre Pean, *Les Deux Bombes* (Paris, Payard 1981), chapters 6–7.
13. Spector, op. cit. pp. 171–3.
14. Benjamin Beit-Hallahmi, *The Israeli Connection* (London, Tauris 1988), p. 204.
15. *Yediot Aharonot*, 3.11.1986.
16. Frank Barnaby, *The Invisible Bomb, The Nuclear Arms Race in the Middle East* (London Tauris 1989) pp. 22, 25.
17. *Observer*, 27.3.1988.

18. Ibid.
19. Jabber, op. cit.
20. Barnaby, op. cit., p. 6.
21. *Davar*, 29.12.1986.
22. *Wehrtechnik*, June 1976.
23. *Newsweek*, 11.7.1988.
24. *Observer*, 23.8.1987.
25. Australian Television, 'Four Corners' 31.8.1987.
26. For a similar argument see Yossi Melman and Dan Raviv, *The Imperfect Spies* (London, Sidgwick & Jackson 1989) p. 402.
27. Seymour Hersh, *The Samson Option* (New York, Random House) p. 198.
28. *Hadashot*, 6.4.1989.
29. *New York Times*, 16.6.1968.
30. Jabber, op. cit., p. 127.
31. Gary Milhollin in *Foreign Policy*, Winter 1987–8.

2. *The Life and Times of Motti Vanunu*

1. *Haaretz*, 14.11.1986.
2. *Yediot Aharonot*, 21.12.1987.
3. *Maariv*, 21.11.1986.
4. *Haolam Hazeh*, 11.2.1987.
5. *Haaretz*, 8.5.1989.
6. *Haaretz*, 5.10.1986.
7. *New Outlook*, September–October 1991, p. 9.
8. Replies to letters from the author to Mordechai Vanunu raising this and other points, sent to him at Ashkelon Jail, were not received.
9. *Koteret Rashit* 19.8.1987.

3. *Devil's Advocate*

1. Frank Giles, *Sundry Times* (John Murray) 1986.
2. *Haaretz*, 5.10.1986.
3. Ibid.
4. Ibid.
5. Ibid.
6. Ibid.

7. *Time*, 12.4.1976.
8. 'The Man from Dimona', *CBS News*, 27.2.1988.
9. Spector, op. cit., p. 138.
10. *CBS News*, 27.2.1988.
11. Barnaby, op. cit., p. xi.
12. Australian Television, 'Four Corners', 3.8.1987.
13. Denis Herbstein, 'Changing Times', *Index on Censorship*, May 1986.

4. *A Tale of Two Papers*

1. Interview by author with Peter Hounam.
2. *Maariv* 21.11.1986.
3. Israel Supreme Court ruling, issued 29.9.1990, Jerusalem, pp. 3–4.
4. Interview by author with Tony Frost.
5. Interview by author with Mike Molloy.
6. Seymour Hersh, *The Samson Option*, New York, Random House 1991, page 311.
7. Hersh, op. cit., page 312.
8. Hersh, op. cit., page 315.
9. Interview by author with Mike Molloy.
10. Interview by author with Mike Molloy.
11. *Yediot Aharonot* 26.2.1988; interview by author with Mark Souster.
12. The *Jewish Chronicle Magazine* 19.9.1986.
13. *The Observer* 27.10.1991.
14. Interview by author with Mark Souster.
15. Extracts from the memorandum from Tony Frost of 26.10.1991 were published in the Sunday Mirror 27.10.1991.

5. *The Mossad v the* Sunday Times

1. Hadashot, 16.11.1986.
2. Ibid.
3. Australian Television, 'Four Corners', 31.8.1987; Melman & Raviv, op. cit., p. 387.
4. *Hadashot*, 16.11.1986.
5. Australian Television, 'Four Corners', 31.8.1987.

6. *Financial Times*, 8.11.1986; *Observer*, 9.11.1986; *Daily Telegraph,* 10.11.1986; *The Times*, 12.11.86; *Sunday Telegraph*, 16.11.1986.
7. *The Middle East*, October 1981.
8. *Hadashot.* 20.6.1988.
9. Thames Television, 20.6.1988.
10. *Sunday Telegraph,* 18.12.1988.
11. Jeffrey T. Richelson, *Foreign Intelligence Organisations* (Cambridge, Mass., Ballinger 1988), p. 196.
12. Ibid, pp. 232–3.
13. Ibid, pp. 205–6.
14. David Tinnin, *Hit Team* (London, Futura 1976).
15. Leonard Spector, *The New Nuclear Nations*, New York, Vintage Books 1985.
16. Weisman & Krosney, op. cit., pp. 125–6.
17. Ibid.
18. Richard Deacon, *The Israeli Secret Service* (London, Sphere 1979), p. 146.
19. *Maariv*, 4.8.1989.
20. *The Middle East*, August 1981.
21. *Yediot Aharonot*, 23.2.1990.
22. *The Independent*, 23.12.1986.
23. *Hadashot*, 16.11.1986.
24. Ibid.
25. *Haaretz*, 21.2.1988.
26. *Hadashot*, 16.11.1986.
27. Ibid.
28. *Yediot Aharonot*, 17.11.1986.
29. *Haaretz*, 6.4.1990.
30. *Hadashot*, 21.3.1988; *Haaretz* 21.2.1988.
31. Ibid.
32. Ibid.
33. *Hadashot*, 16.11.1986.
34. *Hadashot*, 28.4. 1987; *Maariv*, 29.4.1987.
35. *Hadashot*, 16.11.1986.
36. Australian Television, 'Four Corners', 31.8.1987.
37. Ibid.
38. Ibid.
39. Ibid.

40. *Hadashot*, 16.11.1986.
41. *Financial Times*, 6.12.1986.
42. *La Stampa*, 27.12.1986.
43. Ibid.
44. *Haaretz*, 1.2.1989.
45. *Washington Times* 26.3.1987.
46. *Haaretz*, 9.8.1987.
47. Ibid.
48. *Corriere Della Serra* 13.10.1988.
49. *Haaretz*, 16.8.1987.
50. Ibid.

6. *Things Fall Apart*

1. *Davar*, 11.11.1986.
2. *Hadashot*, November 1986; *Jerusalem Post*, 26.10.1988.
3. *Haaretz*, 20.1.1988.
4. Ibid.
5. Ibid.
6. *Jerusalem Post*, June 24 1988.
7. Ibid.
8. Ibid.
9. *Hadashot*, 23.3.1990.
10. *International Herald Tribune*, 18/19.6.1988.
11. *Sunday Telegraph*, 18.12.1988.
12. *Jerusalem Post*, 24.6.1988.
13. *Yediot Aharonot*, 19.6.1988.
14. *Hadashot*, 20.6.1988.
15. Ibid.
16. *The Independent*, 28.7.1988.
17. *Sunday Telegraph*, 18.12.1988.
18. *The Independent*, 28.7.1988.
19. Ibid.
20. *The Times*, 25.7.1988.
21. *The Independent*, 28.7.1988.
22. *Sunday Telegraph*, 18.12.1988.
23. Ibid.
24. BBC World Service, 12.3.1989.
25. FBIS Near East and South Asia, 4.1.1989.

26. *Haaretz*, 16.8.1987.
27. Ibid.
28. Ibid.
29. Ibid.
30. Ibid.
31. Ibid.
32. Ibid.
33. Ibid.
34. *Panorama*, 26.9.1988.
35. Ibid.
36. David Tinnin, op. cit., pp. 56–9.
37. Ibid.
38. *Haaretz*, 21.2.1988.
39. *Haaretz*, 21.2.1988; *Hadashot*, 21.2.1988.
40. *Hadashot*, 16.11.1986.
41. *The Times*, 25.7.1988.
42. Beres, op. cit.
43. *Maariv*, 14.11.1986.
44. Ibid.
45. *Time*, 20.3.1989.
46. Deacon, op. cit. p. 135.
47. *The Independent*, 29.11.1986.
48. Wolf Blitzer, *Territory of Lies* (Harper & Row, 1989).
49. Ibid.
50. *Maariv*, 14.11.1986; *Sunday Telegraph*, 16.11.1986.
51. *Maariv*, 14.11.1986.
52. *The Independent*, 29.11.1986.
53. *Haaretz*, 5.10.1986.
54. Melman & Raviv, op. cit., p. 102.
55. *Israel Shelanu*, 7.11.1986; *Maariv*, 7.11.1986.
56. *Hadashot*, 15.10.1986.
57. Deacon, op. cit., pp. 120, 252.

7. *The Newspaper & The Informer*

1. BBC 'Breakfast Time', 28.11.1986.
2. Australian Television, 'Four Corners', 31.8.1987.
3. BBC 'Breakfast Time' ibid.
4. *Hadashot*, 16.11.1986.

5. Ibid.
6. Interview by author with Wendy Robbins; see Wendy Robbins' article 'Betrayal', *New Moon*, December 1991.
7. *Yediot Aharonot*, 15.1.1988.
8. Ibid.
9. Interview by author with Robbins.
10. Ibid.
11. *Jewish Chronicle*, 13.12.1991.
12. *Hadashot*, 16.11.1986.
13. Ibid.
14. *Haaretz*, 19.11.1986.
15. BBC 'Breakfast Time', Ibid.
16. Interview by author with Robin Morgan.
17. Interview by author with Meir Vanunu.
18. *Palestine Focus*, January–February, 1988.
19. Robbins, New Moon, op. cit.; *Davar*, 14.11.1986.

8. *(3 metres × 2 metres) × 18 years*

1. *Jerusalem Post*, 19.6.1987.
2. *Al Hamishmar*, 11.3.1987.
3. *Hadashot*, 8.12.1987.
4. *The Guardian*, 8.12.1987; *Hadashot*, 8.12.1987.
5. *Hadashot*, 24.3.1988.
6. Ibid.
7. Ibid.
8. *Jerusalem Post*, 28.9.1987.
9. *Jerusalem Post*, 14.8.1987.
10. *Davar*, 28.8.1987.
11. *Jerusalem Post*, 14.8.1987.
12. *Jerusalem Post*, 28.8.1987; *Kol Hair*, 21.8.1987.
13. *Hadashot*, 23.11.1987.
14. *Davar*, 28.8.1987.
15. *Hadashot*, 31.8.1987, 1.9.1987.
16. *Hadashot*, 31.8.1987.
17. *Davar*, 3.9.1987.
18. *Hadashot*, 1.9.1987.
19. *Hadashot*, 24.3.1988; *Jerusalem Post*, 19.6.1987.
20. *Hadashot*, 24.3.1988.

21. *Jerusalem Post*, 4.9.1987.
22. *Davar*, 30.11.1986; *Yediot Aharonot*, 20.11.1986.
23. *Haaretz*, 21.11.1986.
24. *Jerusalem Post*, 23.11.1986.
25. *Hadashot*, 3.5.1989.
26. *Hadashot*, 7.1.1988.
27. *Haaretz*, 29.7.1987.
28. *Haaretz*, 1.9.1987.
29. Appendix to Statement by Amnon Zichroni to the Workshop: Mobilising the International Peace Movement for a Nuclear Weapon Free Zone in the Middle East, Fourth UN International NGO Meeting on the Question of Palestine, September 1987, Geneva.
30. *Davar*, 4.11.1986; *Haaretz*, 4.11.1986.
31. *Hadashot*, 7.1.1988.
32. *Hadashot*, 18.1.1988.
33. *Davar*, 24.1.1988.
34. *Haaretz*, 29.7.1987.
35. *Jerusalem Post*, 28.8.1987.
36. *Hadashot*, 31.8.1987.
37. *The Guardian*, 31.8.1987.
38. *Yediot Aharonot*, 27.8.1987; *The Independent*, 26.8.1987.
39. *Hadashot*, 10.12.1987.
40. *Jerusalem Post*, 28.8.1987.
41. *Maariv*, 5.1.1988.
42. *Davar*, 2.12.1987.
43. *Maariv*, 2.12.1987.
44. Israel Supreme Court ruling, pp. 5–6.
45. *Hadashot*, 25.3.1988.
46. Israel Supreme Court ruling, p. 9.
47. *Hadashot*, 25.3.1988.
48. *National Journal*, 30.9.1989.
49. *Kol Hair*, 16.8.1991.
50. Israel Supreme Court ruling, p. 52.
51. *Davar*, 25.10.1991.
52. *Jerusalem Post*, 10.9.1987.

9. *A Consensus of Silence*

1. *Newsweek*, 11.7.1988.
2. *Spector*, op. cit., pp. 386–7.
3. *Time*, 27.4.1976.
4. Barnaby, op. cit., p. 38.
5. *Haaretz*, 17.12.1990.

Chronology

1. *Spector*, op. cit.

CHRONOLOGY

1954	Establishment of the Israel Atomic Energy Commission
1956	Signing of secret agreement between France and Israel for the supply of a nuclear reactor at Dimona
1958–64	French engineers and scientists construct the nuclear reactor and an underground plutonium processing facility[1]
1973	Nuclear alert at beginning of October Arab–Israel war
1977	
7 August	Mordechai Vanunu starts work as a night controller at Dimona
1985	
November	Vanunu ceases working at Dimona
1986	
January	Vanunu leaves Israel for the Far East
May	Vanunu arrives in Sydney Australia
August	Oscar Guerrero contacts the *Sunday Times* Reporter Peter Hounam meets Vanunu in Sydney
Early September	Vanunu is flown to London and debriefed by nuclear scientist Dr Frank Barnaby
28 September	*Sunday Mirror* publishes 'The Strange Case of Israel and the Nuclear Conman'
30 September	Vanunu disappears in London
Early October	Vanunu taken by ship to Israel from Italy
5 October	*Sunday Times* publishes Vanunu's story

9 November	Israel Government confirms Vanunu back in Israel
1987	
August	Vanunu trial opens
1988	
March	Vanunu is sentenced to eighteen years' imprisonment
1989	
May	Vanunu appeals to Israel Supreme Court
1990	
May	Supreme Court rejects his appeal